The Customs of Mankind

In 2 Volumes

Lillian Eichler

Vol I

GyAN PUBLISHING HOUSE
Delhi-110 007

First Published in 1988 Reprint 2017 in India by
Gyan Publishing House,
5, Ansari Road, Darya Ganj,
New Delhi-110002
Phones : 011-47034999, 9811692060
E-mail: books@gyanbooks.com
Website: www.gyanboks.com

Lasser Type Setting by: Quick Media, Delhi
Printed at : G. Print Process, Delhi

PREFACE

I wandered into a church, one day, for an hour of quiet. There were some people in front, but I selected an obscure corner where I would be alone. In my contemplation I did not notice the church fill up, did not notice the quality of restlessness in the air. It was not until an organ directly above me began the stirring strains of the march from Lohengrin that I realized I was an unbidden guest at a wedding!

It was too late to leave. The wedding procession had started. In the dingy little church I watched the principals try to enact a scene of fashionable splendour. There was a little flower-girl who forgot to strew her flowers before the bride; a page who stumbled and went scurrying after the ring; an usher who persisted in grinning at the unaccustomedness of his high silk hat.

But no one smiled. And when the bride entered there was a sudden, hushed silence, as though everyone had taken one long, deep breath.

I watched her as she walked down the aisle, this little twentieth-century bride. As is the way of unruly imaginations, I pictured her a bride of long ago. Did she realize that she was actually observing certain ceremonial rites that were practised thousands of years ago? Did she realize that the traditions so dear to her heart—so dear to bride-hearts the world over—were based upon the fears and superstitions of primitive man, upon age-old customs that had been handed down to her through many generations?

Why was her wedding gown white? Why not pink, or green, or yellow? Why were there orange blossoms on her veil? Indeed, why a veil at all? And the wedding ring, the bridal procession, the handful of rice—surely they had some meaning.

The ceremony did not last long. In half an hour it was over. The little church was deserted; nothing remained but a trampled rose or two. But something had happened to *me*. I had glimpsed behind the pages of history and saw promise of a treasure rarer than any in the Valley of the Kings!

Like another Lord Carnarvon I set out to explore the pages of the past. I traversed the centuries and came, trembling, upon the cradle of the human race. I stood amazed upon the threshold of life. And mankind passed by in pageant before me! Cities created themselves before my eyes. Tangled masses of folklore and superstition confronted me. But armed with the pick and shovel of the archæologist and the pen of the historian, I did not hesitate to begin my ride across the centuries.

I peeped into the caves of our hairy ancestors and saw their modes of worship. I sat in the gardens of Babylon and watched civilization plant its first precious seeds. I wandered through ancient European wastes and saw new towns lift their faces to the sky. I shadowed Queen Elizabeth; I glimpsed the gaudy ballrooms of Louis XV; I followed Columbus across the sea to America.

Oh, it has been a wonderful task! I have peered into marble palaces and sat with cave dwellers on the hills. I have danced with Indians in young America and dined with savage cave men of long ago. I have browsed in old Egypt, following civilization along the Nile. I have watched customs grow out of the fears, the superstitions, the ignorance of early life. And I have followed these customs through the ages, watching them thread their way into every country, among all peoples, weaving themselves eternally into the pattern of life. I have traced them even to our own polished twentieth-century civilization, marvelling that they should have changed so little in the centuries between.

This, then, is precisely, as the title implies, a book of customs I have traced back to their source the customs which we to-day observe—the customs which we accept without question. Why should black be the colour of mourning? Why not red, or green, or white? Why do we shake hands in greeting, instead of touching noses, or foreheads, or elbows? Why do we throw rice after the bride? Why not corn, or oatmeal, or barley?

In "The Customs of Mankind" I shall concern myself solely with those customs which we to-day observe, which we to-day accept. "The Book of Etiquette," which was so heartily welcomed by the public, tells you what to do on every social occasion. "The Customs of Mankind" tells you not only what to do, but why you do it.

I offer in this volume many "discoveries" that are peculiarly my own. Some of the customs I write about have never before, to my knowledge, been investigated. They are customs that have long been buried in impenetrable mists of antiquity, and that I have snatched from oblivion only through the most painstaking research.

"The Customs of Mankind" has taken me over a period that extends backward for 500,000 years, and over an area that includes practically every country, civilized and uncivilized, in the world. The research entailed the use of thousands of volumes and papers, the most important of which are included in a list of authorities at the end.

I wish here to extend my thanks to the New York Public Library for the use of reference books; and to the Metropolitan Museum of Art and the Museum of Natural History, both of New York City, for the use of photographs that appear in this work.

LILLIAN EICHLER.

CONTENTS

LIST ILLUSTRATIONS

LIST OF HALFTONE ILLUSTRATIONS

LIST OF LINE DRAWINGS

THE CUSTOMS OF MANKIND

Era	Period	Subdivision	Ages / Epochs	Events	Duration	Age
CENOZOIC	QUATERNARY		**1919 A.D.** **Age of Man, A. D.** **B.C.**			
			Iron Age Bronze Age	Holocene	500,000 years	AGE OF MAN
			New Stone Age Neolithic, or upper Palaeolithic			
			Old Stone Age Or Lower Palaeolithic	Pleistocene Glacial Period Europe, Asia, America		
			Dawn Stone Or Eolithic			
	TERTIARY		Pliocene		5,000,000 yrs.	Age of MAMMALS
			Miocene	Himalayas Swiss Alps Pyrenees		
			Oligocene			
			Eocene	Rocky Mts.		
			Palaeocene	Eastern Alps		
MESOZOIC		Late Mesozoic	Upper Cretaceous Cretaceous Jurassic		10,000,000 yrs.	Age of REPTILES
		Early Mesozoic	Triassic Permian Carboniferous	Glacial Period South Africa		
PALAEOZOIC			Devonian		15,000,000 yrs.	Invertebrates
			Silurian	Scottish Highlands		
			Cambrian			
PRE-CAMBRIAN		Archaean			50,000,000 years	ORIGIN OF LIFE
		Archaeozoic		[illegible] Algae Bacteria Earliest Living things		

(Courtesy of New York Museum of Natural History)

THE CUSTOMS OF MANKIND

CHAPTER I

Introductory

In every department of human thought there is present evidence of the persistence of primitive ideas. Scratch the epiderm of the civilized man, and the barbarian is found in the derm. Man is the same everywhere at the bottom; if there are many varieties, there is but one species. His civilization is the rare topmost shoot of the tree whose roots are in the earth, and whose trunk and larger branches are in savagery.

—Edward Clodd.

THE CHILDHOOD OF MAN

THE writer on primitive man and on ancient civilizations does not always know precisely where to start. He walks, for a while, hand in hand with fancy, following wherever it may lead. All history seems to him as but yesterday. And prehistory seems a swaying mass of shadowy forms from which he takes or leaves, according to his purpose.

But he who would build history, not with the ordinary facts of evolution, but with the manners and customs of man himself, has no choice. He is obliged to go back to the very cradle of human existence, to project himself into the daily life of many thousands of years ago, studying man in his infancy, walking beside him through barbarism, through the early gropings for reason, through the dawn and development of religion, through civilization. And he must take the vast store of raw material which he gathers, interpreting it in terms of simple human nature.

No historian or antiquarian can tell you the exact day

when man for the first time stood erect upon the earth and gazed upon a universe that had been created for him. Many have guessed; many have tried to prove, but no one knows the exact period or the exact spot where man first began. We cannot, then, be certain about the origin of man, but we can be reasonably certain about his antiquity.

The earliest type of a man-like creature which has been discovered until now is the *Pithecanthropus erectus*, which means simply the *erect ape man*. Authorities believe that the Pithecanthropus man lived about 500,000 years ago, which was in the Pliocene or pre-glacial period. The remains of this man were found in Trinil, Java, by Dr. Eugène Dubois in 1892.

Regarding the ancestry of man, not all authorities are agreed. H. G. Wells adopts the theory that man's immediate ancestor was a ground ape. This, on the whole, seems the most plausible explanation of the still obscure origin of man, and many scientists and historians are inclined to accept it.

But Henry Fairfield Osborn (one of the authorities who places the age of the Pithecanthropus man at 500,000 years) says, "Man has a long line of ancestry of his own, perhaps two million or more years in length. He is not descended from any known form of ape, either living or fossil."

David Starr Jordan, in his "Footnotes to Evolution," says:

> Man is not simply a "developed ape." Apes and man have diverged from the same primitive stock—ape-like, man-like, but not exactly one nor the other.

One writer on primitive man asks, "Have you noticed that a baby loves to get its fingers tangled up in your hair—always keeping its tiny fist closed, always attempting to grasp everything it can place its hands on? And if there is nothing within reach, it keeps its hands closed tightly in imitation of the act of holding on." This, he declares, would seem to bear out the fact that man is developed from the ape or the primate!

Of course, no one can definitely say when the brute man ended and the human man began. Joseph McCabe, in his "Evolution of Civilization," believes it is safe to say that at least 1,500,000 years have elapsed since the human branch of the tree of life separated from the ape branch. And Sir Arthur Keith, who is one of the leading authorities on the remains of prehistoric man, has a diagram in his "Antiquity of Man" (1915) representing the tree of life, in which the human stem branches off from the anthropoid group in the Oligocene Period. The geologist Professor Sollas says that this Oligocene Period closed about 1,800,000 years ago.

These few but impressive hypotheses are cited merely to bring to attention the long primitive heritage of the human race. Man has an ancestry reaching back, not five or six thousand years, but a half million years at least. Skeletal remains have been found which indicate that in Europe the existing species of man (*Homo sapiens*) goes back at least 30,000 years.

We do not attempt to discuss the origin of man at any great length in this volume, or to refute any of the conclusions already reached by authorities. The subject is so vast that, to discuss it intelligently, would require a volume in itself. We wish solely to give you an idea of the age of man and the centuries in which he has been developing. You know now that, though the compilers of the sacred narrative did not even hint at a prehistoric era, man lived hundreds of thousands of years ago, half brute and half man, ignorant of the simplest arts save, perhaps, the making of flint implements, devoid of love and tenderness, depending upon brute strength for his very existence.

And so, for many centuries, man has lived and dreamed and laboured, leaving for us who follow in his footsteps a record of what he has thought and what he has done, even as we are now leaving for future generations a record of our thoughts and our achievements.

SOURCES OF INFORMATION CONCERNING PRIMITIVE MAN

The reader will ask—and with justice—how it is possible to write of the manners and customs of men who lived so very long ago. What about the people who left no record of their existence—who lived and died in a brief span? What about lands that lifted their faces to the sun, brought forth life, and vanished for ever beneath the surface of the sea? Who knows what forgotten civilizations hide their calcined bones, layer upon layer, beneath the feet that tread on life to-day?

Perhaps there *are* volumes in the history of life that have never been recorded, and thus never will be known. But for our purposes it is entirely sufficient that we concern ourselves with the facts that are known, that are recorded. Whatever has happened of importance in the vast ages that have gone by has somehow left its trace. And, of course, what facts omit, imagination can sometimes supply.

In studying the early history of man and society, the chief sources of information are archæology, anthropology, mythology, and folklore, and later, the sacred writings. The archæologist emerges from the dark silences of tombs, bringing into the light of the twentieth century new truths concerning primitive man. The anthropologist studies the races of the world, studies man as a unit in the animal kingdom, and teaches us to understand the savage as we understand ourselves. Mythology and folklore give us a rare insight into man's method of reasoning, reveal to us the fancies and conceptions of early thought. And the sacred writings, being the first histories, record for ever the manners and customs of life at the very inception of civilization.

Archæology.—The great master key to the understanding of man's primitive condition is held by prehistoric archæology. The archæologist collects and compares the material relics of forgotten races—the axes and the arrowheads, the sharpened bones and woven baskets. With pick and shovel he pierces the darkness enveloping the early history of man. He uncovers the ruins of ancient cities, removing the litter of ages from their bowels. He delves into long-sealed tombs and carries out rare treasures of another age.

Through the findings of the archæologist it is possible to reconstruct the buildings, the utensils, the burial grounds, the clothes—all the material things of man as they existed long ago. And thus we are able to piece together the story of daily life thousands of years ago. Standing at the elbow of the archæologist, we are able to transplant ourselves, project ourselves into the daily life of the old race whose relics lay revealed before us, and so come to know and understand the people of whom we write.

Few localities have attracted a deeper degree of archæological interest than Egypt. The Pyramids and the Sphinx lift their lofty heads into the heavens—and are silent. But on the walls in the palaces and on the monuments are facts that give as clear an index to the life of the early Egyptian as would any definite history.

It was a custom in Egypt to preserve important parts of history and important facts of daily life by engraving and carving descriptions of them on the walls in the palaces and on memorial stones. The inscriptions are in the form of pictures with combinations of syllables added—hieroglyphics, as they are called. Living forms and living scenes were portrayed by the ancient sculptor and painter. This "language of the Pharaohs" is an important source of information for the writer on civilization and on primitive man.

If you have ever viewed the Sphinx at dawn you know what a feeling of awe takes possession of you—as though you stand for a moment at the very beginning of things. Yet, though Egypt is old and gray, though the first phases of civilization are mirrored in the waters of the old Nile, who knows what ancient civilizations await the pick of the archæologist in China, in India, in our own America?

Anthropology.—When a tomb is opened and both skulls and implements are found within it, the archæologist keeps the implements, assorts them, compares them, rendering all information concerning them accessible to future investigators along the same line. The skulls and human bones he hands over to the anthropologist.

In other words, the archæologist studies civilization and the anthropologist studies races. It is the anthropologist who speculates as to the age and origin of man; who takes a bit of skull and reconstructs therefrom the entire man. The anthropologist tells us much about the whys and wherefores of man's customs by revealing the effect upon the nature of man, of climate, food supply, and other external conditions.

At one time individual explorers devoted their time and money to the investigation of prehistoric man and his remains. But since 1880 organized institutions of anthropology have taken the spade out of the hands of these individual explorers, and both the archæologist and the trained anthropologist are now associated.

The science of anthropology makes it possible for us to *visualize* the men of whom we write—see them as, very probably, they actually appeared. The anthropologist gives us a very fair idea of how the *Pithecanthropus erectus* looked, although only a handful of bones were found in Java.

But perhaps the greatest service of the anthropologist is one who writes of the manners and customs of primitive man is his study of existing savage races—the last living link that binds us to our prehistoric past. He goes to the lands that have been cut off from the main stream of the development of mankind, where our savage brothers have lived and bred for centuries. And he tells us authoritatively of their age-worn customs, their habits of life, their primitive beliefs and ceremonials.

Mythology and Folklore.—What the primitive mind lacked in reason it made up in imagination. Beautiful tales and legends have come down to us in the form of mythology

—tales created in the minds of primitive people who sought somehow to explain the phenomena about them. Childlike contemplation of the universe—of the stars, the moon, the lightning, the thunder—brought into being rude bits of fiction, bold nature myths which were gradually elaborated into complex and fascinating traditions.

The word "mythology" comes from the Greek word *mythos,* meaning fable. It is, then, a system of fabulous or fanciful opinions concerning nature, deities, beliefs—concerning man himself. The Indians have exquisite myths about the North Wind, the Hare, the spirit of Dawn. Nothing makes more delightful reading than the mythology of the Greeks—the beautiful myths regarding the beginning of things, the myths and legends of the gods. The tales that filter through Mexican mythology are stiff, cruel. In Buddhist Asia one finds myths that are at once exaggerated and artistic. And the Australians in the shade of the *gunyeh* relate ancient myths that are puerile, obscene, monstrous—born in the souls of savage myth-makers of long ago.

A myth in ancient times grew out of any little incident in nature, was related by the "wise man" of the tribe and promptly elaborated by the imaginative multitude. There is the robin, for instance, with its inexplicable bright-red breast. To the primitive mind, no bird's breast is red without reason. Therefore the tale was fabricated that the bird daily bears a drop of water to quench the flames of hell, and the red is his mark of distinction!

The Chippewas have many beautiful myths concerning man. There was a time when any Chippewa Indian you met would have told you that sleep was caused by Weeng, a giant insect that one could actually see on a huge tree in the woods. It made a soft, murmuring sound with its wings and caused sleep by sending a host of fairies to beat drowsy foreheads with their tiny clubs. A charming bit of mythology, created long ago by some imaginative Indian who sought to explain the mystery of sleep to his fellows.

Since myths go back to the remotest antiquity and carry

with them through the centuries fragments of traditions, beliefs, customs, fears, superstitions, they offer the investigator a valuable source of information concerning early man. Mythology is, in a way, a relic or a history of the thoughts of our ancestors. Myth-makers, in their skill, built up veritable monuments of tradition, preserved by being handed down by word of mouth from generation to generation. Popular myths still exist among civilized peoples in the form of nursery tales such as "Jack the Giant Killer," "Beauty and the Beast," "The Lion and the Mouse," "Cinderella," and others. Many of our present-day superstitions also had their origin in ancient myths.

One might say that mythology is a part of history, though apart from it. Legends are usually confined to one or two particular localities; but myths spread everywhere, drawing their colourful threads through the pattern of life, weaving themselves eternally into the religions of mankind, finding a way into literature and civilization.

Folklore, in its fullest sense, is the remains of ancient mythology—the traditional lore which has survived in a certain locality, among a certain people. Properly speaking, folklore concerns itself solely with the legends, customs, beliefs, and traditions of the folk. Indeed, among unlettered peoples, folklore takes very largely the place of literature, and, like literature, reflects in marvellously accurate pictures the life of the people.

The study of folklore reveals strange relics of thought and of custom, primitive fancies and beliefs that are surprisingly close to the surface of civilized life. In certain sections of Germany and England there are mothers who actually believe that their children will grow up to be thieves if their nails are cut before their first year. Mr. Andrew Lang tells of the widow of an Irish farmer in Derry who, not so very long ago, killed the horse that belonged to her deceased husband. When someone remonstrated with her she said, "Would you have my man go about on foot in the next world?" It seems that there exists in this locality a belief that a faithful horse will find its master if permitted to follow him into the next world. A fragment of a myth, undoubtedly, which found its way into the folklore of the people. Incidentally, it is notable that both in England and in the United States the horse of a dead soldier or distinguished person is usually led behind the coffin to the grave.

It was found necessary in tracing back to their source the manners and customs of man, to study the folklore and mythology of all countries, of all peoples. And you shall see in the pages that follow how both these factors—folklore and mythology—influence in a thousand little ways the things we do and say to-day. They are like mighty links, forged in the furnace of time, binding even us of the twentieth century to a chain of tradition that reaches far back into antiquity.

The Sacred Writings.—When we search the sacred writings as a source of information concerning primitive man and his mode of living, we have reached at last a written history. No longer is it necessary to depend upon archæology, upon folklore and mythology and oral traditions for our facts. We are now able to read what the people wrote about themselves, about their neighbours, about their customs and beliefs.

As you know, the world existed for many generations without a word of history being written—history, that is, as we interpret it to-day. Oral history was carried by word of mouth from one generation to another—a method of instruction, strangely enough, referred to in the Bible:

> Tell ye your children of it, and let your children tell their children, and their children another generation. (Joel, I, 3.)

The oldest existing sacred writings are, perhaps, (with the exception of those from which Moses compiled the earlier chapters of Genesis) the Vedas. These are the sacred books of the Hindus. In the Vedas we find a picture of the simple nature worship of the people of India in their early history.

Moses, as the first historian, teaches us a great deal

concerning the manners and customs of man in the era preceding Christianity. He wrote about 1500 B.C. He wrote for his people and of his people—and of their neighbours in other lands. He built history with the bricks of human nature—and each one of those bricks is pure gold to the student who turns back the pages of the past and reads in the story of life.

To Moses we are very largely indebted for the preservation of the tale of man's creation. Moses—the teller of tales, the leader of men, the prophet, the historian—wrote for future generations to read the inspired tale of the beginning of man.

From 1500 to 500 B.C. the writers of the Old Testament are the only historians. They wrote as though inspired, as probably they were. And though their pens were dipped frequently into the wells of fancy and imagination, these writers wrote truthfully of many things and they give us an excellent picture of the life of their period.

There are other sacred writings from which we glean information concerning man and manners. The Talmud, a commentary on the Bible, clears up many doubtful points. It took many rabbis many years to write the Talmud, explaining in detail the laws of the Bible and making it easier for the Hebrews to understand and follow the laws brought them from the Mount by Moses.

The Scandinavians have some very beautiful myths and legends, preserved for many generations by word of mouth but set down at last in their sacred writings. The Romans have some rare old writings on sacred subjects, as have also the Egyptians. An earnest attempt has been made to investigate all existing sacred writings and obtain from them whatever material would prove valuable in the preparation of this work.

These, then, have been our sources of information. We have studied the relics of other ages as brought forth from the bowels of the earth by the archæologist. We have studied prehistoric man—not as a fossil or a museum exhibit, but as he must have lived and laboured in his daily life. We have followed the threads of tradition into many lands, over vast periods, through labyrinths of folklore and mythology; and we have extracted from these journeys some startling facts which long lay buried beneath the intellectual débris of the generations. And we have delved into the sacred writings for information, coming at last upon written history and its wealth of valuable facts.

We have, in a word, worked our way behind the scenes of life, beginning with the prologue and going through the three great acts, or ages—barbarism, mediævalism, and modernism. The finale is left to the future.

WHAT IS SOCIETY?

The word "society" taken in its fullest sense means people as a whole—human beings. We are all members of society. Only the hermit or the outcast on a desert island can claim exemption.

By his very nature man is gregarious. He may, if food is scarce, eat furtively and alone in some corner; but when his appetite is satisfied and he comes from his hiding place to sit before the fire, he wants some of his own kind near him. After all, isn't this true of all nature? Birds fly in flocks, bees in droves, locusts in great swarms. Sheep herd together, and wolves gather in packs. Nature has created separate species and has instilled in each a liking for its own kind.

During the greater part of prehistory, man had no real social life, owing to the organic struggle—the material struggle for existence. He looked upon his nearest neighbour with fear, suspicion, distrust. He guarded his food and glared at any one who dared approach it. If there was a woman in his cave he watched her too, and probably growled if she so much as attempted to take more than her allotted share of food.

Under circumstances such as these there could be no social life. Man depended not upon humanity but upon nature. The berry tree was of more importance than the man who sat a little distance away before his cave fire.

But nature proved treacherous. There were wild beasts who made it unsafe to search in the woods for berries. There were other, stronger savages who stole the food supply from the cave while the owner was gone—and perhaps carried along the woman, too. There were droughts and winds and storms. To fight enemies such as these, strength was needed. And when primitive man discovered that two were twice as strong as one, he saw the great value *to himself* of joining forces.

Thus did society rise out of the oldest human instinct—self-preservation. If two were twice as strong as one, how very strong five must be! Indeed, five could easily overcome Strong Arm who so persistently stole food and women. Yes, it was a good idea to join forces with one's neighbours.

And so a certain social cohesion entered early life. In regions where the climate is severe and the environment inhospitable, this social instinct came early. Men needed one another. But in the tropical jungles where food of some kind or other is practically always attainable, it developed slowly.

When man began to clan together there was probably always one head clansman, or leader—the strongest and most powerful man among them, no doubt. It was to him that the food supply was brought for distribution, to him that all disputes and problems were brought for solution. Since he had more skins than the others, since he was more powerful and more to be feared, he was treated with a certain amount of deference.

Naturally, there were outcasts in early society. The weak, the sick, the timid, the blind were ostrasized. They hindered rather than helped the clan. They were, one might say, "at the bottom of society." But the tall, strong, powerful man, on the other hand, belonged to the "favoured class." He could club an enemy to death. He could fling a huge beast over his shoulder and carry it to

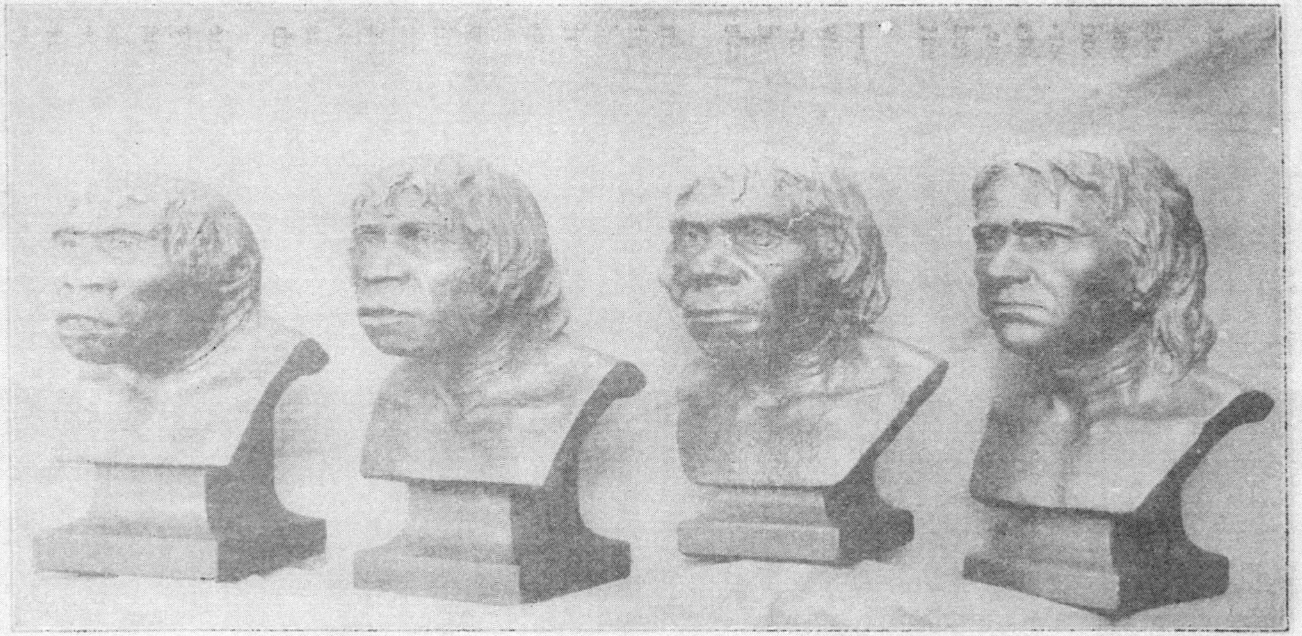

(Courtesy of American Museum of Natural History, New York)

The Four Predominating Types of Prehistoric Man.
Left to right: Pithecanthropus, Piltdown, Neanderthal, Cro-Magnon.

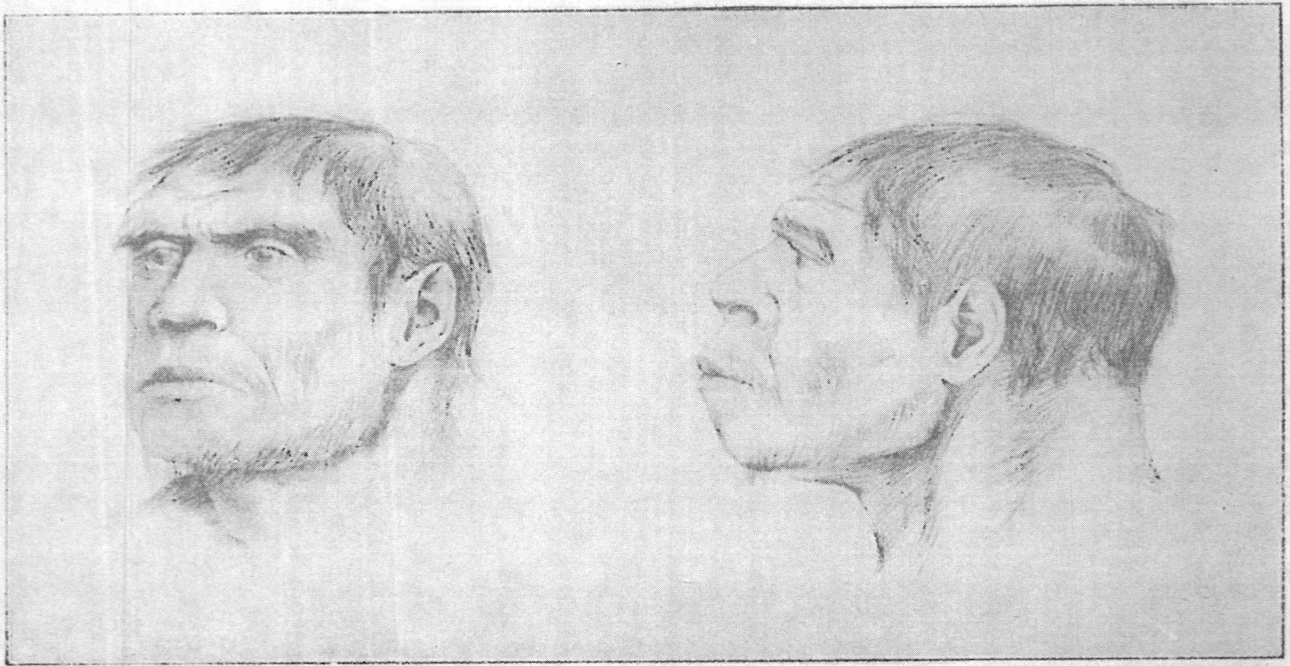

(Courtesy of American Museum of Natural History, New York)

Head of the Piltdown man, drawn by Stirling from McGregor's restoration.

the cave. He could steal a woman from some other clan. He was at the very "top of society."

A thousand external circumstances have been moulding and shaping society since the time of the head clansman. To-day the word society still means human beings, people, but it is generally associated in the mind of the multitude with caste, class, position, wealth. This will be taken up more definitely in a later chapter.

THE EARLY THOUGHT STAGES

History divides times into ages, or stages, of development. There are the four Glacial Ages which are estimated to extend from 500,000 to 35,000 B.C. There are the Palæolithic (Old Stone) Age and the Neolithic (New Stone) Age. There are the great Bronze Age and the Age of Iron.

But the writer on the manners and customs of man finds it advisable to divide time into thought stages. As we study prehistoric man we see reason struggling everywhere to exist. We find man groping about in his crude and child-like way for a reason for things. Freed from the material struggle for existence, he began to think; and it was then that he laid the foundation upon which civilization was later to be built.

The first mankind was, of course, in the lowest status of savagery. There was no articulate speech. There was no knowledge of fire. There was no defence against animals. Restricted necessarily to tropical territories, these early men subsisted upon raw nuts and fruits.

To this writer it would seem that the first great thought stage centred about the discovery of fire. This discovery certainly represents one of the greatest strides forward in primitive life. Man was able to extend his habitat. He was able to include flesh and fish in his dietary. He was able at last to leave the forests and wander along the shores.

The power of fire was probably made known to man

through the conflagration caused by lightning, or through the spontaneous combustion of vegetable materials in a state of fermentation. Living craters, belching fire; or the accidental striking together of two flints, producing a spark which caused a conflagration, may have revealed the secret. No one can know for certain. We do know, however, that man, exercising his power of thought, learned the use of fire and so took a step ahead in process of evolution.

The next great thought stage brought forth implements of defence against wild beasts. It probably took thousands of years for our ancestors to reach that point of intellect which made it possible for them to take the sinew of an animal and use it as a cord to fasten a sharp flint to the end of a stick. That gave them a tooth longer, sharper, and more powerful than the tooth of any animal in the jungle. It enabled man to stab an animal from an overhanging branch, himself in safety.

It is quite probable that primitive man learned of flesh as food by devouring dead animals, or appropriating half-eaten animals left behind by some gorged beast. Now, with the flint implement born of his thought, he was able to kill animals himself and thus be assured a new and valuable food supply. With an implement to kill his animal, and a fire to cook the flesh, he was two great steps in advance of the earliest brute man who wandered in the forests before him.

The flint-tipped spear gave way to the bow and arrow—still in the great thought age which provided man with a means for defence and a means for increasing his food supply. The bow and arrow made it possible for man, the two-legged animal, to bring down birds from the air, to shoot enemies at a distance, himself unseen, to kill any beast in the jungle, no matter how powerful. He could provide himself not only with food but with skins and materials for his home. And this great discovery, which made man king of the jungle, came out of *thought*.

Nature, you remember, proved treacherous to primitive man. There were sunshine and gentle rains; but there were also droughts when there was no water to be had, storms when one could not venture forth for food, seasons when the animals disappeared and he was faced by starvation. If only food could be preserved in time of plenty. If there were only some way to keep surplus food supply for a time when it would be needed.

Groping about for some solution to this problem, man entered the next great thought stage, which developed into the creation of the first crude pot. This marvellous discovery made a great advance upon social conditions. Man, with his new pottery, was able to store away foods for time of famine. It is barely possible that he ultilized his new pots as cooking utensils, in which case they exerted a civilizing influence.

The next great thought stage is associated with the domestication of animals and the use of irrigation in cultivating the soil. The dog was probably the first animal to be domesticated. Whether consciously or not, man exercised great judgment in domesticating the dog, as without it there could be no guardianship of the flocks, no faithful watchman of the herds.

In quick succession there followed the domestication of the sheep, ox, camel, horse. Man became a herdsman. Milk was added to his dietary. And using both ox and horse to help him, he began to plough the ground and prepare it for agriculture.

One can readily see the tremendous influence this great thought stage must have had upon man—upon society. Home came to mean more than just a rock shelter. Pride of possession was born. And man learned the great lesson of industry. The brute man gave way to a newer, finer man who worked and dreamed and thought; a man who recognized his family ties, no doubt, and his duties not only to himself but to society—to the people who lived with him and near him.

From this period onward there appears to have been progress in many lines and a multitude of minor arts and practices were developed. But for the next great thought stage we would select that era in which man's wonderful mind conceived the art of smelting iron. It now became possible to build houses, to make powerful tools and implements, to wall in cities as a means of protection. Nature created iron, but the thought or the mind of man took this iron, smelted it, shaped it into usable form and employed it in a thousand marvellous ways.

Having reached this thought stage, primitive man has a certain civilization. But as yet he has no means of communication. He is unable to make known his ideas or thoughts either to his own people or to his neighbours. The breaking down of this barrier brings us to the next great age of thought in the evolution of man.

Graphic signs were invented for the purpose of symbolizing events and making even the most abstruse ideas tangible. Systems of writing, crude but understandable, were developed. Man achieved a conquest over time—he was now able to transmit by written word the record of his deeds and thoughts to remote posterity.

And so, through many great thought stages man developed into a reasoning creature. Although it was not necessary for primitive man to think beyond the actual and immediate necessities of life, this first enforced thinking stirred man's remarkable brain and set both mind and imagination in motion. It was this power of thinking, of reasoning, of planning ahead, that separated man in his infancy from the lower beasts and made him a conqueror wherever he wandered.

PRIMITIVE IDEAS OF CREATION

In studying the early thought stages of man, it is interesting to notice the various myths or stories of creation that were evolved in the primitive mind. For thousands of years before the rudest kind of picture writing was invented, the mind of man was busy speculating as to where he had come from—even as some of us to-day are still asking whence we came and whither we are going!

The legends of a beginning, of a first man, of a creator of things, were without doubt created in the imagination of some tribal "wise man" and handed down by oral tradition through one generation after another. There may have been a little fact mixed up with the fiction—a natural phenomena, perhaps, or some strange coincidence. But the legends, after much repetition, came to be regarded as truth. Instead of being set down as fancy born in the mind of man, they were set down as history to be taught and believed. We find these myths still lingering among certain tribes and peoples. As with custom, we do not readily give up the old for the new.

It is said that in Australia stories of the flood are exceedingly common among all the tribes. There is one tribe that has a tradition a little different from all the others. Members of it tell the traveller that once a long time ago, *they* had a wonderful hunting ground on the banks of a river where game was plentiful and where the members of the tribe could hunt in safety. Some protective spirit pervaded the place and none of their number was ever killed. But one day when the men of the tribe went to the old hunting ground they found that one bank of the river had disappeared and the sea was flowing in. And the animals had somehow grown scarce; very little food could be found. The men instantly interpreted this as an omen, a warning and they quickly deserted the spot.

One can see precisely what happened in this instance. The river was probably swelled by recent storms and overflowed, meeting the sea. The animals, very naturally, went further back into the forests where they would be safe. But the primitive mind would not have been satisfied with so simple an explanation. Supernatural powers must have had something to do with it!

There are, of course, many variations of the flood or deluge story. The Eskimo believe that the souls of the dead are encamped around a large lake in the sky which, when it overflows, causes rain upon the earth. If at any time the floodgates should burst, a universal deluge would result. They believe also that at one time the world had been tilted over and all men drowned except one. To prove this they tell of the bones of whales which were found on their mountains.

The Mandan Indians have a deluge myth. According to Catlin, they celebrate every year in elaborate pantomime the subsidence of the great waters.

The Minnetarrees of North America believe that at first everything was water and there was no earth at all. Then the first man, the "Never-Dying-One" who is known also as the "Lord of Life" sent a great red-eyed bird down into the waters to bring up the earth. What a huge bird he must have been to bring up the earth in his beak!

The Delawares of North America imagined that at one time they all lived under one great lake where they would still be living to-day if one of their number hadn't discovered a hole through which they all crawled, reaching the surface of the earth at last.

Not all of the North American Indians have deluge myths. Their notions concerning creation are much diversified. Many tribes believed that their ancestors existed within the bosom of the earth, sometimes in human shape, but more often in the form of the rabbit, the woodchuck or the tortoise. These animals were reverenced by the early tribes.

The Mandans had a tradition that they lived at one time in a great cavity of the earth. One day, one of their young men climbed up the side of the cavity to the surface, by means of a slender vine. Delighted with what he saw, he returned and told his people of the upper world. There was an immediate rush to the vine and the people began to clamber up to the surface. Some reached the top, but one careless person gave the vine a wrench and it fell to the ground. There was no further means of escape. Those on the surface established a Mandan village; those in the bowels of the earth continue there to this very day.

The Abipones of South America believed that they had been created by an Indian like themselves. They spoke of him as "grandfather" because he lived so long ago. They fancied that he could still be seen in the Pleiades. Thus, when that constellation disappeared from the sky, they bewailed the illness of their grandfather, their creator. And when he reappeared in May there was feasting and merry-making.

The Greeks, always artistic, have a beautiful tradition concerning the origin of man. They represent Prometheus as moulding the first human beings from clay and giving them life by means of fire stolen from heaven. The Mandans, mentioned above, had a similar tradition. They believed that the Great Spirit formed two figures of clay which he dried and animated by the breath of his mouth. To one was given the name "First Man," to the other, "Companion."

It would be tiresome to allude to the many creation myths which have come down to us. But it is increasingly fascinating to the student to read these myths, and while reading marvel at the almost limitless power of the human imagination.

DAILY LIFE OF PRIMITIVE MAN

Let us now conjecture what daily life was like in primitive times. Perhaps we can steal quietly beside some rough-hewn cave and peer in upon the inhabitants.

See, there is a huge flat rock right in the centre of the cave—a "table," you will probably call it. There is a fragment of rock beside it, and on this a woman is sitting. Do not be afraid. She cannot see you. She does not know you are here. You belong to one age, she to another. Study her carefully, for you will meet her many times in the pages that follow.

Clothing she has none, unless you count the necklace of

claws strung around her neck. Her hair is heavy, coarse, knotted. Her hands and feet are large and powerful. She is gnawing at a bone—her dinner.

Glance quickly around the cave. You see those bright stones and shells? Probably a crude attempt at decoration. And there are some implements of bone—knives, fish hooks, arrows, even needles. That hole in the ground is for food. Between alternate layers of hot cinders are placed eels, herring, oysters—and over all a layer of fir branches. There are also nuts, cherries, and plums stored away somewhere.

Sssh! Here comes the master of the cave. Step aside while he enters. What a fierce, brawny fellow he is! He is carrying a carcass on his back. His hair is coarse and matted, like the woman's. His limbs are heavy and powerful. He looks as though he could crush us all like eggshells. He is very proud of that string of claws, teeth, and bits of carved bone encircling his waist, because he made it himself in the long evenings before the cave fire.

He is in the cave now, showing off the carcass to the woman, boasting, strutting about and beating his chest in his arrogance. Let us leave them for a moment and investigate the outside of the cave.

That rock at the entrance is for protection. At night it is rolled over against the hole to keep out prowling beasts, and the still more dangerous prowling human beings. If an enemy approaches during the day one of those smaller rocks is hurled down the hill on top of him. A safe home, this cave.

The huge heap behind the cave is merely a refuse ground. Here all the débris is thrown, sometimes not only from one cave but from many caves.

Does this give you a fair picture of primitive man in his daily life? These cave dwellers, you know, belong to a higher order of development than the brute men who wandered through the jungles from one place to another. They came only after the lapse of long ages of geologic change.

(Courtesy of American Museum of Natural History, New York)

Pro-Magnon man, from a painting by Charles R. Knight.

(Courtesy of American Museum of Natural History, New York)

Neanderthal man, from a painting by Charles R. Knight.

The first "home" was the place where primitive man brought his game when he killed it, ripped off its hide, made his flint implements, slept, ate, and lived. It is easy to suppose that the family tie was soon recognized instinctively, though in a crude and savage fashion. The attachment between the sexes is an instinct deeply ingrained in the human soul.

The tools and remains of these early cave people are found scattered over a large part of the surface of the globe. Vast numbers of stone implements, shaped by the hand of man, have been unearthed. These tools and implements and "household appliances" give us a definite clue to the wild state of those who made them—give us an excellent insight into daily life as it must have been in those days.

We know that man in the prehistoric centuries was a savage hunter, armed solely with weapons of flint and bone, living in nature-made homes such as caves and grottoes. He frequented the lake and river margins, always remaining near enough the forests to hunt his food. Perhaps he hunted and fished alone, carrying the spoils to his cave and dividing them with the woman and the children who shared that cave with him. But it is not improbable that two or more would hunt or fish in company for the sake of advantages thus obtained in coping with larger game and withstanding the attacks by those who wished to rob them of their spoils.

FEAR AND SUPERSTITION

You know how afraid children are of the dark. It makes no difference whether the child is a little pickaninny on some Southern plantation or a blustering little German fellow on his father's farm. If it is late and there are strange noises, or even if it is absolutely silent the child whimpers and looks around for the consoling companionship of a grown-up.

So it was with all mankind in the dawn of prehistory. Men were like children lost in the dark. They wandered alone and afraid in a land fringed with forests, haunted by huge beasts of prey; a land shrouded sometimes in the darkness of storms, blinded at other times by terrifying shafts of lightning. "Survival of the fittest" was more than a catch phrase in those days: it was the first law of life.

Is it any wonder that men feared, and that out of their fear grew vague superstitious notions? The wonder is that these superstitions have survived and that many of them are observed now, in an age of supposed enlightenment.

William J. Fielding says:

> The first emotions a child has are those of fear and surprise. Before we have the power to love or hate or comprehend, we are *able to be afraid.* This conforms to the defensive reactions of mankind's remote prehuman ancestors, who were protected by this prompting to fear and flee from ever-alert enemies.

What primitive man did not understand he feared. And there was much that he did not understand. The sun and the storm, the breeze and the calm were miracles. The uprooting of a tree by the wind was the act of some evil spirits. The stars were magic eyes that saw everything, and the moon was a god—silent and majestic.

In his fear primitive man entered a state of superstitious bondage. The thunder, the tempest, the sudden attack of mysterious illness, the earthquake, the forest fire—these were more to the primitive mind than the mere natural forces working out their natural destiny. They were evil spirits, and dragons, and powers to be propitiated.

Man particularly feared illness and death. He did not understand them. Why should a man lie suddenly stiff and cold and silent, when no one had harmed him, when no beast had attacked him? Surely it must be due to the evil spirits.

The Navajos, for instance, ascribed death to the devil, Chinde. When death came to the Andaman Islands, the inhabitants shot arrows into the jungle to frighten away the spirits. The Veddas deserted their cave homes whenever any one in them died, as did also the Austrian Blackfellows and other savage hordes. Death was something alien to life and to the living; thus it was formidable and to be feared.

Many savage races even to-day do not believe in natural death, and if a man, no matter how old, dies without being wounded, they believe him to have been the victim of magic. Out of this belief has grown the custom of "sucking out the evil" which exists among savage races all over the world. When a man is ill, he attributes his sufferings to some enemy or evil spirit within him—the spirit which ultimately will cause death. Therefore the lips are applied to that part of the man which is affected and the evil is "sucked out."

This method of treatment is used among the savages of Paraguay and Brazil, among the Eskimo and Indian tribes, among the savages of Australia, South Africa, and elsewhere. Sometimes the witch doctor, or the medicine man, is called in to do the sucking-out, and instances have been recorded when the medicine man extracted a bit of stone or other substance from his mouth and declared that it was the evil that had been causing all the pain!

The age-old nursery remedy of "Kiss it and make it well" is probably a lingering fragment of the custom of "sucking out evil." It seems a natural instinct to put a hurt finger or bruised arm to the lips.

Mr. Harris in his "Life of Charles I" says:

> Everyone knows the mischief superstition has produced in the world; gods of all sorts and kinds; sacrifices of beasts and of men; rites, ceremonies, and postures; antic tricks and cruel torments; with every other thing which, from time to time, has been falsely called by the name of religion, has arose from hence. It took its rise early in the world, and soon spread itself over the face of the earth; and few, very few, there were who were wholly free from it.

The first note in all superstitions is, of course, ignorance—an ignorance to which fear is closely allied. The true origin of superstition is to be found in primitive man's efforts to explain the phenomena about him; his wish to avoid evils he could not understand; his desire to propitiate fate and invite fortune; his attempts to pry into the future.

Being contagious, superstition quickly spread everywhere. What one man feared and suspected, his neighbour was bound to fear and suspect. And once a superstitious notion has taken possession of a people, it is the hardest thing in the world to shake it off.

Egypt, even at the height of its glory, even in its pioneer civilization, was a land steeped in superstition. The people believed in sorcery and in magic. No unexpected happening, no coincidence, was accepted as natural and proper. Some meaning was instantly attached to it.

Nor did Christianity dispel this bondage. The Church has itself been a fountain head of superstition. There is, for instance, the reason given for the trembling of the aspen leaf which, you know, is proverbial. Christ is alleged to have been crucified on aspen wood. Because of this the boughs of aspen trees have from that time "been filled with horror and trembled ceaselessly." This curious myth is actually accepted as truth by many people.

America, having blazed new trails, having built for herself a world within a world, is curiously free from many of the superstitions of the Old World, yet many customs here in America are tinged by primitive belief. It is interesting to see how widely we have deviated from the original meanings of certain customs and superstitions; yet we observe them slavishly, without question.

There very frequently crops up, even in this advanced twentieth century of ours, an example of superstitious reasoning of the kind which fostered the Salem witchcraft delusion. The newspapers, which every morning spread history before millions of people, have a great deal to do with it.

Lord Carnarvon, searching a royal Egyptian sepulchre in quest of funeral treasures that will reveal new secrets of early man, is bitten by a poisonous insect and dies. Instantly the whole world encouraged by the newspapers becomes interested, digs up interesting but obsolete superstitious facts, and boldly declares: "Lord Carnarvon had to pay the price each one pays who dares to touch the Oriental dead."

Reasoning people recognize this as a bit of superstitious nonsense, of course, but not so the multitudes. People put their heads together and whisper that there must be some truth in it. And why? Just because it is man's age-old heritage to fear that which he does not understand, to attribute to some evil power that which he cannot otherwise explain.

And yet, what would modern life be like if we were robbed of all our superstitions? Isn't superstition—harmless superstition—a sort of luxury for the imagination? We would hate to think of a wedding without the handful of rice; of a Hallowe'en without a secret wish before the mirror; of a four-leafed clover that would not bring good luck!

Not even civilization's greatest thinkers have been free from superstition. Rousseau imagined that a phantom walked continually by his side. William Blake, poet, mystic, and artist, insisted that he was a brother of Socrates and that he had talked with Christ. Sir Walter Scott would not visit Melrose Abbey by moonlight because of the superstitious notion that bogies were there. Napoleon was afraid of black cats. Peter the Great had a horror of crossing bridges. Cecil Rhodes would never try on new clothes because of the superstition that to do so would bring ill luck or disappointment.

Thus has superstition, born of the fear and ignorance of primitive man, found its way into all countries and among all peoples, goose-stepping through the ages side by side with civilization, not only creating custom but helping it survive.

THE AGE OF DREAM INTEREST

The great philosopher Nietzsche says:

> In our sleep and in our dreams we pass through the whole thought of earlier humanity. I mean, in the same way that man reasons in his dreams, he reasoned in the waking state many thousands of years. The first *causa* which occurred to his mind in reference to anything that needed explanation, satisfied him, and passed for truth. In the dream this atavistic relic of humanity manifests its existence within us, for it is the foundation upon which the higher rational faculty developed. The dream carries us back into earlier states of human culture, and affords us a means of understanding them better.

People have always been interested in dreams. To the savage mind the dream was a symbol, a sign. We to-day ponder over our dreams and search them for a meaning. We like to believe that the dream is a prophecy, or a warning, or a sign of some kind.

If we could but glimpse behind the histories of nations and the lives of individuals, we would find that dreams have played a conspicuous part in their destinies. Like superstition, dreams early appealed to the imagination of men, and it is now believed by authorities that the elaborate conceptions of mythology, folklore, and tradition are the day dreams and night dreams of young humanity, blended together into beautiful, complex tales.

It is interesting to contemplate the primitive man or woman, curled asleep by the fire, dreaming dreams and seeing visions. What did he dream of? What did he see? His spirit—some part of him—seemed to separate from his body and soared away to some beautiful spot where he joined old friends who were dead or lost. And with them he did the fascinating things we all do in our sleep.

And when he awoke he found himself once again at his fireside, alone, with nothing more tangible than the memory of his dream to prove that he had seen his friends at all. How amazed he must have been! And startled, perhaps, that so extraordinary a thing should have happened to him. Of course, he told his friends and neighbours of his strange adventures, and they told him of adventures they too had had in sleep. They must have thought about it and discussed it with one another; and finally they came to the conclusion that the people in their midst who died (and whom they saw in dreams) were not really dead but had merely departed to another more beautiful world. Man for the first time felt that he had a spirit that could quit the body.

Bad dreams, following too much meat, perhaps, and nightmare with its equivalent horrors, probably brought about the belief in an underworld of bad spirits. Thus man came to have a heaven and a hell of his own imagining, way back in the dawn of civilization. We can scarcely realize what an importance even the simplest dreams had to the savage. They were to him reality; the events that took place in them were to him as real as those that took place in his waking hours.

We can easily see how the man who dreamed a great deal, and who filled in the gaps in his stories with facts of his own imagining, was looked upon with awe and reverence. Men listened to him for hours, and if he warned them against hunting in a certain district or eating a certain food, they heeded his warning. He became a sort of magician, a mystery man, a priest.

In Madagascar even to-day the people throughout the whole island pay a religious regard to dreams. They imagine that their good demons tell them in their dreams what ought to be done and warn them of what ought to be avoided. And have we not books right in this country that portend "to interpret the dreams and visions that come to you in sleep?"

It is no exaggeration to say that dreams have profoundly influenced the customs and manners of man. Not only did man first conceive of a soul—of a detached spirit—in dreams, but since the earliest times man has associated his dreams either with divine or diabolic inspiration. The influence of the dream will make itself felt in many of the customs that are later to be discussed.

SYMBOLISM

Someone once described early life as a "succession of symbols." Everything seems to be a meaning or a sign for something else. Every happening, no matter how trivial, seems a warning, or a prophecy, or a sign. A symbol *is* a sign; symbolical pictures and ideas are a language—the natural language of primitive man and of our own primitive personality.

Symbolism, as a language, is universally understood. To dig a hole in the ground and bury one's hatchet or knife is instantly interpreted as a sign of friendliness, of peace. "Burying the hatchet" therefore becomes a symbol of friendliness, just as smoking the peace pipe with the Indian is a symbol of friendliness. Similarly, closed lips mean silence, and when we wish someone to remain silent we place our fingers to the lips as a symbol of silence. The black cat is recognized as a symbol of evil and disappointment because witches at one time were supposed to use black cats in their divinations.

The whole fabric of religion is held together by symbolism, as we shall later discover. Because lightning flashed down upon the earth in a snakelike zigzag, the early Egyptians worshipped the snake or the serpent. The sea, in early life, served to symbolize the great gulf between life and death. And the fish, because it is able to reach both shores, has for centuries been a most sacred symbol in Christianity. Salt, too, became a symbol of sanctity; not only because it has a preserving power but because the sea is salt. Even to-day holy water is salted.

In the creation of custom, symbolism has played a conspicuous part. In prehistory when one savage fellow met another with whom he did not wish to fight but with whom he wished to join forces, he dropped his weapon and extended his right hand—his weapon hand—as a symbol of friendliness. The original meaning and purpose of this symbol has long since passed into forgetfulness, but we still extend the right hand as a sign, or symbol, of welcome.

Traditions were preserved in Indian life by the "runner" who wandered from tribe to tribe with his tales. He belonged to no one tribe, yet to all of them.

There are existing to-day many formalities in connection with our customs which are really acts of symbolism descended from remote antiquity. This is particularly true in our wedding and funeral customs. Burning candles near a corpse is a symbolic relic of the days when fires were built around a corpse to keep away the evil spirits. The yew tree is planted in the churchyard or graveyard because its unchanging verdure is symbolic of the resurrection.

In our wedding customs, the ring is symbolic of what was once the yoke of man's absolute authority over the bride. The orange blossoms are plainly a symbol meant to bring fruitfulness to the union, the blossoms coming as they do from one of the most prolific of all fruit-bearing trees. The honeymoon tour, beginning with the hasty departure after the ceremony, symbolizes the act of stealing the bride and carrying her away—once an actuality. Symbols, all symbols!

MAGIC IN PRIMITIVE LIFE

In the evolution of the human race, magic rose before religion. Before he coaxed his deities by the soft insinuation of sacrifice, worship, and prayer, man tried to bend nature to his will by the force of spells and enchantments. The idea of courting the favours of nature and the deities by offerings and prayer came only after a long age of magic.

Of all the natural phenomena there are, perhaps none which modern man feels himself less able to control than the rain, the wind, and the sun. Yet primitive man believed all of these to be under his control, believed he could influence them at will. Systems of magic were formulated for the purpose of driving away storms, lightning, wind; for inducing rain; for causing the sun to shine.

The magicians of the twentieth century are the inventors and scientists who make artificial lightning, who have made it possible to fly across the continent in twenty-four hours; who use friendly microbes to kill those that injure us. But the magicians of primitive times were the savage rain doctors who attempted to wring showers from cloudless heavens, medicine men who sucked illness from the body and sent the evil spirits scurrying through magic incantations, sorcerers who played upon the child-like, credulous minds of the multitudes.

Controlling the Elements.—Magic might be defined as an elementary process of reasoning. Primitive man did not understand the storm. He was afraid of it. Therefore he shot poisoned arrows at it to drive it away. The Namaquas particularly feared the storm and considered it an evil spirit who had come to harm them. They would gather together and shoot their arrows into the sky, certain that the storm would become frightened and leave. They combated the storm as they would any human enemy.

Many primitive tribes believed they could control the wind, make it blow or be still, according to their wishes. There were many elaborate ceremonials for this purpose. In New Britain when a sorcerer wished the wind to blow in a certain direction, he threw burnt lime into the air, chanting a weird song. If a Hottentot desired the wind to stop, he took one of his fattest skins and hung it on the end of a pole in the belief that by blowing the skin down the wind would tire itself and lose all its force. Travellers tell us that this custom still exists among certain Hottentot tribes.

The Payaguan Indians of North America feared the wind that threatened to blow down their huts. Whenever a fierce wind blew down upon them, they rushed against it with firebrands, believing that in this way they could stop its flight.

In his book, "Die Völker des östlichen Asien" (vol. IV, p. 174), Bastian tells of a pass in the Peruvian Andes known as Andahuayllas where one can see two old iron rings, each on a great ruined tower. The towers stand on opposite hills, and in days gone by it was the custom to stretch a net from one tower to the other by means of the iron rings. The purpose of the net was to catch the sun.

Why they should have wanted to ensnare the sun we do not know and can only guess, but the fact remains that they actually did attempt to catch it and built tall towers for this very purpose.

The Bank Islanders have a unique method of "making sunshine." They take a very round stone, called a *vat loa* or sunstone, wind red braid about it and stick owl feathers in it to represent the rays. Singing the proper magic spell, they hang this mock sun in a high tree. No matter how dark and cloudy the day may be, the sun is expected instantly to make its appearance.

• *Making Rain by Magic.*—In torrid climates where rain is of extreme importance it has been an age-old custom among savage tribes to "make rain"—that is, force rain to fall through magic and sorcery.

In Halmahera, near New Guinea, there is a ceremony for making rain in which a wizard appointed by the people plays a conspicuous part. He takes a branch from a certain kind of tree and dips it in water. Chanting magic words, he scatters the moisture from the dripping bough over the ground. Rain is expected to follow. If the rain does not follow, it is the wizard and not the method that is blamed.

Mock thunder and lightning form part of the rain charm in Russia and Japan. In a village near Dorpat, in Russia, when rain was wanted it was at one time the custom for three men to climb into the fir trees in an old sacred grove. One drummed with a hammer on a kettle or cask to imitate thunder; the second made sparks fly by knocking two firebrands together and thus simulated lightning; the third had a bunch of twigs with which he sprinkled water from a vessel. All phases of a rainstorm were imitated in the firm belief that an actual rainstorm would be precipitated.

It was the custom of the natives of the Japanese Alps to climb to the top of Mount Jonendake, one of the most imposing peaks in the range, and roll down great masses of rock as part of their ceremony for rain. They also built bonfires on the cliffs in crude imitation of lightning.

The Zulu rain doctors, on the other hand, had a ceremony for frightening lightning from the sky. They themselves were afraid of it; through magic they tried to make the lightning fear them. The rain doctor stood alone on a small mound, a branch of some tree in his hand, and whistled into the sky. The lightning, hearing his magic whistle and seeing the staff in his hand, was supposed to become frightened and run away.

The Greeks and Romans, like other peoples, sought to obtain rain by magic. Even to-day, when a drought has lasted for a long time it is customary for the Greeks in Thessaly to send a procession of children to all the wells and springs in the neighbourhood in a picturesque ceremonial for the purpose of inviting rain. At the head of the procession walks a pretty girl, adorned with flowers. At each well she is sprinkled with water while all the other children sing magic rain hymns. A similar custom is observed in certain sections of Bulgaria and Roumania.

In Arcadia, when the corn and trees were parched with drought, the priest of Zeus dipped an oak branch into a spring on Mount Lycæus. The water, troubled by the branch, sent up a misty cloud from which rain fell upon the land. One sees here the early gropings of primitive science, seeking for a means of expression.

It was mainly in torrid countries, and in lands where droughts frequently occur, that rainmaking was practised. In the tropical island of Java where there are rainfalls in abundance, ceremonies for the making of rain are unknown. But it is interesting to observe that there are ceremonies for the prevention of rain. The rain doctor of Java exerts his professional powers in regulating the behaviour of the rain clouds.

A curious mixture of religion and sorcery, of sacrifice and magic is evident in the rain magic practised by the Athenians. To avert drought and dry heat, they sacrificed meat to the seasons. This meat was boiled, not roasted as ordinarily. The Athenians probably conceived in some dim way the idea of transmitting water to the deities through the meat, which had been boiled in water, and that it would be sent down to them again in the form of rain.

Punishing the Deities.—In savage life, and this is true even of existing savage races, deities are created for the sole comfort and pleasure of man. They are expected to do man's bidding. They are feared only in proportion to the amount of coincidence which has made them seem powerful.

Therefore, it was quite customary among savages to punish recalcitrant deities and gods. In several Japanese villages it was the custom to destroy the image of a god and hurl it ignominiously into the parched ricefield, if it remained deaf to the pleas for rain. The Chinese used to make a dragon of paper or wood to represent the rain god, and carry it around in procession. But if no rain fell, the procession ended in the tearing to pieces of the mock dragon. The Feloupes of Senegambia, even to-day when they want rain, are in the custom of dragging their fetishes around the fields until rain falls.

Sir James G. Frazer in his most fascinating "Golden Bough" tells an interesting story concerning this custom of punishing disobedient gods. He tells us that about the year 1710 the island of Tsong-ming, which belongs to the province of Nanking, was afflicted with a drought. The usual attempts were made to soften the heart of the local deity by burning incense sticks and making offerings. But when these attempts proved futile, the viceroy of the province became impatient and sent word to the idol that if rain did not fall by a certain day, he would have him turned out of the city and his temple would be destroyed.

The threat had no effect. The skies remained cloudless. And the enraged viceroy ordered the temple shut up and the doors sealed. The people were forbidden to make offerings of any kind to the obdurate deity. This seemed to have the desired effect, for rain began to fall soon after, and the god was reinstated!

It is amusing to note, in this connection, how very careful the early Greeks were to keep their gods sober. They made it a rule to pour honey, but never wine, on the altars of their sun god. They realized how much depended upon this god, and how important it was that he remain strictly sober.

The Uses of Imitative Magic.—By the term "imitative magic," used frequently by Sir James G. Frazer, is meant the working of magic by means of images. Thus, among the Battas of Sumatra, if a woman wants a child a doll is made of wood and this the woman holds in her lap while the wizard chants some magic words to induce birth. The wooden image of a child is used by many tribes in magical ceremonies to induce childbirth.

Some authorities refer to this type of magic as "mimetic magic." It is based upon the principle that like produces like. The most widespread and familiar use of this type of magic is in harming or destroying enemies by making images, or effigies, of them, and injuring or destroying the image at will.

The Malays believe that the most effective method of causing the death or illness of an enemy is to stick a pin into the heart of a wax figure or image of him. If he wishes to cause dissension between a husband and wife, the Malay makes two wax figures resembling them, breathes upon them and puts them on a shelf back to back. He imitates in effigy what he would like to happen in reality. This custom is still observed among the Malays.

The Ojibwa Indians have a similiar custom. They believe that as the image suffers, so does the man. A world-wide superstition of the civilized races to-day is that a magic sympathy exists between a man and any severed portion of his person. We often hear a man whose arm or leg is amputated complain of pain in the missing member. This would appear to be a remnant of the imitative magic of other days.

Regarding the Ojibwa Indians, a wooden image of the

enemy is made and a needle is run through its head or heart. The belief is that the person against whom this magic is directed will be seized with pain. If it is intended that the enemy be killed, the image is burned or buried, magic words being uttered over it.

The savage has a superstitious dread of the magic words used in the ceremonies for injuring or destroying enemies. These words, used in imitative magic to wreak vengeance or destruction upon an enemy, correspond to nothing in modern life so much as the curse. The modern man of primitive personality will curse his enemy, and will feel relieved and satisfied at having done so. Isn't this a survival of imitative magic?

The man of to-day who is roundly cursed by some enemy will probably shrug his shoulders and grin; but not so the savage against whom a magic curse is uttered. So dreaded were the words directed against the person whose image was destroyed in savage life, that men and women have actually been known to die of fright. This was a form of psychology unconsciously employed by the savage mind.

Imitative magic was early used in hunting and in sowing. In the Interior of Sumatra it is a custom among the women who do the sowing to allow their hair to hang loose. The purpose of this is to induce the rice to grow luxuriant and have long stalks. In ancient Mexico it was customary to give festivals in honor of the goddess of maize. During the festival the women wore their hair unbound, shaking it and tossing it in the dances, the pantomime being a subtle plea to the goddess to make the tassel of the maize grow as profusely as the women's hair.

In British Columbia, if the fish do not come in due season, the Indians have a wizard make an image of a fish which is placed in the water with great ceremony. Care is taken to place it in the direction from which the fish are expected to come.

A missionary who spent two years in British Columbia tells of an occasion when he actually witnessed this primitive type of imitative magic. The Indians of this region subsist largely upon fish. There was a great scarcity of fish during one particular season, and the Indians could not understand it. Formerly, at that particular season there had always been an abundance; now there was practically none. They had a long conference and finally came to the conclusion that magic was needed to induce the fish to come.

Accordingly, they made a wooden image in the form of a swimming fish and with much ceremony placed it in the water. The following day there was a terrific rainstorm, and when the rains cleared away the fish began to come in vast numbers. It seems that some obstruction upstream had held them back, and that the rain had removed this obstruction. The missionary, having proved this later to his entire satisfaction, tried to explain it to the Indians. But they refused absolutely to reason. They were mad with joy. They had practised magic, and the magic had worked. They made huge wooden images and placed them as offerings in the water. So it has always been: civilized man seeks for a cause; savage man accepts without reasoning.

In the "Golden Bough" Sir James G. Frazer tells of a tree in Central Australia which is known as the Blind Tree. The natives have a tradition that this tree sprang up to mark the spot where a blind man had died years ago. They believe that if it were cut down all the people would become blind. It serves a very definite purpose in imitative magic: if one native wished to deprive another of his sight, all he need do was go to the Blind Tree, rub it, and make his wish. The enemy would instantly become blind.

Primitive man, like the savage of to-day, evidently was not interested in whether or not his imitative magic achieved the result desired. He was probably satisfied to torture the image, feeling certain that the person must have felt the torture also, whether he showed signs of it or not. It was a personal satisfaction. Burning in effigy, piercing

(Courtesy of the American Museum of Natural History, New York)

"Dawn of the Stone Age."

An interesting exhibit at the American Museum of Natural History.

(Courtesy of American Museum of Natural History, New York)

Prehistoric Swiss lake dwellings, erected over flowing water for purposes of sanitation and defense. A model by M. Götzinger.

clay images with pins, melting waxen figures before fire, satisfied his barbarous egotism—and undoubtedly kept him from doing mischief.

Imitative magic played a part in medicine also. For instance, a Dyak medicine man who wishes to cure someone who is ill will lie on the ground and pretend to be dead. Other medicine men will bind him up in mats, take him out of the hut, and deposit him on the ground. After an hour or so the medicine men loosen the bindings and the pretended dead man imitates the process of coming back to life. As he recovers slowly, the sick man is supposed to recover with him. So potent is superstition that in many cases the sick man does actually recover.

The Servian and Bulgarian peasants practise a curious bit of imitative magic, as amusing as it is curious. The women take the copper coins from the eyes of a corpse, wash them in wine or water, and give the liquid to their husbands to drink. This renders the husbands blind to the wives' faults!

We have mentioned these instances of imitative magic, and of primitive magic for the control of the elements, to show the firm hold that this type of reasoning had taken upon the mind of man before religion took its place. It would seem that man has never quite overcome the love of magic. There is always a lure in the supernatural, the uncanny, the ghostly. The spirit of make-believe which is ever present in children would appear to be a survival of the make-believe in primitive life. Did you ever know of a boy who didn't love to "play Injun," or a girl who didn't enjoy fussing over her dolls and pretending they were real?

Magic is part of our primitive heritage, and we should be glad to accept it as such. The miracles of modern science are simply magic of another sort—a reasoning magic instead of the superstitious magic of primitive man.

THE BIRTH OF FAITH

No one can possibly estimate the part faith has played in the humanizing, the civilizing, of man. Faith has led us away from blind superstition and fear; it has delivered us from cannibalism, from human sacrifice, from all the horrors of primitive life. It has, in a word, changed us from beast to man.

Faith was born when man for the first time realized the futility in attempting to force nature to do his bidding. A little shrewder than his fellows, he probably saw that the magical ceremonies, the sacrifices and incantations, the pleas and offerings, did not really produce results. Why cling to beliefs that were so often contradicted by experience? The silent procession of the stars seemed in no way affected by his incantations; the rain still fell; the sun still rose in the morning and still set at night; man was still born and still died.

It was not as easy as it might seem to detect the fallacies at first. If rites were observed by a certain tribe to help the sun rise in the morning, those rites would be accepted as worthy of perpetual observance, for the sun never failed to rise. The primitive mind did not reason that the sun would rise even if the rites were omitted.

But the things that didn't happen balanced those that did. Rain sticks failed to produce rain. Wizards used all their professional skill in vain attempts to control the storm and the wind. Slowly there came to primitive man realization that it was not he who guided the earth and the heavens in their course. He realized that friends and foes alike succumbed to a force stronger than any he could wield; that men were as puppets in the palm of a destiny which they were powerless to control.

How like a child primitive man must have been as he felt himself cut adrift from his ancient moorings! We can see him groping for a reason for things, doubtful, half afraid. Step by step we see him yielding his place as ruler of the elements. Now the rain, now the wind, now the thunder, now the sun—we see him accept them one by one as powers greater than himself, greater than the greatest tribal chief.

And it was then that man prostrated himself, entirely and absolutely, before the awe-inspiring, powerful, unknown being who ruled the universe without consulting the people who lived upon it. It was then that there was born in man a great, overwhelming faith in the mighty power that traced its handiwork on all sides. The trees, the mountains, the sky, the moon—man himself—were all masterpieces of this unknown's creation and dependent upon him for existence.

With this belief, with this faith, came peace. There was a great transition from magic to religion. But do not think that this change came quickly or suddenly. It required long ages of development, as did all of man's greatest steps in evolution. It is plain that the distinction between the natural and the supernatural must have been blurred in the early stages. Primitive man must have sought desperately to understand the higher power of which he now was vaguely conscious. It was not enough to have faith: he needed something tangible to which to pin that faith.

To the primitive mind nothing existed that could not be seen and touched. Eager to worship the power in which he now had faith, but knowing not what that power was, early man floundered about helplessly. He sought the unknown power in the familiar things about him. And there grew up a profusion of primitive religions, strange worships, all based upon mankind's first crude faith.

Like all things he did not understand, primitive man feared the power which he could not control. It probably startled him to think that some of the very things he used in his daily life were the abodes of that power—perhaps the power itself. Of course, it is easier to fear that which we cannot see or feel, so man began to build totem poles and create idols and fetishes as shells to house the spirit of the power or powers he worshipped.

This newer kind of worship—though still primitive—was entirely different from the blind, unreasoning magic and ceremonial that had gone before. Although primitive man beat his fetish and coaxed his idol, there was, nevertheless, a certain faith in that fetish or idol. In the earlier magic and ceremonial, man had attempted to bend nature to his will; now he coaxed his god—which, you understand, was merely the shell that housed the great unknown power—to intercede for him and persuade the unknown to furnish him with all good things.

There is probably no subject in the world about which opinions differ so much as religion—its origin, its development, its nature, and its meaning. Many writers believe that faith came only with Christianity, and they will probably scoff at this association of faith with the earliest forms of worship. Nevertheless, this writer believes that the primitive man who worshipped his fetish or his idol had faith. And because he had faith, his worship was a religion—a crude and savage religion, of course, but one that recognized a power higher than himself.

Ralph Waldo Trine says, "There is a golden thread that runs through every religion in the world." Doesn't he mean faith by that golden thread, and doesn't that thread go back to the time when man stood upon the brink of a new understanding and realized for the first time his own littleness?

THE FUSION OF MAGIC AND RELIGION

As has already been indicated, religion did not begin as a simple, logical thing. It began as a slight, and only partial, acknowledgment of powers superior to man. The perfect submission to one divine will in all things came later, when the jumble of quasi-religious ideas gave way to a deepening sense of man's littleness as compared with the vastness of the universe.

There runs through human thought a persistence which is astounding. What man once believes, he is loath to discredit. And habits are even more enduring than beliefs. Early man, believing utterly in his magic and his magical ceremonies, accepted his new faith with awe and fear; but he did not throw off the beliefs and customs which had preceded this faith. Magic simply faded into the background, but remained. And its influence has tinged all religions that have since developed.

One can easily understand how a confusion of magic and religion followed. Man became aware that he needed protection and advice, that he needed guidance and knowledge. In the eternal manner of "supplying the demand" there rose hosts of "wise men" and prophets, wizards and magicians, medicine men and sorcerers. Shrewd, cunning, perhaps a step in advance of their time, they played upon the simple credulity of their fellows. Themselves unable to understand the power which guided the universe, they invented modes of worship—strange, symbolic, tinged and alloyed with the stuff of which magic is made.

The acts of worship, devised by dreamers, magicians, priests, satisfied the souls of the people. They did not question the rites and ceremonies which they were obliged to practise. Their wizards and sorcerers were "wise men," were they not? They knew the way to please the gods; they knew how to coax them and frighten them and even, if the occasion demanded it, deceive them.

In ancient Egypt the magicians claimed the power of compelling even the highest gods to do their bidding. In India the sorcerers believe, even to-day, that they have power over the mightiest deities. How differently the history of the world might have been written had the magicians and sorcerers become more powerful than religion and the Church!

In the early fusion of magic and religion, the functions of the priest and the sorcerer were frequently combined. Religious and magical rites were performed simultaneously. Man was content to get what he wanted, whether by prayer or by incantation. It is but natural that fragments of magic should have survived in religion—fragments that are actually part of the worship of the civilized world to-day. We cannot study any existing religion without finding evidences of magic cropping up.

Professor Maspero remarks that "we ought not to attach to the word 'magic' the degrading idea which it almost inevitably calls up in the mind of the modern. Ancient magic was the very foundation of religion." Indeed, one might say that the age of magic represents one of the landmarks in the path of man's progress.

THE EVOLUTION OF RELIGION

"Religion," says H. G. Wells, "is something that has grown up with and through human association, and God has been and is still being discovered by man."

The beginning of religion and its development run on parallel lines with the development of the human race. All religions, it would seem, have built their structure around the emotional life of the people—fears, superstitions, traditions, magic ceremonials all being utilized. And if the magical and superstitious elements of religion have changed little, it is probably because there has been very little change in man's primitive personality.

Religion has played such a large part in the humanizing of man, and in the creation of his customs—social as well as secular—that a brief study of its origin and evolution is necessary in introducing this work. The subject is not an easy one to handle. To write of religion in any of its phases is to be drawn into a maze of widely varying notions and beliefs which have been accumulating from the earliest times. Almost everyone who has ever written of religion has advanced some favourite theory of his own. It is doubtful whether any two students of religion have ever had the same notion as to its origin, its exact and precise beginning.

But *can* one give an exact and precise fact concerning the origin of religion? Can one make any definite assertions at all? Who knows when religion started, or where it started, or how many times it came to the surface of savagery only to be buried once again under the barbarity of primitive reasoning? Since the very dawn of life man has poked timidly into the great unknown, accepting the fancies of his mind as facts. Who can be clever enough to judge how much of that fancy was faith—how much of it possessed the essence of true religion?

We must, then, throw all dogma to the winds. We must write of religion just a little differently than any one has before. Instead of concerning ourselves to any great extent with the great, familiar religions of mankind, such as Buddhism, Christianity, Judaism, Confucianism, we must search the simple faiths of man, starting with the first crude forms of worship, and see how these simple faiths have influenced thought, custom, civilization.

In other words, instead of presenting the various beliefs of the many writers on religion, or the interesting but unproved theories which have been advanced, we must present facts, truths, from the history of man himself. This will give us not only a better understanding of our primitive ancestors, but a finer, clearer, more beautiful conception of religion and all it has meant to man in his march through the ages.

The Oldest Forms of Religious Worship.—It would appear that there is nothing, either visible or imaginable, that man has not worshipped at some period in his development. There have been gods of every name and shape, of every nature and form. Man has worshipped trees and stones, flowers and fruit, the earth and the sky, the sun and the moon, saints and snakes, living men and dead ancestors. The gods, idols, deities, and objects of worship which we encounter are bewildering in number.

Groping about helplessly in a hostile world, vaguely conscious of a power greater than himself, primitive man very early felt the need for worship. But worship of what? The curiously marked stone over which he stumbled and on which he hurt his toes; the tree into which he climbed and thus escaped the jaws of some jungle beast; the stars at which he gazed at night, and which seemed somehow to motion and beckon to him; the reflection of himself in the water. He worshipped the things which were close to him, the things he could see and hear. Particularly did he worship the things he feared, and the things that hurt him, like the stone over which he stumbled.

One of the oldest forms of religious worship of which we have any definite knowledge is nature worship. Primitive man must have speculated a great deal about the living things he saw all about him. And out of this speculation grew many kinds of nature worship, including the curious Phallic worship which we shall presently discuss.

Nature worship is what the name implies—the worship of nature pure and simple. Primitive man worshipped the sun and the rain which made things grow; he worshipped the moon, the planets, the stars, the elements.

Early man believed that the changes of the moon portended change in the lot of mortals. Therefore, he feared the moon more than any other natural object. The Bushmen, as an instance, had a superstitious dread of the moon and its changing aspects, believing that it could cause great damage to the earth and to man. Yet they have this curious tradition concerning it: Having incurred the wrath of the sun, the moon (which is in reality a man, according to their age-old belief) has been knifed until nearly destroyed. But having implored mercy, he is permitted to grow from the small piece until he is large and full and round again, at which time the stabbing process begins all over. Strange contradictions such as this occur frequently in savage life. The moon is feared; yet it is the sun which is actually doing the damage.

At a very early period religious ideas gathered around the tabu. The tabu (a word of Polynesian origin) is a magical or religious prohibition. Certain places, persons, animals, things are endowed with a magical or sacred

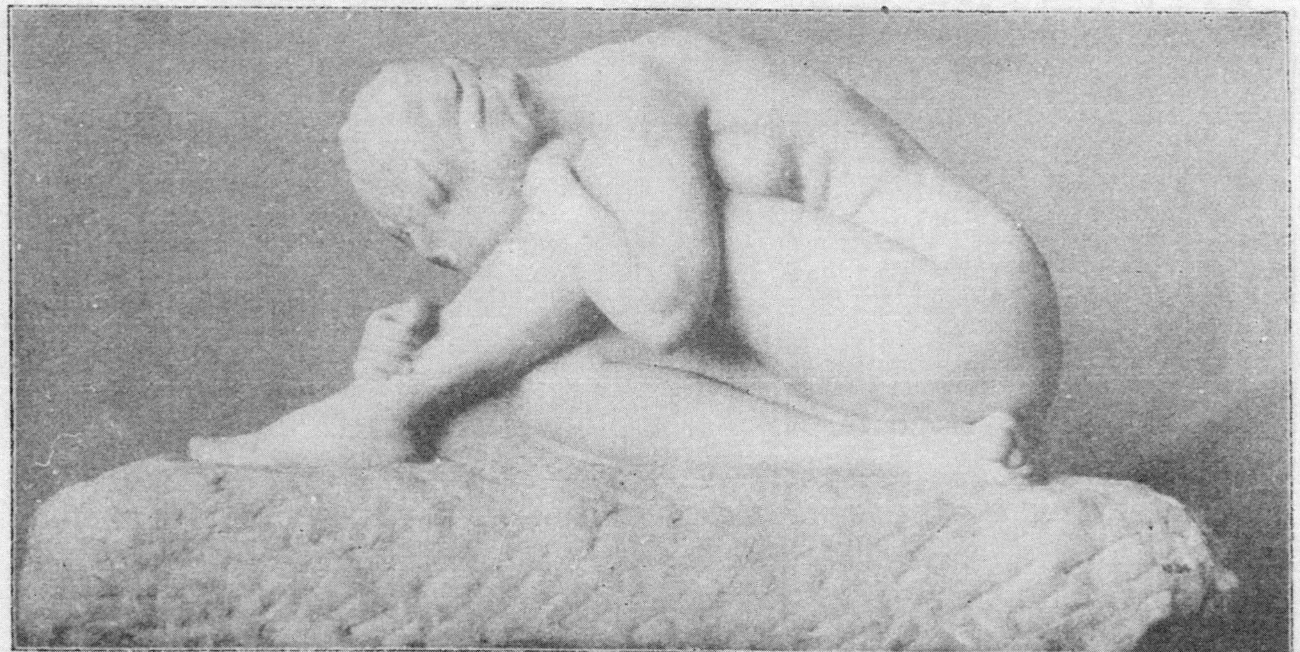

(Courtesy of Metropolitan Museum of Art)

A 20th Century conception of Eve, by Margaret Hoard—American.

(Courtesy of Metropolitan Museum of Art)

"And She Shall Be Called Woman"
An interpretation of the Creation, by Thomas Blake.

power, and mere man is forbidden their use or association. Thus the spear of the chief was tabu to the other members of the tribe. The bear, being worshipped by some tribes, was tabu in those tribes as food. A series of ritual acts, of worship, grew up around these early tabus and were retained long after the reason for them was forgotten.

Animism (a term made popular by Tylor) is a primitive form of religion in which conscious life is attributed to all objects, including rocks, trees, stones, fire, water. The worship of stones was widespread, possibly because of the belief that the spirit of the dead entered the stone and dwelt there. Thus in Central America when a man of importance died, a stone was put into his mouth to receive his soul. The worship of sacred stones is common in India and, to some extent, in China to-day. Many North American Indians also worship stones, prominently among them being the Pueblos. The Pueblo Indian firmly believes that his success in hunting depends entirely upon the cold stone which he carries with him.

Tree worship is very ancient. It was practised by practically all the Aryan peoples of Europe. The Druids worshipped the oak tree. The oak tree seems also to have been sacred among the Greeks. Among the Swedish peasantry there is a tradition that a leafy branch stuck in each furrow of the cornfields will insure an abundant crop. Many authorities believe that the Maypole was once the May tree, and that it had its origin in tree worship still observed by European peasantry.

Creating Tangible Gods to Worship.—It is interesting to note how very little reason primitive man required for creating a god or a deity. One wonders how these early ancestors of ours kept track of all the idols of fetishes they worshipped, of all the stones and trees and animals to which they felt they owed reverence! It must indeed have been confusing, unless—as is sometimes the case—the medicine man or magician memorized the tabus and the gods and conducted the rites and ceremonies for the people.

It is to be noted that very rarely did one tribe or one people have but one object of worship; it was more usual for one tribe to have many objects which required worship of some sort or other.

An excellent illustration of how deities are created even to-day by savage men is mentioned by Lichtenstein in his "Travels" (vol. I, p. 254). He relates that the king of the Koussa Kaffirs, having broken off a piece of a stranded anchor and carried it around with him, died soon afterward. Thereupon all the Kaffirs looked at the anchor with awe and reverence, considering it alive. They saluted it respectfully whenever they had occasion to pass near it. The mere finding of an object like an anchor would have been sufficient reason for primitive man to have set up that anchor as his god.

In Yucatan it was anciently the custom to place an infant on the ground on a sprinkling of ashes and leave it there overnight. The following morning the ashes were examined, and if the footprints of any animals were discovered that animal was chosen as the child's lifelong deity. Sometimes the infant disappeared—carried off, no doubt, by a beast—in which case the parents believed the deity to have claimed the child as an offering. They promptly made offerings of thanks to their own gods!

Man made a god of the animal that supplied him with the food; of the axe that protected him from his enemies; of the skins that kept him warm. He was never at a loss for a god, never searched very long for something to worship. But this early worship was not entirely due to the demands of the soul; it was due largely to a profound fear of impending evil and a desire for good.

Thus it was not enough for primitive man to have a god to worship. He must see that god, touch it, punish it if it did not do as was desired, pray to it, make offerings to it. It must be a *tangible god*. This accounts for the idols, totem poles, amulets, fetishes, and other objects of worship which were created in such great profusion.

The Fetish.—A fetish is simply some material object in which a god or a supernatural power is supposed to dwell. As a form of worship it represents the lowest type of idolatry. The fetish worshipper puts a spirit into everything he can see, hear, touch, taste, smell, or imagine. This type of worship still exists among many savage tribes.

Very probably, fetishism grew out of magic. The possession of a fetish is supposed to give the owner a certain power over some spirit or demon. The fetish, in other words, acts as a sort of charm or amulet worn or carried on the body and portending to protect from evil influences and disease. We must recognize it as a form of religion because it reveals a glimmer of faith, a suggestion of man's subservience to what he believes is a higher power.

The word *fetish* is of Portuguese origin, a corruption of *fetico* which means an amulet or a charm. De Brosses, a French writer who published a book entitled "Du culte des dieux fetishes" in 1760, termed all "terrestrial and natural objects apparently worshipped by the negroes 'fetishism' and this cult he denominated 'fetishism.' "

The fetishes are of various sorts. Sometimes the reed of a certain plant, the root of a certain tree or the horn of a certain animal is used as a fetish. The claws and teeth of animals, and slips of wood fantastically notched and carved, are frequently used. Among the Kaffirs the witch doctors and fetish men furnish the fetishes, which, among these people, are supposed to protect from the evils of witchcraft.

Among the Indians fetishism was, and is, common. Frequently it happened that an Indian dreamed of an idol or a fetish in a certain grotesque form and when he awakened he proceeded to make it according to the pattern of his vision. Similarly, the Negroes of Africa frequently made their own fetishes, although ready-made fetishes in the form of claws, teeth, etc., are often noticed by the traveller among these people.

The Negro of Guinea beats his fetish if his wishes are

not complied with. This is an example of the endeavours of the savage to make a slave of his deity. On the surface this would seem like the very opposite of religion. But, on the other hand, these same people hide the fetish if about to do something of which they are ashamed.

Strange fragments of fetishism have found their way into civilized life. The little ivory pig which the modern man wears on his watch chain is probably a relic of fetishism. Aladdin's Lamp is nothing more or less than a glorified fetish. And the many "lucky charms" which are offered for sale in any novelty shop are simply fetishes in a modern guise.

The Totem.—The fetish is a single object. The totem is usually a class of objects. In its stricter terminology the totem denotes the object or objects from which the family or clan derives its name.

The savage regards his totem with superstitious respect. He believes that there exists between his totem and himself a certain intimate and sacred relation. Therefore it is almost universally customary among savages to refrain from eating the animal or animals which appear in the totem pole. And marriage within the totem name is considered incest, punishable in many instances with death.

The reason for not eating the totem animal is explained by some authorities as having to do with the fact that savage man believed himself descended from that animal. For instance, the Bakalai believe that if a man eats his totem animal the women will give birth to animals of the totem kind. And the Omahas believe that the eating of the totem will bring sickness, perhaps death, to the women and children.

In Australia totemism is almost universal. Clans are named from their totems, and the totem animals are not eaten. Totemism is found also among the American Indians, and the traveller can see many grotesque and fantastic totem poles throughout this country which date back hundreds of years.

The relation of totemism to civilization cannot fail to be of interest to the student. The totem tended—tends—to consolidate a group of individuals. Thus, supposing the Cockatoo Indians and the Crow Indians are food groups of the same totem; the people of both groups are considered brethren because they are "one flesh." This consolidating of groups, this organizing of societies under certain totem kins, could not fail in early times to have had an appreciable effect upon the civilizing of man.

Sir James G. Frazer, in his delightful work called "Totemism" traces the derivation of the word totem to an Ojibwa (Chippewa) word, the exact spelling of which is somewhat uncertain.

Cannibalism and the Worship of Animals.—Under the heading "Strange Cannibals—They Are Deeply Religious," a New York newspaper recently published the following bit of gruesome information:

> A cable message says France worries about cannibalism in the Kamerun, the part of Africa that France took from Germany after the war. Down there certain blacks, a secret society, call themselves "Leopards," and act the part.
>
> Wearing leopard skins, they lie in wait, kill their fellow blacks and devour them.
>
> The man-eating is part of their religion, curiously enough. Another interesting fact is that the cannibals are the finest specimens among the natives. Plenty of proteid and vitamines explains their physical superiority, according to scientists.

It is not strange or curious that man-eating should be part of the religious worship of these savages. They are merely carrying out an instinct bred in their souls—and appetites—many generations ago. Their fathers and grandfathers and great-grandfathers before them were cannibals. Far from being a form of depravity practised by only a few peoples, cannibalism marked the life of nearly all peoples in primitive days.

Probably cannibalism began as a solution to the food problem. Man was certainly easier prey to man than the huge beasts—at a time when no weapons were known.

But we have records culled from all corners of the world showing that men killed and ate their elders; mothers even ate their children, and savages ate their dead relatives as a form of religious and tribal ceremony. Thus, although cannibalism doubtless originated in a bodily need, imaginative man soon gave it an emotional and religious meaning.

Among the Lhopa of Sikkim, in Tibet, it was customary to eat the bride's mother at the wedding feast. (There always *has* been a prejudice against mothers-in-law!) Among the Chavante, on the Uruguay, mothers ate their babies when they died, believing that by doing so they regained the tiny souls. In the Solomon Islands victims were actually fattened like cattle. On the Upper Congo cannibalism was practised for thousands of years as the result of an instinctive passion for cannibalistic feasts. Among these peoples the love of human flesh became as strong as the opium habit.

In this contemplation of cannibalism, which is necessarily a part of our study of man, it would be comforting to remember that all things are relative. The Maori people, who are cannibals, have never been guilty of torture or deliberate cruelty. They are struck with horror when they hear of the thumbscrews and rack of Christendom; they cannot understand the "roasting alive" of Joan of Arc. To apply "live coals which pain exceedingly" to a person is cruelty, but to kill a person and cook him for consumption is another matter.

Frederick O'Brien, in his "White Shadows in the South Seas," tells how the Marquesan ponders over the problem of Christianity, attempting to understand the "magic" of the missionaries. These cannibalistic people see no harm in their mode of life, but they try wholeheartedly to understand the worship of the white man. Their confusion between barbarism and religion is sometimes amusing. According to O'Brien, they ask; concerning resurrection:

What would God do in cases where sharks had eaten a Marquesan? And what, when the same shark had been killed and eaten by other Marquesans? And in the case of the early Christian forefathers, who were eaten by men of other tribes, and afterward the cannibals eaten in retaliation, and then the last feaster eaten by sharks? There was a headache query!

There is a phase of cannibalism which probably preceded the eating of animals, and out of which the worship of animals doubtless grew. This is the once world-wide custom of eating a man to gain such properties as strength, swiftness, courage, etc., from him. The savage of prehistoric times ate his slain enemy to acquire his strength and other good qualities.

In this connection, the Bechuanas had a solemn ceremony of eating the flesh of an enemy killed "following the ancient superstition that eating human flesh inspires courage and by degrees renders the warrior invincible." It is said of the notorious Matuana that he drank the gall of thirty chiefs in the belief that it would make him stronger than any man. And the ancient Russians, if certain writers are to be credited, ate their fathers believing to gain thereby their strength and wisdom.

If this type of cannibalism preceded the eating of animals, it is easy to see how the next logical step would be the eating of certain animals for the qualities which they possessed, and the prohibition of other animals for the opposite reason. Thus the Amaxosa drank the gall of the ox to make themselves fierce. The Hottentots ate the flesh of lions to gain that animal's courage and strength. But the Hottentots even to-day will not eat the flesh of hares, believing it will make them timid. Similarly, the Dyaks of Northwest Borneo forbid their young men and warriors the flesh of venison; only women and old men are permitted to eat this flesh, as it renders those who eat it as timid as the deer.

This idea that a person imbibes the characteristics of the animals he eats is widely distributed. We find it in Australia, in Africa, in certain sections of South America. The Malays of Singapore will give a large price for the flesh of the tiger because they believe that the man who eats tiger flesh acquires the sagacity, strength, and courage of that animal.

The countless pictures of animals which have been discovered in palæolithic caves are not sporting pictures, not the products of idle moments of amusement. The latest belief is that they are religious pictures—pictures that have a certain spiritual significance. Primitive man, in his conceit, liked to believe that he was descended from the lion whose strength he admired, or the tiger whose agility he envied. He made of these animals a god, and in eating the god he believed that he became one in common with him.

Thus eating certain animals became a sort of tribal, religious rite. This would seem to indicate that sacrifice was not originally offered *to* the god; adopting the opposite theory, the god himself was sacrificed and gave his strength, his spirit, his life to the people. This is a curious twist of religion which has not yet been developed to its fullest possibilities. Perhaps some day a writer on religion will trace its influence through the centuries and find instances of it in our own forms of worship.

But this is not a history of religion or a book on theology. In connection with this work it will suffice if we touch merely upon those important features of early and primitive religion which influenced our own religions and which help us to a better understanding of early man. Animal worship, which we shall now consider, is an extremely ancient type of worship, still existing in many parts of the world. Some of our customs, not only religious but social, are directly traceable to animal worship.

How did animal worship grow out of animal-eating, you ask? It is reasonable to suppose that man, believing himself descended from the animals he admired—and therefore eating them to be one with them—gradually came to hedge around these animals with certain tribal tabus. Ultimately the animals became sacred and as such took part

(Courtesy of Metropolitan Museum of Art)

An interpretation of Adam and Eve in the Garden of Eden.

(Courtesy of American Museum of Natural History, New York)

Hunting the cave-bear in primitive times. A painting by W. Kuhnert.

in the tribe ceremonial. From this it was just a step to the tabuing of those animals as food. They were worshipped; they were incorporated into totems. Totemism, we find, is one of the most widely distributed modes of showing respect to animals.

Animal worship was very prevalent in America, The North American Indians worshipped the bear, the bison, the hare, many species of birds, the buffalo. In Brazil the jaguar was worshipped. In Mexico the owl was feared as an evil spirit.

The ancient Egyptians were greatly addicted to animal worship. Even now the natives on the White Nile will not eat the ox, according to Sir S. Baker. In India animal worship has flourished since early days, and there is to-day a sacred cow that is worshipped and fêted. Eagles, toads, dogs, fish, horses, leopards, lizards, monkeys, serpents, sheep, buffalo, cattle—all have been worshipped at some time or other by savage peoples.

The cult of the white elephant is familiar to all students of religion. In Siam it is believed that a white elephant contains the soul of a dead person, perhaps an ancient god. When one is taken, the capturer is rewarded and the animal is baptized, fêted, worshipped. At death it is mourned for like a human. The cult of the white elephant is found also in Cambodia, Indo-China, in Sumatra, Ennares, Southern Abyssinia.

It was only when man came to realize that he was really superior to animals that he began to make gods in his own image. The Egyptians appear to have been the most prolific of all idol or god-makers. The man-like gods of ancient Egyptian worship are bewildering in number.

Kings as Gods.—H. M. Tichenor, in his "Survival of the Fittest," says:

> Religions are the reflex of the state of society that produces them. The gods are largely the images of the ruling and exploiting classes.

This is very largely true. When great serpents were a dreaded power, serpents were worshipped. When lions and leopards were feared, lions and leopards were worshipped. When kings became powerful not only they were worshipped, but gods were imagined that sat on thrones and wore crowns.

Thus in Egypt we are confronted by a religion which worships kings as gods. The daily life of the kings of Egypt was regulated in every detail by precise and unvarying rules. Traditional tabus had to be observed. Since the welfare and existence of the people were bound up in the king, the man god, the life and health of this god were naturally of great concern.

Very frequently in early society we find that the king or priest was thought to be endowed with supernatural powers. The control of nature was believed to be more or less under his control. While, under favourable circumstances, this might have been a mighty nice thing for the king, when there was bad weather, when the crops failed, or under similar calamities, his very life was in danger. He was held responsible. In ancient China the king was frequently killed in time of drought. The Greeks of the Homeric Age believed that a good harvest or a period of prosperity was due entirely to the king, and rewarded him accordingly.

The Phallic Worship.—We cannot leave the subject of religion without a brief survey of Phallic worship, a curious and interesting type of worship which grew out of nature worship. It was practised by the Egyptians, the Phœnicians, the Greeks, and the inhabitants of Asia Minor in the early periods of civilization.

In the Phallic religion the generative organs are worshipped. Our Phallus-worshipping ancestors sanctified the functions of the body which gave them the most pleasure, and which reproduced their own kind. We can understand how early man stood in awe of the mysteries of nature, speculating in his crude fashion as to the source of life. The generative organs were the obvious physical basis of procreation; therefore they were venerated.

Symbolism played a large part in Phallic worship. There are still in existence to-day remarkable specimens of original phallic symbols—crosses, talismans, amulets, etc.—all symbolic of the phallus. The steeples on the churches, the horseshoe over the door, the pyramids and obelisks, arts, architecture, literature, language—all show the influence of our Phallus-worshipping ancestors.

In the National Museum at Washington one can see large stone phalli which were dug up in Tennessee, Georgia, California, and other sections of the United States and Mexico; and H. M. Tichenor, in his "Primitive Beliefs," tells us that a phallic image in the form of a pillar is still to be seen in the ruins of Solomon's temple.

These relics of Phallic worship remind us that a section of mankind is still searching for the answer to the eternal question—Whence did we come and whither are we going? For many the riddle of creation has not yet been solved, and man still hopes for, but is not sure about, immortality.

Conscience and the Soul.—This brings us to our final contemplation of religion. We have not really made a study of religion, for we have not even touched upon Judaism, which has given something to almost all existing religions; upon Buddhism which numbers more followers than almost any other faith; upon the religious systems of the Greeks, the Romans, the Japanese; upon Christianity, the fabric of which contains threads, fibres, that reach back into ancient paganism.

We have, however, made a study of religion in its relation to man—his manners and customs, his early modes of reasoning, the beginning of his faith. We know now that Christianity did not flash upon the world in a finished state, but grew up step by step in the process of evolution and adapted itself from many other forms of worship. Many of its sacred symbols were borrowed from pagan peoples.

Above all, we know now what the early religions, the early forms of worship, crude and savage as they may seem, have done toward holding the social fabric together.

Worship of nature, of totems and fetishes, of animals, of man gods and gods created in the image of man all have helped change man from a selfish, wandering two-legged beast to a home-loving, kin-loving, worshipping member of a group. No matter how savage or brutal the form of worship may have been, no matter how ridiculous it may seem to our twentieth-century way of reasoning, we must remember that the very act of worship tended to solidify or consolidate the group, and thus played a large part in holding together the early fragments of society.

Let us now glimpse the conscience of man and see what has been happening to it through these centuries of development. Had man a conscience at all in his primitive state? Did it bother him? Did he ever feel the least bit of remorse at having killed and eaten his enemy, at having beaten and forsaken his aged father on the march to newer and more plentiful hunting grounds?

Conscience, by its very nature, belongs to the higher stages of civilization. Yet this writer cannot help believing that a certain quasi-conscience existed in the savage mind which was steeped in fear and superstition. The conscience that is born of fear is not conscience in its truest, finest sense; yet it would appear to be the undeveloped conscience of an undeveloped mind.

Do you recall the story of Peter the Great, the Tsar who founded the power of Russia? It is interesting enough to quote. While the Tsar was sleeping a would-be murderer twice pressed the trigger of a pistol held against his head. And twice the pistol missed fire. Within the mind of the man who had come to kill, something spoke. Was it fear of an unknown? Was it conscience? We do not know. Nevertheless, he wakened the Tsar and, telling him that he had come to the palace to kill him, said, "But God would not permit it. He sends me to prove his love of you. Now kill me."

The man doubtless believed what he said. Thus was conscience born of fear, as it might have been born any number of times in our savage ancestors, who feared not one but many unknown powers. The Tsar did not kill the man. Instead he told him to go away in peace. If, as the man had indicated, he was God's special envoy to show His special esteem to the Tsar, the Tsar would lose that esteem by killing the envoy. In other words, the Tsar was as superstitious and as awed by the coincidence as the would-be murderer.

Is it not possible that conscience was early awakened in primitive man through just such superstition as this? And that conscience advanced as civilization advanced, the one keeping step with the other?

As we study religion in its many phases, and browse for a moment along the byways of religious reasoning, we cannot help seeing that there was growing up in the lives of men, everywhere, from the earliest times, a certain something which tended to bind them together mentally and emotionally—a certain something which seems to hold together the bricks of human nature from which civilization is built.

That "something" we would call simply *soul*. We do not know any more about it to-day than our prehistoric ancestors did. Perhaps that is why it is so fascinating to study the primitive notions concerning the subject of the soul.

Readers who are acquainted with Dante know of the idea that the dead have no shadows. The poet did not invent this. It is a piece of traditionary lore. From the very earliest times men have regarded their shadows as their souls. This belief exists even to-day among the Benin Negroes. The Basutos believe that if a man walks at the brink of a river and his shadow falls upon the water, his life is in danger. A crocodile may seize it or it may drown. Therefore there exists among these people a superstitious dread of walking near the water.

With many peoples, this conception of the soul being identical with the shadow flourishes. The Greenlanders say that a man's shadow is one of his two souls—the one which goes away from his body at night. The Fijians also believe that a man has two souls, and the shadow is called the "dark spirit" as distinguished from the other. But the reflection in the water is not considered a shadow among the Fijians. On the contrary, they consider it the true likeness of the man—and hence his "light spirit."

Among the primitive peoples, the soul was conceived to be a facsimile of the body. The reason for this belief can readily be seen. In his dreams man saw friends he knew to be dead, people probably who had been devoured by animals. Yet he saw them whole and alive in his dreams. This inevitably led to the belief that there existed an incorporeal part of man—a part which survived the dissolution of the body.

Of course, the conceptions of the soul varied with different peoples. The shadow theory is found in Tasmania, North and South America, classical Europe. The Nootkas of British Columbia regard the soul as a tiny facsimile of man living in the crown of the head. Many peoples conceived of the soul as a bird. Various tribes of North American Indians, for instance, believe that the soul is a bird enclosed in an egg and living in the nape of the neck. When a man dies they say that the shell has broken and the bird has flown away.

The belief in a soul, gradually but nevertheless at an early date, brought about the idea of a future life. And the idea of a future life, of an immortality, has been man's sustaining hope through the centuries.

OUR ANCIENT HERITAGE

The foregoing pages give but the briefest outline of man in his infancy. For untold ages man has been thinking, wondering, hoping, scheming, struggling—sometimes progressing and sometimes regressing—but always slowly evolving from savagery to civilization. We to-day can but dimly realize what a painful and prolonged struggle it must have been to humanity to reach the present point of civilization.

The world has progressed tremendously since the beginning of the Christian era, and particularly in the last few hundred years. Civilized man has accomplished through science what primitive man attempted to accomplish through force and through savage worship. He has conquered the forces of nature—compels those forces to serve him. He has actually harnessed the lightning from which early man fled in terror, and he has achieved many other amazing triumphs.

But we who reap the harvest of a newer and more advanced age should not forget that we stand upon a foundation built for us by the generations that have gone before. We owe a debt of gratitude to the numberless and nameless men and women who lived and toiled in the ages before us and who have made us, to a very great extent, what we are.

After all, can we afford to ignore our savage ancestors, can we afford to be contemptuous of their share in human progress? The amount of new knowledge which any one age, no matter how remarkable, can add to the great common store is comparatively small. What are two, or three, or even four thousand years compared with the countless generations in which man has been developing? What can the few thousand years of recorded history mean beside the million or so years of unrestrained animal activity—the years during which our ancestors evolved from beast to man?

Primitive man was the true pioneer of civilization. What we of the twentieth century are prone to call by the name of "civilization" is just a thin film of idealism spread over the top of a million years or so of human savagery. Stripped of that idealism, stripped of its conscious glory and triumph, life is very much the same as it was thousands of years ago. It is the purpose of this work, primarily, to prove that this is true.

We are like heirs who have inherited a fortune which has accumulated through many generations. That fortune is in the form of folklore and traditions, customs and beliefs, habits and impulses. As Mr. Frazer points out, our resemblances to the savage of yesterday are still far more numerous than our differences from him. Many of the customs, impulses, and ideas which we are inclined to look upon as original and intuitive have been bequeathed us by our savage ancestors, who acquired them by age-to-age experiences.

The Relation of Primitive to Modern Society.—"As creatures of emotion we are hundreds of thousands of years old; as reasoning beings we are but of yesterday," says Edward Clodd in his "Magic in Names" (p. 10). It is the mode of life that has changed; human nature is very much the same, fundamentally, as it was when civilization was young.

Thousands of years ago any savage would have felt honoured to be selected by his people to accompany their dead chief into the next world. To be buried alive with a man of such tribal importance as the chief pleased the ego of the savage. To-day men are not buried alive to accompany other men of importance into the next world. But thousands still shout in frenzy as two civilized beings try to pound consciousness out of each other in the ring. And of those thousands it is doubtful if there is one who would not feel honoured by the suggestion that he carry a valise or some other article for the winner.

Thus do our savage ancestors slumber within us. There is, indeed, a "solid layer of savagery beneath the surface of society." And the long ages that have gone before show our own culture in the making. Unless you have turned special attention to this subject and studied it carefully, you cannot realize that a mass of pagan and primitive ideas exist in our code of social life, exercising a living hold upon the popular mind. Primitive life has bequeathed us traditions, customs, and beliefs; we have accepted them as our own.

In primitive life it was a symbol of peace to drop the weapon and extend the hand—unarmed. From this crude beginning developed our handclasp.

Dr. James Harvey Robinson, in his "The Mind in the Making," says that there are four historical layers underlying the brain of civilized man. They are the animal mind, the child mind, the savage mind, and the traditional civilized mind. All these old minds, he says, contend with the higher mind that has been evolved. In an instant a man can become an animal, a child, a savage. Sometimes the child mind is always predominate, and we have an imbecile. Sometimes the savage mind is always predominate, and we have a criminal. But on the whole it is the traditional civilized mind that predominates—a mind rich in a heritage of age-old tradition, a mind that still accepts without reasons, that still is tradition-bound and custom-bound.

Many authorities have adopted the theory that the individual in a few months passes through changes that have taken the race millions of years to undergo. William J. Fielding, in "The Caveman Within Us," declares that man is still chained to the cave man within him, still chained to primitive levels. Beginning with the age of one year, he says, the mind of the civilized child is a crude but unmistakable outline of the prehistoric evolution of the race.

We know, of course, that the young child is a savage. He has all the emotional reactions peculiar to the savage. He likes to tie cans to the tail of the neighbourhood cat. He likes to tear the legs from a frog, the wings from a fly. He likes to paint his face and pretend he is a strong and fearsome Indian. And even as an infant he likes to wield a stick, banging away to the right and the left, much in the manner of his club-using ancestor. Contemplate, if you will, upon the rattle. Is it not necessary to the child's natural emotional instincts?

> These are all primitive pastimes [says our authority], and all of them still fulfill the rôle of an emotional outlet for the primitive cravings of modern man. Children are dominated by these primitive emotions; normal adult persons who have succeeded in adapting themselves to their social environment have learned to conform, more or less, to certain general requirements of our civilization; but within

every individual, under this surface conformity, there remains intact all the old mechanism of the primitive savage.

"Surface conformity"—a happy phrase; but notwithstanding this "surface conformity" to the time we live in, there is a remnant of primitive man still within us—within the very best of us.

The Veneer of Civilization.—Despite the great scientific triumphs of recent years, despite the great strides forward which recently have been taken by mankind, civilization has just begun. That is, civilization in its twentieth-century interpretation; for basic civilization began when man first cooked his food, and made pottery in which to preserve it, and learned to speak, and write, and think. The real story of civilization, it would seem, lies in the millions of years still remaining for man on this plane.

What we call civilization to-day is merely a "slight coat of cultural whitewash"—a veneer over the surface of impressions, emotions, impulses, instincts, superstitions, fears that have been accumulated by man during his ages of struggle with the forces of nature. We move to-day upon a thin crust of culture which at any moment can be swept away. The recent war is an excellent example of civilization reverted to savage instincts, of restraint swept away, of intense and startling emotional reaction.

As Freud explains, it is not that people sink so very low in time of war; it is that they are never so high in peace times as is popularly supposed. Let the modern man hear the primitive call of the tom-toms, let his blood pulsate to the blare of the war spirit, and in a flash centuries of civilization vanish. War unlooses all the primitive passions and emotions of man which are held in check during saner times.

This is true also of the crowd or the mob. Give it the least excuse or incentive and the mob will become wild, will start any sort of savage riot. As Mr. Martin very cleverly expresses it, "The crowd is a device for indulging ourselves in a kind of temporary insanity by all going crazy together."

Yet this very "crowd," under ordinary circumstances, insists upon going in the beaten track. Man has an inherent inclination to imitate the past. He is resentful and astonished at every new discovery. He laughs at a Columbus who says the earth is round, and jeers at a Fulton who would make a boat move by steam. Even to-day the man who departs from the beaten track, who dares to blaze new trails through the mazes of custom, receives little better consideration than did Friar Bacon or Galileo or the many others who have tried to tear down the walls of custom in the generations gone by.

This brings us at last to the great, fundamental purpose of this work—the study of customs and their origins. Custom, in savage life, is a chain which man breaks at the risk of death. Shall we who live in an age of enlightenment accept customs, like the savage, without reason? Or shall we know at last precisely why we do things, why we say things? Why do a thing if you do not know why you do it? Isn't it immensely more satisfactory to *know* exactly why you do such and such a thing—your *reason* for adhering to a custom which is ages old and which has no twentieth-century significance?

The Survival of Custom.—The term "survival of custom" appears to have been originated by Sir John Lubbock, who wrote the "Origin of Civilization." No better term could be used. Custom *has* survived, and it will probably go right on surviving as long as man patterns himself by his neighbour. The things that we consider customary and conventional are simply the things that others around us are doing, and that others before them have done.

The human race has always clung to the established customs and traditions. The habits and customs of man are almost as enduring as the flint knives, the stone monuments, and the clay pottery which tell us of the daily life of his primitive ancestors. Many old customs still survive in our social life, curiously obtruding the past into the present. These we shall study in detail in the following chapters.

Custom is the unwritten law of life. We have only to look around us to see how potent custom is. It dies hard. It survives the shocks by which kingdoms are overthrown. Early civilizations were born and perished time after time; races achieved the highest degree of culture and sank back again into obscurity; but each succeeding system of society invariably borrowed some of the custom and the formality of the preceding order. Thus, once a notion, a tradition, or a custom was fairly started in the world, it lived on from generation to generation, preserving some form and colour of identity.

Many meaningless customs which we to-day observe had at one time a practical or ceremonial intention. Why do they survive when the original meaning has long since fallen out of popular memory? Superstition, of course, has a great deal to do with it. People are afraid to ignore the age-old customs which have been handed down to them. It is much easier to observe a custom and laugh about it than to ignore it and be troubled by tiny fears of evil influence. Customs are, in a sense, sacred, as any savage will still tell you to-day, in the jungles of Ceylon or in the hinterlands of Australia. "Remove not the ancient landmarks which thy fathers have set," say the sacred narrators. (Proverbs XXII, 28.)

But how is it, you ask, when races had to learn their lessons all over again, when people lived for a brief span and disappeared forever, when civilization flourished in remote corners of the world—how is it that we find such a striking similarity of custom wherever we go? The uniformity which pervades the thoughts and customs of the world to-day is indeed remarkable. Strange reversals occur only here and there—such as where white is the colour of mourning, or where to turn one's back on a person is a sign of reverence.

Mr. Lang explains why we can pick up threads of similar customs in widely different countries, among widely separated peoples who do not even speak the same language.

> In the moderate allowance of 250,000 years [he says], there is time for stories to have wandered all around the world, as the Aggry beads of Ashanti have probably crossed the continent from Egypt, as the Asiatic jade has arrived in Swiss lake dwellings, as an African trade cowry is said to have been found in a Cornish barrow, as an Indian Ocean shell has been discovered in a prehistoric bone cave in Poland. This slow filtration of tales is not absolutely out of question. Two causes would especially help to transmit myths. The first is slavery and slave-stealing; the second is the habit of capturing brides from alien stocks, and the law which forbids marriage with a woman of a man's own totem. Slaves and captured brides would bring their native legends among alien people.

In prehistoric time there must have been much transmission of myth. And with myth went custom. Primitive man travelled, as is indicated by the similarity of axes and arrowheads discovered on both the old and new continents, and with him he carried his local traditions and customs.

It frequently happened that conquerors patterned themselves after the conquered, borrowing their customs, habits, traditions—even their language. The Franks in Gaul, for instance, became Latinized. The Romans who conquered Athens were governed by their new environment. The Hyksos conquerors of Egypt were subjugated by its customs, its civilization. Somehow the old feeling always prevails.

But coming down to our own day—what, precisely, is custom as it concerns us? Custom is mob thought, is it not? Custom is made up of many customs. We submit to the tyrant—for custom is a tyrant, you know!—through a vague desire to "hunt with the pack," to be one of the crowd. We do not wish to appear strange or conspicuous or queer. We are half afraid to give offence, to cause confusion. We dare not break down a belief. We do the thing that everyone else does because we are afraid to do otherwise.

That is custom. A funny thing—yet it holds the fabric of social life together. It makes it easier for us to mingle with one another, to understand one another. It keeps the thin veneer of civilization above the layers of savagery that slumber in our souls.

"The iron age of the world belongs to the past, its golden one to the future," says James A. Farrar. Perhaps by studying the past we can glimpse the future—and see a bit of the gold that is promised.

We wish to make one fact absolutely clear before leaving this Introductory Chapter. We have not attempted to give the complete story of man from the dawn of life to the present day. Man passed through many stages of development—all interesting and all important. But this is not a history of man and how he has developed or what he has accomplished. It is a *book of origins*—a history of the manners, customs, traditions, and superstitions of man. Therefore, only that part of the history of man has been sketched which has direct bearing upon his manners and customs.

CHAPTER II

Searching the Sources

Trample out Minoan culture, it shoots up again in thousandfold splendour in the glory of Greece; crush out Greece, the whole world is fertilized; give the Roman world up to the fury of barbarian hordes, and the outcome is Modern Europe. We see one race stepping into another's place in the van of the march, but nothing of the continuous inheritance is lost. Every treading down of the seed results in a harvest richer than the last. Chaldean, Egyptian, Greek, Roman, European, bear the torch in turn; but the lampadophoria of human progress is continuous. In the progress of evolution races and nations count for no more than do individuals. Like individuals, races, empires, civilizations pass away,—but humanity proceeds onward. —Robert Briffault.

THE EARLY CIVILIZATIONS

HOW would you like to take a rocking-chair journey around the world? How would you like to visit, in their native lands, the people from whose myths, legends, customs, and traditions we have so generously borrowed?

Here is a brief geographical survey that will carry you into lands strange and distant, among races civilized and uncivilized. You will learn to know who the Fijians are, and the Hottentots, and the Bushmen, so that when we speak of these people you will know and recognize them.

Our journey starts with the very birthplace of civilization, Egypt—the "gift of the Nile." It was in Egypt, shut in by the Red Sea and the desert, by the Mediterranean and the mountains, that the first precious seeds of culture and civilization were planted. Here one finds a highly advanced form of picture writing on papyrus—from which our word "paper" is derived—and a method of ploughing the fertile grounds very similar to that used by many peoples to-day. There is in the Necropolis of

Memphis a scene showing two ancient Egyptians ploughing with oxen yoked to a clumsy wooden plough.

No one knows when the Nile cut its way across the desert, dividing the fertile land and forming what is now Egypt—the country that forms the northeast extremity of Egypt. McCabe places the time in the Neolithic (New Stone) Age, possibly 10,000 years ago. The monumental history, a rich source of information concerning early civilization, begins with Menes, the first Pharaoh.

Parallel with the ancient beginnings of civilization in Egypt is a similar beginning in Sumeria. The Sumerians, who are of doubtful and mysterious origin, shaved their heads, wore woollen garments and wrote on clay. They

Courtesy of the Metropolitan Museum of Art.

fertilized their fields; they built tower-like temples; they were, in a word, a highly advanced and civilized people.

Among the first civilizations we must include that of the Phœnicians, a seafaring Semitic people of antiquity. Their colony of Carthage, which at one time had a population of a million, was founded before 800 B.C. But even before 1500 B.C. the Phœnicians had two great settlements—Sidon and Tyre—on the African coast. They were great traders and had a large trade in slaves, metals, precious stones, and woven goods with all the Mediterranean peoples. The Phœnicians were advanced in many arts, and they had an alphabet and system of picture-writing of their own.

Another of the oldest civilizations is the Chaldean. The Chaldeans dwelt in what is now a desolate valley on the western frontier of Persia. The capital of the Chal-

(Courtesy of Metropolitan Museum of Art)

Fishing and fowling skiff of ancient Egypt. Model from the tomb of Mehenkwetre.

(Courtesy of Metropolitan Museum of Art)

Fetish drums of the French Congo.

dean Empire was Babylon—named for the great ruler Babylon who engineered the Great Canal which, centuries later, was still an object of wonder. This Chaldean civilization followed the Assyrian civilization with its capital city of Nineveh. For many centuries power swayed between Nineveh and Babylon, wars were fought, sometimes the Babylonians and sometimes the Assyrians were more powerful. But finally the Medes and the Persians joined forces with the Chaldeans and in 606 B.C. took Nineveh.

The Chaldean civilization itself did not last very long. In 539 B.C. it collapsed before the attack of Cyrus, who founded the power of Persia.

To the southeast of Persia is India, another of the older civilizations. The ancestors of the Hindus appear to have branched off from the Persians, pushing north into India, conquering as they went, and finally occupying the whole peninsula. They seem to have entered the Punjab about 2000 B.C. A simple Aryan people, they tilled the land and herded the flocks. By 1000 B.C. they had a fairly advanced civilization.

Now let us leave India by way of Bombay and cross the sea into Arabia. Arabia is the peninsula to the southwest of Asia and is between Egypt and Persia. Commercial intercourse between Arabia and Egypt by way of the Persian and Arabian gulfs existed thousands of years ago.

Egypt is a land of monuments. Arabia is a land of men. But like the monuments of Egypt, the men of Arabia are unchanged. The Bedouin of the desert possesses the same mode of life, the same traits of character as were possessed by his ancestors.

Leaving the land of the Arabs, famous more for its horses than for its civilization, we advance north and enter Palestine, the land of the Palestines or the Philistines. This land was peopled originally by the descendants of Canaan, grandson of Noah, who divided the land among his eleven sons. The occupation of Palestine by the Canaanites continued for more than seven centuries. Besides them there were the Philistines, descendants of Misraim from Egypt.

We must not forget to visit Abyssinia, the grand tablelands and mountains of ancient Ethiopia. We will find Abyssinia to the southeast of Egypt, an inland country. Civilization found an early start in this land, known to the ancients as Ethiopia. Its northern limits reached at one time to about Syene, and there was a very intimate connection between Egypt and Ethiopia in early times. Occasionally the two countries were under the same ruler. The arts and civilization of Egypt naturally found their way into Ethiopia, now known as Abyssinia.

The Abyssinians are a superstitious people. They have many curious customs which have somehow obtruded themselves upon the civilizations of other countries. As a kingdom, Abyssinia traces its royal lineage back to the Queen of Sheba.

Now let us sit on our magic carpet of fancy and fly into China, the land of time-worn customs and traditions. Here we find a people of great conservatism, and a civilization of bewildering antiquity. Here we find also a society founded upon filial piety—the teaching of Confucius; we find Buddhism and its countless followers; we find ragged remnants of aboriginal tribes. The Chinese are perhaps the most prosaic of all Asiatics. In many things they are our exact opposites. We could tarry long in this land of strange people—but see! The whole world beckons.

Browsing through Africa.—We have glimpsed the early civilizations. Now let us take a leisurely journey through all the countries of the world, as they present themselves, instead of skipping here across an ocean, there across a continent, jumping seas and bays and gulfs at random!

Let us start with Africa, since it cradled the first civilization. On this continent there are still many savage races—even many aboriginal tribes that have been untouched by civilization. At a very early period the Semitic, Ethiopic, and Nigritic races emigrated into Africa—from the beautiful land at the head of the Persian Gulf—and traced their course down the Nile and the eastern coast of the continent.

Starting at Port Said, we glide down the Nile through Egypt and through the northern part of Abyssinia. Directly to the east we see Somaliland. Here we find remnants of the ancient racial stock known as the Hamite. Below Somaliland is East Africa—a land which is not particularly friendly to the traveller. But come! These remnants of ancient tribes are harmless. They are savages to us and we are savages to them, but they will not molest us if we do not try to interfere with their age-old customs. Zanzibar is on the coast, and its tribes are most interesting. How the people do love gaudy decoration!

Here we are in Mozambique, seat of an ancient kingdom. See how the Zambesi River cuts it clear in half. Along the shores of this river are remnants of the Native Empire. Suppose we chat for a moment with some Mozambique women. They tell us they have no grievances. They are equal with the man in every respect. They may sell, fish, barter, rule. They engage in the same occupations as the men, are exposed to the same hardships. And they like it—can conceive of no other arrangement.

These strange people who use live birds for ornaments are the Zulus. They are extremely superstitious and strangely gentle and kind for a savage race. They love dancing, as do most savage peoples.

Now we enter a great stretch of territory known as the Congo and inhabited by the Congo Kaffirs. This spot was once the scene of great slave-trade activity. The Congo Kaffirs are interesting people, are they not? They believe so absolutely in their fetishes and in their rain doctor. What a superstitious people they are!

But we are to visit some people now who are even more superstitious—people very little removed from their primitive state. They are scattered through Central and South Africa. As we go among them we realize that here are the aboriginals—that civilization has swept by them without their knowing it.

Among these dregs of races we find the Hottentots and the Bushmen, both of which are supposed to be descendants of the tribes which first settled in southeastern Africa. Now, you see, they dwell for the most part about the Cape of Good Hope, having been driven into this section by the more powerful Kaffirs.

The Bushmen are a savage and cruel people. They are extremely small in stature, you see, and they seem very crafty; but the Bushmen have been found to be courageous, intelligent, and trustworthy. Despite their savage nature, they will die themselves rather than have injury done someone who is dependent upon them for protection. Bushmen mothers are noted for their devotion to their children.

Here comes a rather timid Bushman fellow. Let us ask him to entertain us. His dance is grotesque, weird, is it not? And how cleverly he can imitate the cries of birds and beasts!

The Hottentots were once considered the parent family, but it is now believed that these people are merely an offshoot of Bantu-Bushman blood. Like the main branch of the Bushman, these people have fallen out of the line of march and are still a savage and undeveloped fragment of mankind. There are some authorities who insist that we do not yet know the true origin of the Hottentots, that they are a superior race and may even have wandered southward from Egypt. But this has not yet been proved.

These Hottentot people who eye us so curiously are more intelligent than their Bushmen cousins. They are taller in stature, you notice. Some of them have embraced Christianity. These people have an extreme love of music and dancing, and they have included dancing in their ceremonials since the earliest times.

What are those three stalwart young Hottentots doing over in that corner? Let us investigate. Yes—they are actually shaking dice! It is good of them to let us examine these dice. They are made, you see, of the bones of animals. It is an old custom among the Hottentots to shake dice to discover what their success will be in warfare.

Leaving the interesting Hottentots, we come to another remnant of the Bushman family—the Bechuanas. These people are also South African aborigines. There are also the Senegambians, who are zealous merchants and who have a curious way of combining business with religion. And there are the Negroes of Upper Guinea, who are savage and superstitious and have many fetishes. They love display and gaudy ornamentation. Their celebrations, at both weddings and funerals, are weird, noisome, primitive.

Crossing North Africa we meet a wandering tribe of Berbers—the "bandits of the desert." They are reputed to be cruel, suspicious, and very treacherous, but do you wonder at it? They were driven from their fertile territories along the great Mediterranean Sea, into the Atlas Mountains, into the Sahara Desert. They were scourged by the Romans, the Vandals, the Arabs, the Phœnicians. But they are still Berbers of pure blood and proud bearing, and though they look upon us with suspicion and hatred, we can find it in our hearts to admire them.

There are many other tribes in Africa. We cannot possibly visit them all. There are the Pygmy tribes and the tribes of the Bantu group; There are the Namaqua and Koranna who belong to the Hottentot family. There are the pure Negroes and there are the tribes of Semitic and Libyan extraction. Wherever we go we find fetishism, superstition, and overwhelming fear of the unknown. Old customs and traditions remain; no one has the courage to tear them down.

Good-bye, Africa, land of the aborigine! We are off to visit the Islands of the Indian and Pacific Oceans.

The People of the Islands.—Here we are on the great island of Madagascar, directly opposite Mozambique and only a few hundred miles from the African coast. Wasting no time, we go directly to the central province and meet the Hovas, a people of great antiquity and rich in rare traditions.

And now across the Indian Ocean to Sumatra, to Java, to Borneo, to the Philippines. We wander among the old Malayan tribes and find remnants of ancient religions. queer marriage and burial customs, strange fancies and beliefs. We linger for a while with the savages on the Andaman Islands in the Bay of Bengal and marvel at their age-old customs and ceremonials.

Sailing below the Equator we come at last upon New Guinea. These people who gather in silent groups to greet us are the Papuans. Notice the crispness of their hair; it grows in tight, separated ringlets. It is said that to arrange these ringlets into one huge mop at the top of the head, the Papuans invented the comb.

Now we're sailing through the Pacific, to the island of the Polynesians. We find these people on the Hawaiian, Fiji, Samoan, Friendly, Caroline, and Marquesas Islands; and as we linger a while among them, we come to understand the origins of many of our customs.

The most savage Polynesians we meet on the Fiji Islands. Until recently they were cannibals. Even to-day they have very little regard for human life, and it is whispered that cannibalism and human sacrifice still exist in certain secret ceremonials. The men on these islands do not tatoo their bodies but paint them.

Among the Fiji Polynesians a curious system of caste exists. A man's dignity and standing is judged by the number of wives he has. There is a low society and a high, and the two are as distinctly separated as the low and high society of civilization.

Let us visit a group of Polynesian people who are more civilized than the Fijians. They are on the Friendly, or Tonga, Islands. The islands, you notice, are well named. The natives are indeed friendly; they welcome us with offerings of food and send their chief to greet us.

On Samoa Island we find a race of warriors. The natives are passionately fond of flowers, and both men and women always have a flower behind the ear. The Polynesians, we discover, have no very definite religion, but we realize at once how grossly superstitious they are. They firmly believe in their amulets, charms, and fetishes. They have an elaborate system of tabu.

With a little thrill of anticipation we embark for the Hawaiian Islands. Here we will find some old and fascinating customs! Here we will hear of some ancient legends and traditions! But we find these islands more civilized than any others in the group of the Polynesia. There are twelve islands, constituting a kingdom and governed by a native. But we find many native superstitions still existing, many native customs still observed. Custom and superstition do not die easily.

In the Polynesian group we find Society Island and Cook Island. We browse for a while in picturesque Tahiti, made familiar to us by the paintings of Paul Gauguin, who lived and died among these people and whose dust lies somewhere beneath our feet. No one knows where; the grave was never marked.

Another picturesque island, made familiar to us by O'Brien in his "White Shadows in the South Seas," is Marquesas. The Marquesans are a friendly and hospitable people. We dare not refuse the breadfruit they offer us, for that would seem to them an insult. This breadfruit and the milk of cocoanuts constitute their diet, with fish added in the fishing season. The Marquesans have many old legends and superstitions, and it is curious to note that they have a deluge myth. As we sit upon the *paepae* in the shade of the trees they tell it to us. And as we listen we realize that here we have struck the origins of some of our very own customs!

Leaving the friendly Marquesans we come to the Maoris, the primitive inhabitants of New Zealand. The Maoris have had practically every superstition, passion, vice, custom which we attach to savagery. For that reason, and because they cannot survive the approaches of civilization, these people are doomed to an early extinction.

The Maoris are cannibals. But as has already been indicated (see p. 50) they cannot be accused of deliberate cruelty or conscious torture. To them flesh was food, as it still is to-day. They "eat their man" but they kill him before they cook him. It was recently reported that a trade in human flesh actually existed among these people, now unable to indulge in cannibalism openly. The desire for human flesh in the Maoris is in some instances as strong as the desire for opium.

From New Zealand it is not so very far to Tasmania. This island, known at one time as Van Diemen's land, is only about one hundred and twenty miles from the coast of Australia. The Tasmanians are extinct now, but let us visit the island, anyway. Perhaps we can find someone who will tell us of the traditions and customs of these people.

And from Tasmania, you know, it is just a step across the channel into Australia, the museum of antiquity.

A Journey through Australia.—Australia is the only continent which is entirely in the southern hemisphere. It includes New South Wales, Victoria, Queensland, South Australia, Western Australia, and Tasmania.

Wonderful treasures of facts and inferences have been extracted from Australia. The dwellers in the interior are savages, untouched in many instances by civilzation, and observing to-day customs, rites, and ceremonials that are centuries old. It is because these people have survived but little changed throughout the ages that the modern investigator is able to learn from them much that is useful and enlightening concerning the origins of certain customs.

Now that we are here in Australia, we can understand to a certain extent why early civilizations did not begin here, could not thrive here. In a prehistory when there were no powerful ships, when man had no means of knowing where he was or how far from the opposite shore, Australia was cut off from all the rest of the world. Egypt had communication with Abyssinia, with Arabia, with Persia, with India. Having planted its first seeds in the soil of Egypt, civilization spread quickly, and we find old races falling and new ones rising up to take their places all over the world.

But Australia was alone, cut off from the world. Perhaps some wandering tribes reached it by way of New Guinea and the Torres Strait. But on the whole it has been the aborigines—the native, primitive, original races—who have lived and fought and intermixed and bred in Australia.

As we journey through this continent we are amazed at the amount of superstition that exists. It is very probable that the native Australians are the most superstitious people in the world. All their customs are tinged with fear of the supernatural; the very history of the country is written with the gloomy pen of superstition.

Let us sit for a moment on this peculiarly notched stone and listen to the tale that our guide tells us. He is not a native—if he were he would never sit on this stone. The natives believe it to be the home of an evil spirit who haunts the graves of the dead. But our guide merely shrugs his shoulders, grins, squats on the sacred stone, and beckons for us to follow. And he tells us this tale.

Many years ago a party of convicts escaped from a prison in Victoria. They wandered far into the country, but unlike the native savage they were unable to wrest food from nature. All perished except one. Journeying still further into the interior, half dead from exhaustion and lack of food and water, he came at last upon a grave. With the body had been buried food to accompany the spirit into the next world, and the spears of the deceased. The convict realized at once that this was the body of a chief who had just died and been buried.

He partook of the food—a crime punishable by death at the hands of the natives—and took the spears as a means of self-defence. As later developed, they served a far more satisfactory purpose.

Leaving the grave and wandering down the bank of a river, the man came upon some members of the tribe who had just buried their chief. Recognizing the weapons and believing the white stranger to be the "honoured chief jump-up" (resurrected) they fell upon their faces and welcomed him as the new chief.

The convict made the most of this opportunity and played upon the superstitious minds of the people. He was adopted and lived with the tribe for thirty years, ruling them with kindness and wisdom but obtaining from them the utmost respect and obedience.

"And that," said our guide with a flourish, "is the kind of superstition that still exists upon this continent. All these natives—every tribe you meet on your way to the coast—are guided by superstition first and reason last."

Which we find to be absolutely true as we continue our journey to the coast. We meet many savage tribes, and as we marvel at their curious customs and beliefs we cannot help wondering what *they* would think if they were suddenly transplanted to the heart of New York City!

Through Asia.—As we leave Australia and journey up through the Indian Ocean, we come to Ceylon, an island to the southeast of India. We stay for a while with the Ceylonese, learning much about their customs and beliefs; and then we cross into India, to begin our ride across the vast Asiatic expanse.

Archæology in Asia is in its infancy, and the beginnings of Asiatic civilizations are still obscure. We know, however, that commercial intercourse existed between Egypt and India at a very early date, and probably some of the early civilization of the Egyptians seeped through to India.

In India we are impressed by the complex system of "caste." The Brahman must not pollute himself by mingling with or touching, the lower classes—the "outcasts."

Going westward we meet the Siamese and the Burmese, and come across many aboriginal tribes. These people have changed very little; they still observe the old rites and ceremonies of their ancient ancestors.

Now we enter China—queer, fascinating, age-old China with its narrow streets and its rich temples and its solemn, majestic idols—the China we find it hard to understand because so many of its customs are the exact opposite of ours. Stand aside for a while and watch this strange procession. It is the trousseau of a bride being carried to her new home. There are foodstuffs in those baskets, and furnishings for the new home, and gaily embroidered jackets. It would be fun to see the bride. Perhaps she is not so very different, after all, from our own bride. But we will meet her later. Let us hurry on, now, to Japan.

We are instantly impressed, in Japan, by the superstitions of the people. They tell us many rare old legends and traditions to which we could listen forever—but we must hurry across the frozen stretches of Siberia, the country which occupies the whole of Northern Asia. This vast stretch of land extends from Turania and the eastern Asiatic plateau to the Arctic Ocean, and from the Ural Mountains to the Pacific. The Siberians, we find, are no longer barbarians but show the influence of Russian and Chinese civilization. But we can still find a hoary old native who knows all the traditions of the land.

Crossing Siberia quickly, we come to the Caspian Sea and cross into Persia. We meet a Persian nomad and he tells us of the customs of the country. The women, we soon discover, are remarkably clever, but they are superstitious, also, and they will not ignore the customs that have been handed down to them. Next to Persia are the Afghans—a most hospitable people. If there is food in Afghanistan no one need go hungry, no matter how poor he may be; the people will share their last morsel. They are particularly cordial to us, who are strangers, and they beg us to partake of their very best.

From Persia we cross into Turkey, the land of the Tartars. The northern routes of travel from the Caspian Sea to India, via Herat, are still in the hands of the Tartars who are probably the descendants of the savage Huns who, history tells us, spread ruin and desolation over a great part of the ancient world.

We notice, while we are in Turkey, that the veil is to some extent disappearing. But most of the people adhere tenaciously to their old traditions and customs. We wander by the old mosques and wonder who built them, and when. We are curious to see a harem, but our guide tells us it is forbidden. We meet Hebrews and Syrians, Kurds and Armenians, Arabs and nomads. We see crazy huts where no civilized person would want to dwell, and near by we see splendid mosques that lift their faces proudly to the sky.

And so, coming down through picturesque Arabia and out into the Arabian Sea, we complete our Asiatic journey.

We see at once that we have made a mistake. We should have gone through Arabia first, then through Turkey and north into Greece. Here we are in the Arabian Sea, whence our next journey should be through Europe; but this being the age of miracles, we merely hop into a 'plane and are whisked across the Red Sea, across the Mediterranean, to Gibraltar!

Glimpses of Europe.—Our first trip is through Spain and Portugal. We are delighted with the beautiful old gardens of Spain and listen enraptured while our guide tells us about the rare relics that have been unearthed at Carthage. Here and there we see the influence of the Roman and the Celt. And we meet a caravan of colourful Spanish gipsies who dance for us the sinuous dances of their forefathers and tell us beautiful old legends that have been handed down to them through many generations.

We leave Spain with regret, but come with joy and pleasure into France. Here is the birthplace of Fashion. Here is the country where culture made its greatest strides. Here is the land of the guillotine, and the *sans culotte,* and the *causerie.* These are the streets where French dandies made merry and here is the little town made famous for its exquisite tapestries. Shall we wander into Normandy and chat for a while with the peasants? What a wealth of romantic folklore they have. It is with regret that we leave them and go at last into the huge boot that is Italy.

But our regret does not last long. We are soon completely beneath the spell of beautiful old Italy. Let us first go through the Catacombs—the vast, underground tombs that house the ancient dead. But let us remain close to our guide; it would never do to be lost here! Now we will visit the buried cities and contemplate the forgotten civilizations that lie beneath our feet. You are restless. You want to see the Pantheon, the Vatican, Rome! You want to see Venice rising from the sea. You want to visit Milan, and Pisa, and Sicily.

Having browsed through Italy to our hearts' content, we cross the Alps into Switzerland and wander through the quaint, simple villages. Here we find a great love of sports. And we see lake-dwellings that somehow take us back over the centuries and make us think of primitive days.

Now we are in Germany, land of great universities, scientists, and leaders, land of inimitable folklore and mythology, land of the Rhine and the Lorelei. We hurry through Berlin, through Hamburg. We marvel at the examples of high caste and low caste that we see everywhere around us. There are two distinct societies—a high and a low—and they are kept strictly apart.

Let us hurry through Austria, through Bulgaria, through Serbia, through Roumania, through the Netherlands so that we can come at last to Greece. Here is a country that serves as a link between the old and the new. The Greeks were for centuries the nucleus of the world's best literature, architecture, thought. Poets still acclaim the "glory that was Greece." Athens still retains in ruins some traces of the masterpieces of architecture and sculpture which characterized her former splendour. You seem to feel this, do you not, as you stand in the shade of the Acropolis?

We must stay a little while in Greece—a week-end at least. There is so much to see, so very much that teaches us about ourselves. The museums of Athens are rich in antiquities; we shall visit and examine them all. And there are the Parthenon and the great temple of Minerva—was it not worth this journey across the world to see them?

Before we leave Greece, we must learn all we can about its folklore, the teachings of its early philosophers, its Olympic games. Our guide tells us of the ancient wedding customs and burial customs. He knows all the legends and traditions. Wonderful Greece! Beautiful, classical, enduring Greece! Your glory and grandeur can never be erased from the pages of time.

What is that island to the south of Athens? Our ship draws near and we see that we are approaching Crete. The pick of the archæologist has scarcely scratched the surface of this mysterious island. Who knows? Perhaps some day it will be proved that civilization had its first and most illustrious start here, passing north into Greece and south into Egypt. Authorities believe it possible. And the recent Cretan excavations make us wonder.

Let us now cross back to Constantinople, across the Black Sea to Odessa—and Russia. We are in a gigantic land. We meet Slavs, Cossacks, Circassians, Georgians, Hungarians, Bohemians. We see many forms of religious worship, and are surprised to see ancient forms of image worship still practised in certain sections. The people who just passed us on the road are peasants. They live in small, sometimes one-roomed houses. They represent one class of Russian life; the government and the wealthy people represent another.

Russia extends westward to the Ural Mountains which separate Europe from Asia. If we were to continue westward we would probably meet some of the strange wandering tribes of the frozen regions of the Arctic. Among them are remnants of the Tartars and the Mongols, and there are, of course, the Samoyeds, who still cling to their ancient religion. This religion is a bewildering combination of witchcraft, spiritualism, idolatry, and sacrifice. Neither Russia nor China has been able to change the mode of life of the Samoyeds. They cling to every tradition and custom that has been handed down to them, and they live in the old manner of their ancestors.

We are now in the Arctic regions, near enough to visit the old Scandinavian countries—Denmark, Norway, Sweden. These countries are peopled by men who like to believe in the mysterious and the supernatural. A mass of traditional lore—impressive and picturesque legends—has been bequeathed them by their forefathers, and they accept all this lore as truth.

Iceland, Finland, and Lapland have also a wealth of folklore and tradition. We travel through these countries quickly, finding not a moment dull. The Lapps, we notice, are the most round-headed people in Europe. Let us talk to that mother with her round-headed baby. Our guide will act as interpreter. This is what he tells us: when a Lapp child is born a reindeer is set apart for him. This, with its progeny, forms the foundation of his future fortunes and he never can be wholly without property. Only for a boy child? we ask. No, no, indeed, the mother hastens to assure us. Her child is a girl, and she has put aside two reindeer, if you please! A sensible way of starting a trousseau, we decide, as we continue on our way.

To conclude our European journey, we cross the North Sea into Britain. The Britons belong to the Aryan races. The term "Aryan" means noble, of good family. It is a Sanskrit word and is believed to have come from the root *ar,* to plough. This same root is found in the word *era,* which is Greek for *earth.* The Aryans, because they ploughed the ground, considered themselves the noblest of human races; and eventually the word itself came to signify that which is noble and honourable. Various European countries are included under the Aryan races. Most historians, however, use the name Indo-European which means exactly the same as Aryan and conveys a much clearer idea of the races included therein. We have visited all the Aryan races with the exception of the Britons.

England is the land of the lord and the lady, of the vassal and the peasant, of nobility, feudalism, peasantry. It is the land of Shakespeare and of Dickens, of King Arthur and Robin Hood. There is probably no other country that has so largely influenced our own manners and customs, although we ran away from all that was England and English.

The Irish, Scotch, and Welsh have also influenced our customs. These people are rich in tradition, and their customs are very largely concerned with the observance of these traditions. How threads of tradition from Great Britian crossed the ocean and patterned themselves into American life will later be seen.

Off to the Newer World.—History likes to speak of America as the "New World." It is new, indeed, if one judges only by the written records. America has no written history, no written records whatever, previous to its discovery in 1492.

Nevertheless, we have every reason to believe that the native American races—the Indians, as they are familiarly known—have a great antiquity. No one knows precisely when the Indians separated from the main branch of mankind, but J. W. Dawson says man very possibly reached America before the mastodon disappeared, indicating that there was an ancient American population of which very little is known. If this is true, and many authorities believe that it is, there was an ancient American race coeval with the oldest cave men of Europe. Like the cave men, these people possibly were swept away before the advent of the more modern races.

(Courtesy of Metropolitan Museum of Art)

Ancient Egyptian amulets, cross, and silver ring.

(Courtesy of Metropolitan Museum of Art)

An Egyptian amulet of the 12th Dynasty. Prototype of the cross.

(Courtesy of Metropolitan Museum of Art)

Amulets, Egyptian, 26th Dynasty.

An interesting conjecture is made by Daniel Wilson in his "Prehistoric Man." He assumes that during the early primitive scattering of the infant races, the Mongol and the American went eastward, and the Indo-Europeans went westward. They met after an interval of thousands of years, coming from opposite directions and having made a complete circuit of the world.

One of the most conclusive proofs concerning the antiquity of man in America was the finding of fossil human remains estimated to be not less than 10,000 years old. ("Types of Mankind," Professor Agassiz, p. 352.) These remains were found in a calcareous conglomerate of the coral reefs of Florida.

The name "Indian" was given to the American aborigines by Amerigo Vespucci, after whom the country itself is named. He believed, as did many others after him, that Columbus had reached the eastern shore of India and that the inhabitants were therefore "Indians."

Aren't you eager to make your journey through this land of the Indian, our own America? Let us leave at once, and starting with Alaska (the doorway through which the Indian entered, according to some authorities) trace our course through the North American continent.

From Alaska to Panama.—Who are these strange people we meet at the very doorstep to the American continent? They are the Eskimo, our guide tells us—an Indian people who inhabit the arctic coast of America from Greenland to Alaska. The Algonquins gave them their name, he informs us. They called these people Eskumaget, which means "raw eaters."

The Eskimo call themselves Innuit which means "men." They are untouched by any foreign influence; their tales and traditions extend back for thousands of years. The women do the hardest work and are the slaves of the men, not even being permitted to eat in their company. In summer the Eskimo live in conical skin tents; in winter they usually live in half-underground huts of stone, turf, earth, and bones which are entered by long, tunnel-like passages. These passages can be traversed only on all fours.

We need not traverse the great distance along the upper coast of Canada to Greenland, for we will meet only this same type of people. The Eskimo are found in broken tribes from East Greenland to the western shores of Alaska. They are never far inland. They are divided into Greenlanders, Labrador Eskimo, the Iglulik or Central, and the Western.

How do these people live? we wonder as we gather around a roaring fire. The country allows no cultivation. The ground is almost perpetually frozen. There goes a fellow with his spear—let us ask him. Sometimes they hunt, he says; more frequently they fish. Most of their food comes from the water. That, then, is why we do not find them far inland.

Let us leave this land of Arctic nights, of snow and ice and primitive people. Going down through Canada we find remnants of the old Indian tribes: the Algonquins, the Chippewas, the Flatheads, the Navajos; but they are fast disappearing, and only now and then do we meet a real full-blooded Indian who knows all the legends and traditions of his people.

In the United States we find it still more difficult to encounter any full-blooded Indians—except on the reservations set aside by the Government. We visit several such reservations but leave strangely disappointed. The Indians have been Americanized, we tell one another. They are not true representatives of their race.

America, and particularly the United States, is unique among the countries, as we very quickly discover. To this continent have been attracted the people from practically every corner of the globe—the French, the English, the Irish, the Dutch, the Spanish, the German, the Italian, even the Chinese and the Japanese have left their native lands and made their homes on these shores.

Among the tribes of North American Indians whose customs have contributed to those we shall discuss in the pages that follow are the Apaches, the Sioux, the Cheyennes, the Dakotas, the Arapahoes, the Shoshonees, the Utes, the Kiowas, the Pueblos, the Hurons, the Iroquois, the Cherokees, the Creeks, the Seminoles, the Choctaws, and the Chickasaws.

Shall we visit the Great Lakes before leaving the United States? Here we are—right at the edge of Lake Michigan. This was once a great Indian territory, you know. Not so very much indication of it now, is there? But perhaps our guide will be able to find the spot where an old Indian totem pole stands. Yes, he finds it. At least four hundred years old, he says. What weird, grotesque figures, yet each little line and curve had a distinct meaning to the Indian race that worshipped it.

We are off for Boston, home of our Puritan fathers. This bustling town was the first centre of culture and civilization in the "New World." Many of the traditions and customs of the "New World" were cradled here. Town of memories, of traditions, of freedom's first note!

And here is New York, great melting pot of the world! Here custom is made for the rest of the nation. Here is a people curiously free from custom and tradition, yet as custom-bound and as tradition-bound as any native Indian tribe! Here is a city that is a little world in itself, yet that has borrowed its customs, its manners, its very people, from every corner of the globe. Here we find caste, and culture, and progress, and religion, and superstition—a little bit of everything that we have found in our journey around the world.

Good-bye, New York! We are off for Mexico where progress has not been so rapid and where we can still find traces of primitive peoples.

An old man stops us on the road. Do we want to hear of the old deity Quetzalcoatl? And of an ancient, lost civilization? We are delighted and we ply the man with questions. He takes us to a place near Palenque and shows us the great white temple dedicated to Quetzalcoatl. It is still and desolate, here in this wild, subtropical country; the temple has not known the sound of human voice for generations.

We enter, awed and silent, as though we stand upon the threshold of some great discovery. Our old man of the road seems a prophet in his ragged clothes. He tells us that the temple was erected, not to some fanciful idol or creature of the imagination, but to a man who actually lived and laboured among his people. He taught them how to smelt and forge metals, how to write, how to cut precious stones. He even taught them a code of manners. But a stronger, cruder people came and wiped out this infant civilization.

We go out into the glowing noonday and our old man shuffles away. He refuses the gold piece we offer him.

Our guide amuses us with fanciful tales of Mexican grandees. He has a wealth of Mexican mythology which he gladly relates. He tells us of the Aztecs. We wander through the rocky, picturesque land, coming here and there upon remnants of early peoples who seem entirely untouched by any civilizing influences. They still live in the manner of their forefathers and appear quite satisfied with their lot.

Leaving Mexico we come to Guatemala, that part of the continent which lies between Mexico and Colombia and which is now designated as Central America. It comprises the British Honduras, and the six independent republics of Guatemala, Salvador, Honduras, Nicaragua, Costa Rica, and Panama. Here, too, we find remnants of several old tribes, in their native state and untouched by civilization.

From Panama to Cape Horn.—Having browsed so long in old worlds and among primitive peoples, it is a curious treat to come to the Panama Canal, engineering triumph supreme. We gaze at it with awe and pride, and we cannot help remembering the Kaffirs and the Hottentots and the Namaquas we have visited.

Stretching below the Panama Canal lies the continent of South America. The peoples we shall meet are the Patagonians, the Brazilian Indians, the Amazons, the Caribs and the Arrawaks, the Mozcas, the old Incas, the Chilians, the Ecuadorians.

We go through Colombia and Venezuela, through Guiana and Ecuador. Everywhere we see traces of superstition, we see people bound by the customs handed down to them through long generations. We go through South Brazil and come upon some aboriginal tribes; we cross Bolivia and enter into Peru.

We stand now upon the ground where the Incas fought the Spaniards, where Pizarro tried to teach Christianity to the proud and haughty Inca chief, Astahuallpa. Here was the great massacre of the Inca hordes—the wiping out, by the Spaniards, of a gentle and advanced people. Our guide shows us the wall where the first Inca fell.

Meditating upon the sad fate of the Incas and upon the greed which caused exquisite goblets, ewers, and vases to be melted for their gold, we leave Peru and wander through the narrow strip of land that is called Chile. Gone are the native tribes; the old order has given way to the new. We come upon bustling seaports and come only rarely upon a true native who can tell us of the Chilian customs and traditions of other days.

To the west of Chile is Argentina with Patagonia at its southeastern extremity. From Patagonia come several of our popular customs which are later to be discussed. And in Patagonia we can still find primitive tribes in their native state, although they are quickly becoming extinct. The Patagonians are believed by many to be the tallest known people and the few we meet seem to carry out this contention.

Now north to Uruguay where we chat for a while with some keen, stalwart natives. And farther north into

Paraguay where we meet natives of another sort—canny, suspicious, tradition-bound, as natives are everywhere.

So ends our journey around the world. You are back, now, where you started—New York, if you live in New York; Portland, if you live in Portland; Springfield, Oshkosh, Memphis, or wherever you happen to be.

You know now the area from which our customs, traditions, superstitions, and lore have been culled. You have met, in their native lands, the people who will tread their way through the pages that follow. Man and the world are revealed before you.

CHAPTER III

Origin and Development of Etiquette

Out of the past we have come. Into it we are constantly returning. Meanwhile, it is of the utmost importance to our lives. It contains the roots of all we are. . . . It contains the record or ruins of all the experiments that man has made during a quarter and a half million years in the art of living in this world. —Cassius J. Keyser.

THE FIRST HUMAN RELATIONSHIP

"ETIQUETTE," says Mrs. Lydig Hoyt, "really means civilization—life as we live it to-day as distinguished from what it was in the days of the primitive."

We hope that by this time the reader has gained a clear and definite conception of what civilization really is, what it means, how it started, how it developed through the long ages of life. Etiquette is just a thread drawn through the many-coloured fabric of civilization. An important thread, of course, since it helps hold the fabric together; but by no means the only thread.

"Just try to imagine what our life would be like without etiquette!" pursues the author from whom we quote. "It would mean, for instance, more difficulty in boarding trolleys and subways, in driving automobiles. We'd all still be eating with our hands only and goodness knows what other things we would be doing!"

To this writer it seems that we would be doing precisely what man has been doing since the beginning of time. We would be inventing our etiquette, creating it in our daily life, living it. Etiquette, if regarded simply as ceremonial, is just another word for pride or caste. But if regarded as custom, habit, as the accepted mode of life, it becomes—

as it actually is—a fundamental factor in the evolution and development of man.

And by "custom" we do not mean the custom of the moment—the fashion or the whim of popular fancy. Since the very dawn of life man has had habit forced upon him by various external influences—the conditions under which he lived, the forces with which he had to contend, the instincts which he blindly obeyed. Thus did his mode of life induce special habits.

These habits passed into custom; custom passed sometimes into ceremonial, sometimes into religon, frequently into law. Custom, then, as we interpret it, means the habits of life as observed by mankind throughout its existence—the things we do, and say, and feel without stopping to think about them.

Taking etiquette in this broader, truer sense, let us trace it back over the ages and see how it served as the first human relationship. What were the first rules of etiquette, which means, in other words, the first laws of life, the first habits of man? When did they start, and how did they spread?

Primitive Etiquette Based on Fear.—In his primitive state man feared more than he reasoned. He feared the huge animals that roamed everywhere, and he found himself a safe home in some cave, rolling a stone against it at night to keep out intruders—the first door. He feared the elements and tried to read the stars—the beginning of astronomy. He feared unknown beings and wore the teeth and claws of animals he had killed to warn these beings of spirits that he was strong—the beginning of charms and of ornamentation.

But more than anything else, perhaps, man feared his own kind. Man was easy prey to man in those days, and food was sometimes scarce. It became one of the first habits of life, therefore, to carry always a crude club as a weapon. Fancy leads us astray, for a moment, as we contemplate the sword which followed the club, and the cane which followed the sword. Don't you, in your own circle of acquaintances, know someone who never feels quite comfortable and at ease unless he is swinging a cane?

Fear, then, is one of the first instincts which shows its influence upon the habits of man. As soon as our savage ancestors met each other, they growled; and having growled, they raised their clubs; and having raised their clubs they fell upon each other. "To the victor belonged the spoils," and it usually happened that one of the fellows was hungry.

Man, however, reasoned as well as feared, although fear came first. Sometimes two savages would meet, and neither being hungry nor particularly frightened, they would eye each other, make a wide circuit, and disappear in opposite directions. Reason spoke. Why kill each other when both were well fed, when each was satisfied to pass on without injury to the other?

At another time, perhaps, they would come upon a great beast of the jungle—both at the same time. The instinct of self-preservation strong within them, they would fall together upon the beast and between them kill it with little trouble. Reason spoke again. Two could kill a beast more quickly and with less trouble than one—then why not hunt together? Why not be friends instead of enemies?

This occurred not to one man, but to many men in many widely separated places. Thereafter, when one savage fellow met another with whom he wished to be friendly, he held out his bare right hand—the weapon hand—as a symbol, or sign, of peace. The other fellow understood; symbolism is the simplest language of mankind. They joined forces, hunting, eating, and probably living together in the same cave.

The custom of holding out the right hand as a sign of peace, or welcome, or greeting, still exists. Our handclasp very possibly had its origin in this age-old custom. And you see, don't you, how it grew out of fear; how it was a habit of life forced on early man by the conditions under which he lived.

The Early Need for Friendliness.—In a world peopled with strange creatures of fancy and haunted by terrifying beasts, primitive man soon found a certain comfort in association with his own kind. The lone huntsman became a clansman, and in the clan were formulated the first laws of primitive society.

It is easy to see how the clan originated, or gathered, around the strongest and most powerful fellow in the vicinity. He became the head clansman, the chief. Mr. Strong Man, we shall call him. He would be proud of his power, disdainful of the weaker men about him. He would have possessions that were tabu to the others.

And Mr. Strong Man, conceited as man has been since the beginning of time, would demand some visible signs of fear and subjection from the men he permitted to join his clan. If they wished to hunt with him, join in the great feasts with him and find protection and comfort in his clan, they must be subservient to him. In other words, they must salute him as their superior.

Thus out of fear for Mr. Strong Man, mingled with a desire for friendliness, evolved forms of obeisance. This was probably the very earliest appearance of caste, or social differentiation.

Few of the ceremonial customs of courtesy which we observe to-day have originated in recent times. Most of them are vestiges of the past; they have grown out of the slow evolution of social life. And most of them are traceable to their genesis and early form, as we shall presently see.

The First Forms of Obeisance.—Early man realized that if he did not sufficiently honour Mr. Strong Man certain dire happenings would follow. Therefore he took pains to show his respect, to show that he realized Mr. Strong Man's importance.

One of the earliest forms of obeisance was kowtowing.

The word derives from the Chinese k'o-t'eu, a term meaning "to knock the head on the ground." Kowtowing, as a method of saluting a superior, was known not only in China, but was a widespread custom throughout Africa. The king of the Brass people, they tell us, never spoke to the king of the Ibos without acknowledging his inferiority by getting down on his knees and striking his head several times against the ground.

The Egyptians had a similar custom known as senta, which means, literally, "breathing the ground." To do homage to a person of importance they would fall to the ground and kiss the earth. The Coast Negroes, possibly borrowing the custom from their Egyptian neighbours, were accustomed to prostrate themselves before superiors and kiss the ground three times. On the lower Niger the people fell to their knees and struck their foreheads against the earth.

Many forms of obeisance, still in use to-day, evidently had their origin in acts to show absolute submission. These forms would be used in times when all chance of escape was gone, and having become a habit would gradually grow into custom. Thus among the Sandwich Islanders even to this day falling on the face is a mark of respect, originating, no doubt, as a mark of submission.

Among the North American Indians it was the custom for two people, when they met, to sit down about twenty yards from each other and simply look at each other without speaking. After a few minutes they would rise and walk on together. But if a person of importance approached, the other fellow would sit down and remain seated while the other passed on. To remain standing would have been a breach of conduct and the offender would very likely have been punished.

Thus were forms of obeisance and homage originated to flatter the vanity of the strong men, the chiefs, the leaders of tribes and clans. And thus, also, was born caste which has probably had more influence upon our manners and customs than any other one factor.

CASTE AND THE CREATION OF CODES

The influence of caste has been felt by mankind since the earliest times. Wherever there have been men with more skins, more wives, more earthly possessions than others, there has been caste. Wherever there have been men with more brute strength and consequently more power than others, there has been caste. Wherever there has been nobility, and peasantry, and fashion, and wealth, there one is sure to find evidences of caste.

And caste brings custom. Those who belong to the upper—the more powerful or influential—castes, demand homage and recognition from those beneath them. Cyrus, we are told, beheaded two of his inferiors because they omitted to place their hands inside their sleeves, when saluting him. And Charlemagne, you remember, pleased his vanity by forcing subject kings to serve him at table.

Caste forms grades or classes of society. It separates one whole society of mankind into many stages or levels, into many kinds of societies. In other words, caste divides. And as it divides, it brings into being certain ceremonials. These ceremonials in time become customs. And these customs, be it noted, bring together again, consolidate, standardize. It is a complete cycle: caste—custom—society—and caste again.

The first definite instances of caste centre about royalty. The word king itself represents a definite grade or caste of society. We cannot think of the word without immediately associating it in our minds with ceremony, pomp, power—caste.

Royalty has always been surrounded by pomp and ceremonial from the cradle to the grave. Every monarch, no matter of what date or country, has called upon his subjects for marks of respect and homage. There would be a strict hereditary etiquette, handed down through one royal generation after another.

Out of this royal ceremonial would naturally grow certain forms and certain restrictions. These restrictions would serve to frame in and emphasize the separateness of the royal person and the inferiority of his subjects.

The Food Tabu.—It is related that when the King of Persia gave dinner parties he himself sat at a separate table in another room where he could see his guests, but where he would be unseen by them. This is a custom of great antiquity.

In primitive times it was believed that evil could enter the body with the food. As the king had enemies who envied him his power, he took extraordinary precaution. No one was permitted to touch his food, and no one was permitted even to see him eat it.

Thus if any man or beast saw the King of Loango eat, that man or beast was instantly put to death. A tradition says that the king's own son was killed for this reason. Similarly, it was a capital offence to see the King of Dahomey at his meals; the King of Tongo ate in secret; and the King of Abyssinia never permitted any one near him when he dined.

Having established this tabu for superstitious reasons, kings, priests and men of power continued it and carried it to extremes because they realized that it separated them from the inferior classes or castes—gave them a certain importance. And presently we find the tabu of not eating together spreading among other peoples outside of royalty and becoming one of the main features in certain systems of caste.

In Tonga, for instance, there are ranks and orders that cannot eat and drink together, no matter what the occasion. In Uripiv (New Hebrides) the males are divided into ten "castes" which are determined by age, and these castes may under no circumstances eat with one another.

The same custom is found among the Hindus, a people

of many caste separations. The Paharias regard themselves as superior to the Keriahs and will not eat or drink with them. The young Bedouin boy shows deference and respect to his father by refusing to eat in his presence. Members of different castes will not eat food that has been cooked in the same vessel. To eat together is one of the "grand tests of identity of caste" among the Hindus.

In New Zealand it was forbidden the slave to eat with his master, just as to-day, among some Eskimo people, it is forbidden the woman to eat with her husband. The Atiu Islanders refuse, to this day, to eat with the missionaries; and the Papuans will not eat food that a European visitor has touched.

And so it continues one people after another creating castes within their own communities and establishing restrictions to emphasize their own power. And so it will continue until the end of time as long as there are different castes or grades of society.

The food tabu may seem strange to us. Yet in modern life many instances of "unwritten laws" against eating together can be pointed out. In England the servant who drinks his master's champagne or sits at the table with him outrages all sense of caste propriety. And there is a caste consciousness even among the servants, for the upper servant refuses to eat with the others.

Nor do we have to go to England to see modern examples of the food tabu. Where is the wealthy American who will dine with his chauffeur in public, no matter how democratic he otherwise may be? And where is the chauffeur who will want to dine with his employer? He will feel embarrassed, ill at ease, conscious of the fact that he is out of caste.

This caste consciousness exists, whether we will admit it or not. We cannot escape it. It is a part of our primitive personality, just as is the desire to imitate, or the love of the magical and the mysterious.

Between the Sexes.—The difference between the sexes

has always been a basis for caste. In primitive life, the woman was subordinated. Because she did not fight side by side with the warriors, because she did not hunt or fish and therefore had to depend upon the men for food, she fell into a lower social position.

Here again we find the food tabu. In many African tribes it was a capital offence to eat with a woman. Even to-day a Uripiv Islander who eats with a woman runs the risk of a sudden and mysterious death. It simply is not done; it is not the custom.

In Barotseland, which is in Northern Rhodesia, Africa, the natives explain their custom of eating separately—men with men, women with women—in this fashion: A man is naturally stronger than a woman, and owing to this superior strength he might be tempted, in his hunger, to snatch the largest and choicest morsels of food. Therefore they dine separately so that the woman is assured her share. Naive and amusing, but not true. They eat separately because all their ancestors before them ate separately; because it has been for generations the custom to do so.

Savage people of long ago kept the young women of the tribe hidden. They were tabu to the warriors, and it was only when they reached a certain age that they were permitted to "come out into the sun" and be married. Survivals of this custom are seen in our chaperon and "coming out" party.

In many tribes it was considered a serious breach of conduct for a man to see his mother-in-law, talk to her, or have any association with her whatever. She belonged to a different tribal caste and was therefore tabu. Thus if a Wemba sees his mother-in-law approaching he at once retreats; if he is forced to meet her face to face he keeps his eyes fixed on the ground and walks on without greeting her. (Perhaps that mother-in-law joke is staler than we think!)

In Tasmania it is a natural custom for a man to look

aside while a woman is passing. This is an ancient form of politeness observed by many savage races. In that country it is also prohibited to speak of sexual matters in the presence of a third person.

There were many tabus in early life that later became forms of politeness. Thus, at one time the wives of the chiefs in Tonga were not permitted to be seen by any other men. Now they may walk abroad with attendants, but never without attendants. We see a suggestion of our chaperon in this custom. In Loango girls were at one time kept strictly secluded; they were tabu; they remained secluded until their parents found a suitable husband for them. To-day a vestige of this ancient custom is seen not only in Loango but among other savage peoples. The youths are not permitted to speak to the girls except when they are in the presence of their mothers. A strange sort of etiquette to exist in savage life!

The early Romans, advanced in courtesy as in all things, treated the women with so much honour and respect that it was prohibited to say the least immodest word in their presence. When a Roman met a woman in the street he always gave her right of way. Even the magistrates observed this custom.

In later civilizations, the association between the sexes brought about elaborate codes of courtesy and chivalry. This is particularly noticeable in France and in England, where the romance of the Crusades, the reign of Chivalry and the gallant tournaments at which "knights found courage in their ladies' eyes" added a distinctly courteous flavour to social life.

Respect for the Aged.—Although some savage tribes have been known to desert and even kill their aged members, many peoples are known who, since earliest times, have treated their aged with marked deference. The Eskimo, the Bushmen, the Australians, the Fuegians, the Veddahs, the Dyaks, the Caribs—all show courtesy and honour to the old among them.

(Courtesy of American Museum of Natural History, New York)

A totem pole of Alert Bay.

The savage believes that there exists between his totem and himself a certain intimate and sacred relationship.

(Courtesy of American Museum of Natural History, New York)

Pygmy Group, Central Africa.
The care of the fire is very important. It must never be permitted to die out.

In Central Africa there are numerous savage tribes, and they are believed by many even to-day to be devoid of all natural affections. Yet there is a group among them members of which have been known to carry around for years an old, feeble, palsied man, showing him the greatest tenderness and attention.

We find many strange contradictions in savage life. Frequently we find barbarity coexisting with habits of refinement within the same tribe. The Ahts until recently deserted their sick and aged, and they are still known occasionally to sacrifice one of their number to the gods. Yet these very same people keep small mats of bark strips for strangers to wipe their feet with, and after meals they offer their guests water for washing their hands and mouths.

An interesting code of politeness exists among the Kikuyu. The girls stand aside for the warriors; the warriors in turn stand aside for the old women. Caste created this code, of course; the girls do not hunt or fish and are dependent upon the warriors for protection; therefore they belong to a lower social order and must show deference to the warriors. But the older women have brought warriors into the world and have served the tribe for many years; therefore they belong to a higher caste than the young girls and are treated with respect by everyone in the tribe.

A Masai warrior dare not greet an elder until the elder has greeted him.

Mabuiag boys are instructed not to stand upright in the presence of old men, but to crouch—a sign of respect.

In Asia, among the Mongols and the Kalmucks, a woman must not speak to her father-in-law or sit down in his presence.

Among the Mpongwe the young may never approach the old without crouching and baring their heads. So potent is custom that even when passing the huts of elders the young Mpongwe instinctively lowers his head.

A Corean and a Pueblo Indian never smoke before their fathers. It is considered a mark of disrespect to do so.

A Wemba may not ask his senior for a smoke; but, as Elsie Clews Parsons so naively points out in her "Fear and Conventionality," "he can sit down near the older men and look wistful."

Thus do we find respect for the aged one of the first traits of savage life. Wherever desertion of the aged has been known, lack of sufficient food and other external conditions of life forced the custom upon the people. But on the whole, we find a surprising degree of respect and courtesy towards older people among the savage races.

The ancient Egyptians, according to Plato, inculcated respect for old age. They required, as we do to-day, that the young rise upon the approach of the old. We are informed that, like the Israelites and the Lacedæmonians, they were required at all times to give place to their superiors in years.

Coming to early European history we find that this respect for the aged, far from disappearing, has increased and has become definitely a part of social life. The young were required to pay marked deference to all older people, beginning with their parents. Even a prince was not permitted to sit at table with his father until he had distinguished himself by valour.

The Castes of Early Society.—Many factors served to divide early society into castes, or classes. There was, of course, royalty which always surrounded itself with elaborate ceremonial. And as important, if not as impressive, as royalty was the temple system or the religious system—the priests, scribes, magicians, wizards, seers. Primitive civilizations grew up around these people and many of them accumulated vast properties and treasures.

Wealth, of course, has always been one of the greatest dividing factors—caste-creating factors—among men. In early days property consisted of rights in land, except, perhaps, for a few movables. Kings granted great tracts of land to their favourites, largely as a matter of pampering their own vanity. And these favourites, once warriors or attachés of the court, became powerful landowners.

Now we come to the artisan class—the makers of pottery, the weavers, the carpenters, the craftsmen. There is no doubt that at some time or other crafts or professions were in most countries hereditary. Thus in the Fijis the carpenters from a separate caste and it is customary for the son to step into his father's place and continue in the craft of carpentry. In India, as in other countries, craft guilds were formed which further divided the people into classes or castes.

At the base of social life we find the largest and most essential class in the community—the peasants, the serfs, the tillers of the soil. These are the people who cultivated the land, who gathered together for safety and formed villages, who took care of the flocks. And these are the people who were then, and who have been through the ages, the most superstitious, the least informed. Therefore they are the people who have accepted the customs of their forefathers without question, and who aped the customs of those above them.

There have been many, many other castes of society, but it would be tiresome to mention them all. There have been the soldiery and the seamen, the merchants and the retailers, the servants and the slaves. Early life was divided into countless castes; there existed high and low even within castes. A study of these early castes or divisions of society enables one better to grasp and understand the social problems of to-day.

Caste and Titles.—"Judging from what has happened since history has been organized," says Frederic Marshall, "it seems reasonable to suppose that in early times kings invented themselves first and then invented titles in order to illumine their glory. Menes was a title in himself for his name signifies 'the conductor.' "

History tells of many battles that have been fought for

titles. A whole book could be written on the subject on titles alone. The man of title considers himself on a plane removed from other, lesser peoples; he feels himself surrounded with glory and pomp. There is no satisfaction quite as great as titular satisfaction.

Mr. Marshall tells an interesting little story in his book "International Vanities." We quote it here because it bears out our assertion that titles pamper the vanity of man, that man will go to any extremes to gain the title he covets.

> Napoleon met one day an old soldier with one arm. He stopped and said to him, "Where did you lose your arm?" "Sire, at Austerlitz!" was the reply. "And were you not decorated?" asked the Emperor. "No, Sire, I was forgotten." "Then," rejoined Napoleon, here is my own cross for you; I make you a Chevalier." "Ah, Sire," exclaimed the soldier, "Your Majesty makes me Chevalier because I have lost one of my arms; what would your Majesty have done if I had lost them both?" "I should have created you an officer of the Legion," answered Napoleon. Thereupon the soldier instantly drew his sword with his remaining hand and cut off his remaining arm!

There have been all sorts of titles since titles were first created. There have been court titles which include king, emperor, tsar, and the lesser court titles such as duke, earl, count, etc. It is said that the word "duke" was invented in 1130 by Louis, third Count of Thuringia. He adopted the title in order to distinguish himself from the crowd of counts around him. Sultan, it is interesting to note, means "mighty man."

Next to the court titles are the religious titles. These include the Pope, bishops, vicars, etc.

Titles of courtesy come next, and they form one of the largest branches of this subject. It is possible that titles of courtesy grew out of titles of court—just as the word courtesy itself grew out of the word court in the time of Philip the Good, Duke of Burgundy. These titles of courtesy include sire, monseigneur, lord, lady, etc. Each has a history of its own.

The origin of Lord and Lady is so interesting that we

cannot resist the temptation to give it here. The Lord was simply the loaf-ward, the guardian of the loaf or the food, the band that kept the house together, that is to say, the houseband—later, the husband.

The lady was simply the *loaf-kneader*, the maker of the loaf, the one who attended to the domestic duties. The spinster is one who does not become a loaf-kneader (or lady) but sits at the distaff and spins or winds the thread.

Gabriel Tarde believes that titles had something to do with the development of politeness, that the deference of one titular caste toward another helped make men polite, brought customs of courtesy into being. We like particularly this paragraph, which we quote from his "Laws of Imitation":

> Politeness is merely reciprocity of flattery. We know beyond a doubt that the desire of the petty potentate for ambassadors, of the marquis for pages, of the courtier for a court, that the general need of being flattered, waited on and saluted like a nobleman, was the secret factor which little by little, in France and elsewhere, made every man polite. It began with the court, then reached the city, then the chateaux, and then all classes to the very lowest.

THE DEVELOPMENT OF ETIQUETTE

Most authorities are agreed that the Orient was the seat of early culture and that manners are oriental in their origin. This may be true, but it did not take long for manners to spread everywhere. Although we find early sproutings of culture and of cultivated manners in China, Persia, Japan, and the Caliphate of Bagdad, it was not until later, in Spain, France, and other European countries, that etiquette took any serious form.

The origin of the Golden Rule as we interpret it, and which is, after all, the true basis of all etiquette, is accredited to Confucius, the sage of China (550—478 B.C.). Several times he expressed that rule in his writings: "What you do not like when done to yourself, do not do to others."

You will be interested in the story of Confucius' birth.

He was the son of the old officer Heih. That officer, when over seventy years of age, sought an alliance with one of the three daughters of a certain man of the Yen clan. Heih had nine daughters and one son who was crippled, and he did not want to die until he could leave a strong male offspring to carry on his glory. This desire for male offspring was very strong in early man.

Ching-ysai, the youngest of the three daughters of the Yen clan, in the manner of all Chinese children said it was for their father to decide the case. As Heih was of most illustrious descent, the father said, "You shall marry him, then." Accordingly she became the bride of the old man, and in the next year the mother of the sage, Confucius.

Heih died not very long after, and Confucius grew into manhood aware always of the gentle, inspiring presence of his young mother who taught him kindness, piety, courtesy, love. Her influence remained with him throughout life.

As the sage of China, Confucius taught his followers the virtues of kindness and gentleness, even as his mother had taught him these virtues in youth. He taught his people to respect the aged and help the infirm; he instilled in them a love of peace; he gave them their Golden Rule. He is reported to have said, "All virtues have their source in etiquette."

Confucius travelled a great deal, and with him went his disciples. It is easy to see how they spread the gospel of courtesy and politeness, how they carried etiquette wherever they went. To Confucius, then, we owe the first distinct code of etiquette, of manners; and to him we are indebted for many of the customs that later will be discussed.

Caste in Japan has always been, and still is to-day, very great. Every particular caste has its own peculiar "I"—a pronoun which no other caste may use.

The Japan of the seventh century was divided into two great classes—the governing class and the supporting class; but each of these two classes was divided into many grades or castes. The higher ranks and offices were accompanied with definite grants of rice land to be held during tenure of office. People of other ranks were exempted from payment of tributes.

Because of the many castes existing within the governing class, all rules and details relating to address, title, ceremonial visits, etc., involved problems of precedence and importance in rank. This brought about a minute, tedious, and extremely verbose politeness which is found in both Japan and China at the present time. The Chinese particularly have an "academy of compliments" by which they regulate the number of bows and words to be used on any occasion. Thus ambassadors before appearing at court sometimes practise these ceremonies forty days in advance!

Meaning of the Word Etiquette.—There are many conflicting opinions as to the correct origin of the word etiquette. What does it mean? Where does it come from? What is its relation to modern life?

Some authorities believe that the word etiquette derives from the Greek stichos which means order, rank. Others claim for it a French origin.

It is possible that the word is a corruption of the Latin phrase *est hic questio inter N. et N.* This was a formula placed by procurers on their law papers, similar in meaning to our legal formula N. *versus* N. The primary French meaning of the word etiquette in the sense of ticket originated probably with this formula.

Etiquettes, or tickets, became popular in France and were fastened upon the outside of parcels and documents to indicate their contents. And later we find *etiquettes* distributed among the people who are to be presented at court. The purpose is obvious. These *etiquettes*, being printed rules on what to do and what not to do, were intended to keep people from making blunders before the royal personages.

Garrick Mallery, writing in the *American Anthropologist*, says:

As *etiquettes* were fastened outside of documents or parcels to indicate their contents, so *etiquettes* were given to people on ceremonial occasions to tell them where to stand and what to do. Thence grew up the secondary use of the term as descriptive of the ceremonies themselves. Therefore the slang phrase of approbation "that's the ticket" is etymologically correct.

The Extreme Etiquette of Spain.—It was in Spain that etiquette attained those extremes which are to-day so difficult to understand. Men and women ceased to be human beings with a will: Frederic Marshall says, "They became machines of reverence, everybody had his place marked out and was kept mercilessly in it. The number of steps and the depths of bows which each person was to make on entering the royal presence, the width of cloaks, the length of ribbons, and perhaps more than all, the elaborate division of offices and functions, were fixed with a precision of which examples exist nowhere else."

The people of Spain took up ceremony and reverential courtesy as a duty. Even the beggars asked each morning of their colleague: "Señor, has your Courtesy taken his chocolate?" As for the grandees, they considered themselves above the universe and all the men within it!

The court etiquette of Spain was elaborate and complex to the extreme. It is related that on one occasion the Queen fell from her horse, caught her foot and hung by the stirrup, unable to extricate herself. This happened in the presence of a number of attendants who made no move whatever to assist her. They couldn't, you see, because the grand equerry whose particular and peculiar privilege it was to unhook the royal ankle on such occasion was absent!

A passerby, noticing the Queen's plight, released her. Whereupon he received several doubloons for his service, but was condemned to banishment because of his indiscretion! Such were the extremes etiquette had reached in the Spanish court.

Mr. Marshall relates still another instance which is interesting enough to quote. Philip III, finding the fire too hot for his royal well-being, told the Marquis de Pobar to

During the age of chivalry knights raised the visor to indicate friendliness. An interesting phase in the development of our custom of raising the hat.

put it out. But unfortunately the Marquis could not presume to do so. Fire extinction was the peculiar privilege of the Duke d'Useda who was at that moment hunting in Catalonia. The King would not give way to the fire, since the fire was bound by etiquette to give way to the King. He sat majestically still before it, got erysipelas, and died.

It would appear that precedence was a matter of life and death in the Spain of this mad period. To enter a room before a person higher than you in rank, would have been a sin inexcusable.

Ambassadors sought to increase the importance of Spain by fighting for precedence in foreign countries. Thus in 1661, it is related, the Spanish envoy attacked the carriage of the French ambassador in the streets of London, hamstrung his horses and killed his men. He went on joyfully to the palace, proud at having done his duty and prevented his rival from getting to court before him.

Bielfeld tells a similar story of two envoys, one from Genoa and one from Brandenburg, who, being unable to come to terms as to which should be the first to be presented to the French king, made this stipulation: He who reached Versailles soonest on the day of the reception would take precedence over the other.

The shrewd Prussian went to Versailles the night before and sat on a bench in the palace until dawn. Arriving early, the Genoese saw the Prussian, recognized the trick, and slipped quietly through the door of the King's bedroom which, for the moment, had been left ajar. He began delivering the necessary salutations, but the indignant German rushed in after him, pulled him back, and began delivering his own little speech!

Still another tale is told of two ambassadors who met face to face on the bridge at Prague and who stopped there for the entire day because neither would permit the other to pass. They felt it would have been a disgrace to their respective countries to allow the other to go by first.

This extreme type of etiquette, this incessant struggle

for precedence, not only in diplomatic circles and at court, but among the people of the cities, was conspicuous for about three centuries. We find it as extreme in France as in Spain, but we find French etiquette gradually taking on a newer note, a finer, saner, more advanced significance.

The French Etiquette.—France has always been the land of chivalry, of elegance, of politeness, of manners. There have been times, of course, when France, like other countries, suffered reversals to barbarism through war and through court tyrannies; but on the whole, France has held the banner of culture and courtesy high.

The great mediæval social system known in history as chivalry was founded in France during the eleventh century. This system of chivalry revolutionized the manners, morals, tastes, amusements, ethics of France, and, later, of England, Italy, and other European countries.

The system of knight errantry, or chivalry, began about the middle of the eleventh century and was originated by some nobles who had become ashamed of their lives of brigandage. At the age of seven every boy of noble birth was apprenticed to some great lord as page and trained to knighthood. He was taught honour, chivalry, truth, refinement. The highest ideals were inculcated in him. Frank Alvah Parsons says:

> This system may properly be said to have sounded the death knell of heathen barbarism and to have marked the beginning of Christian civilization as we know it to-day.

During the next three centuries many external conditions changed the manners and customs of France, making them heavy, formal, dull. There were the Crusades, in themselves most romantic and with a delightful history, but bringing into France new and strange tastes and customs. And there were the wars which threw the country into chaos. The decline of the spirit of mediævalism and chivalry at the end of the fourteenth century was followed by the gradual decay of the ideals and the courtesies that began in the time of Henry I.

In the sixteenth, seventeenth and eighteenth centuries in France there were books which gave the rules of conduct. These books of etiquette were known as the *Civilités*. Two such *Civilités* are now in the hands of an English art collector. One is dated 1695 and the other 1782. They are both occupied to a great extent with the civilities of the table, and one may see in them precisely how Paris dined in the 17th and 18th centuries.

At the close of the 17th century it still seemed necessary to remind the host that he must not chastise his servants at table, and the guest that if he swallows his wine too rapidly he may choke himself, "which is impolite and inconvenient." According to these *Civilités* you sit down to table with your hat on, removing it only if your health is toasted "by a person of quality." And how, we wonder, did they judge these "persons of quality"?

Every *Civilité* of the 17th and 18th centuries enjoins you to go to dinner with your hands clean. Apparently there is only one towel, for the *Civilité* requests that "a dry corner be left for the person who is to use it afterward."

Furthermore the *Civilité* exhorts the man of polish not to scratch himself in company, not to snuff the candle with his fingers, not to blow in his soup, not to return the meat to the dish after smelling it, not to talk with his mouth full, not to pocket the fruit at dessert. These rules of conduct give us an excellent insight into what social life must have been like in the 17th century. The *Civilités* warned the people only against those things they actually did, those habits and customs which actually existed.

But let us leave the fascinating and naïve *Civilités* for a while and see what has been happening at the French court. Court etiquette reached its height in France under Louis XIV. He was a great king and he had a magnificent court. His reign was the most striking politically, socially, and morally that France has ever known. He came into his sovereignty in 1643 and reigned for seventy-two years.

As in Spain, a great deal of ceremonial surrounded court

life. Louis XIV himself wrote a book concerning court ceremonial, and all courtiers were enjoined to obey the rules. Precedence was a matter of great importance. It found its way even into the streets, where it became a subject of frequent dispute. The narrowness of the Parisian streets made it impossible for large coaches to pass each other; when two met, therefore, that of the lesser dignitary was obliged to go back to the last crossroad. One can see how this occasioned arguments. Long pedigrees were recited, claims set forth, and strangers called in to settle the matter of precedence.

At Versailles the importance of etiquette reached such a point that it was carried to almost incredible extremes. The catch phrase of the time was *"Toute la femme est dans la reverence,"* which meant that the manner in which a woman curtsied—in other words, the manner in which she followed the etiquette of the times—revealed her true qualities.

It is related of Louis XIII that, being on one occasion obliged to visit Richelieu, who was ill at Tarascon, he lay down on the bed beside him. He was, after all, the sovereign; Richelieu a subject. Therefore it was impossible that Richeieu lie in bed, though ill, while Louis stood or sat beside him. Therefore, he took his place on the bed beside the sick man, and so preserved the royal dignity! Louis XIV visited Maréchal de Villars in the same manner when the Maréchal was lying wounded at Malplaquet.

France of the Revolutionary period is a France in which we do not like long to dwell. We glimpse man's primitive personality coming, for a moment, to the surface of life after long years of civilization. We see the pent-up furies of the people finding savage expression in the mass, the mob. Castes were destroyed; petty precedences and ceremonials were wiped away. And the titles that but a moment before had been proudly flaunted, became handles of death.

Yet out of this madness, out of this savage chaos,

emerged France—the Republic. And now we come to the new régime with its newer code of etiquette.

The famous "Book of Ceremonial" originated by Napoleon still exists. It is a bulky collection of 819 articles concerning etiquette, and it was intended to anticipate every possible situation and supply directions for meeting every emergency. It is as elaborate as that of Louis XIV, on which it was based; it is even more elaborate than that of the Second Empire, for which it served as a model.

Concerning the compilation of the Book of Ceremonial, in which several people besides Napoleon had a share, Madame de Staël says:

> Whoever could suggest an additional piece of etiquette from the olden time, propose an additional reverence, a new mode of knocking at the door of an antechamber, a more ceremonious way of presenting a petition, or folding a letter, was received as if he had been a benefactor of the human race.

Napoleon applied to many of the surviving members of the Bourbon court for information. It was partly with their aid that the "Book of Ceremonial" was compiled. But Napoleon, in the main, framed his own etiquette and always assigned to himself the first and most important place.

In matters of precedence Napoleon was stubborn. It is related that in 1808 the "Almanach de Gotha" for that year had just been printed with the regular alphabetical arrangement of the reigning houses, beginning with the Anhalt duchies. The Emperor indignantly suppressed the edition and required the whole to be reprinted with his name on the first page.

At St. Helena Napoleon gave his reasons for having compiled the bulky code of etiquette and ceremonial. He said:

> I was rising above the level of the crowd, and it was indispensable to create myself an exterior, to compose a dignity and a gravity, in one word, to establish a ceremonial; otherwise I should have been

daily tapped upon the shoulder. In France we are naturally inclined to ill-timed familiarity; we are instinctively courtiers and obsequious at the outset; but if not repressed, this familiarity soon ripens into insolence. (Las Cases, "Memorial de Sainte Helene," vs. IV, p. 271.)

Here we have the reason for all ceremonial, for all form, for all rules of conduct. It is the "rising above the level of the crowd" and the desire to be apart from that crowd and protected from its crudities that results in the creation of codes.

France of the late 19th century is polished, cultured, leader of the world in fashion and in social matters. From this 19th-century France, as from the France of Louis XIV, we borrow many delightful customs which shall presently be discussed.

In England and America.—England with its knights and ladies, with its vassals and lords, its peasants and royalty, was from the very first a country of forms, observances, and ceremonials. As a maritime nation it was very naturally one of the greatest promoters of maritime ceremonial, such as the firing of guns, the dropping of sword points, the presenting of arms, the lowering of sails, etc.

In early times, salutes given in the open sea consisted in a certain number of cannon shots between ships of equal rank. In cases of inequality, the inferior side was expected to add some sign of respect and homage—strike or hoist its flag, furl its upper sails, change its tack. But in the time of James I, England, in her pretension to possess the high seas, insisted that her maritime supremacy be recognized by the instant disappearance of the flags and sails of all other ships. The English vessels were to offer no greeting in return. This attitude led to many wars. To-day salutes are obligatory to no one, having become pure acts of courtesy.

In manners, customs, and fashions France has always been the "feminine" country—England the "masculine." Early England was crude, though courtly, borrowing some of its customs from Spain, France, and Italy, but being largely sufficient unto itself and deigning to ignore the customs of the countries around it.

Courtliness and chivalry began in England at about the same time that the great system of chivalry made itself felt in France. In the time of Richard Cœur-de-Lion (1189—1199), England's most generous, impulsive and lovable king, there were gay tournaments, rich banquets, elaborate court functions. Romance lurked in Sherwood Forest. And "knighthood was in flower." The courtly manners and customs of the time reflected the spirit of the people at court and in the cities.

Mediæval England was an England of castes and caste restrictions. The Barons and the Lords wore silks and velvets: the peasants who dared to ape them were punished. We read, for instance, of a needlewoman of the 13th century who was compelled to sweep the streets for a week because she had the audacity to make herself a cap like the one worn by her lady!

As mediævalism decayed, the Renaissance was born, nurtured, and developed in Italy. Its influence upon the manners, customs, morals, and arts of the whole world cannot even be estimated. In England, the Renaissance appears to have inspired a period of luxury, grandeur, and magnificence which vied with that at the French court of the same period.

During the reign of King Henry VIII etiquette received an impetus but was still extremely crude. Table manners were nearer those of the savage than the civilized level. Yet remnants of barbarism were gradually disappearing from the customs and the manners of the English people.

At the beginning of the 17th century there appears to have been a great aping of the customs and fashions of France. With the ascension of Charles I to the throne, court manners became stately and dignified and throughout the kingdom there was a careful regard for the niceties of dress, for little politenesses, for courtesy and consideration toward others.

Toward the close of this century Lord Chesterfield makes his appearance. He gives us a clearer insight into the manners and customs of his period than any other writer. He teaches us not only of the customs of England, but of France, Germany, Italy, and other European countries.

A few excerpts from Lord Chesterfield's famous letters to his son will reveal to you a great deal concerning the manners and customs of the late 17th and the early 18th centuries. This son to whom Lord Chesterfield wrote was illegitimate. It was the Lord's mission in life so to educate and cultivate this young man that his inferior birth would not be held against him. Despite his letters, so devoted, so persistent, and so enlightening, the boy turned out to be a great disappointment.

Lord Chesterfield in one of his letters to his son asks:

> By the way, do you mind your person and your dress sufficiently? Are you be-laced, be-powdered, and be-feathered as young fellows are, and should be?

As his son visited many different courts and was educated in several countries, Lord Chesterfield had occasion to write him several times concerning the customs of these countries. He wrote at one time:

> A man of the world must, like the chameleon, be able to take every different hue.

And at another:

> Take care to inform yourself if there be any particular customs or forms to be observed, that you may not commit any mistake. At Vienna men always make courtesies, instead of bows, to the Emperor; in France nobody bows at all to the King, nor kisses his hand; but in Spain and England bows are made and hands are kissed. Thus every court has some peculiarity or other, of which those who go to them ought previously to inform themselves, to avoid blunders and awkwardness.

During the 18th century we find practically all of Europe suffering from "Anglomania." All countries and peoples attempted to copy the English mode of life, the

(Courtesy of Metropolitan Museum of Art)

The kissar, a Central African stringed musical instrument made from a human skull and the horns of a gazelle.

(Courtesy of Metropolitan Museum of Art)

Kettle drum of the Mandan Indians, North Dakota. Reproduction made by a Mandan boy at Indian school in Carlisle, Pa.

English fashions and manners. Even France fell under this influence.

Beau Brummell, immortal dandy of England, appears at the beginning of the 19th century. His real name was George Bryan Brummell, and as a "dandy" he became the ruling spirit of the English noblemen. He had a remarkable personality—was at once witty, charming, sarcastic, flattering. He frequented the best clubs and the most exclusive houses; his manner gained for him a wide acquaintance and unparalleled popularity.

The secret of Beau Brummell's influence is to be found in his magnetic personality. His insolence appears to have been amazing. On one occasion, we are told, he ordered a duchess to leave the ball-room backward because her back offended his taste! On another occasion he deliberately "cut" a young colonel whose name was on everyone's lips because "Who ever heard of his father?"—he said. Yet, no one ever heard of *his* father.

Beau Brummell and his associates became, nevertheless, the finest connoisseurs of good living. Beau Brummell showed exquisite taste in all that concerned dress. He changed fashions to suit himself. He wore his hair short and without powder, and instantly his admirers aped him. He shunned the bright colours of the period and wore dark, perfect-fitting clothes. Although there were many other "dandies" during this period, no one could manage to appear as distinguished looking as Beau Brummell and he became known as the best-dressed man in London. We will discuss more definitely in later chapters the influence of Beau Brummell and his associates upon the manners and fashions of the world.

Etiquette received a great impetus during the Victorian Era. The Queen set the pace for elaborate functions and rich attire and, as always, the people attempted to imitate the court. The Victorian Era made itself felt even across the sea in young America.

What has been happening in America while the world

has thus been developing in matters of culture and fashion? During the early colonization etiquette was negligible, of course. The early struggle for existence was a great leveller of castes and classes, and everyone worked together for the general good. There was a wholesome simplicity, an inspiring generosity, a kindliness and thoughtfulness toward one another.

Before the colonies declared their independence there was an influx of French and other foreign ideas. From France, Italy, Holland, England emanated much that we ourselves are. After the Revolution, peculiarly enough, the social ideas and ideals of the United States were distinctly English. The Colonial style was the English style; the young nation could break away from the power of the older nation, but not from the influence of its manners and customs.

Washington set the pace for diplomatic simplicity in the United States, although there was a certain courtliness. A contemporary of France, visiting the young nation, reports of Washington: "He was as gracious as a king."

During the first hundred years of its existence, the United States was a forcing house for the customs, whims, fancies, fashions of all the world. We imported our customs with our clothes and food-stuffs, although we prided ourselves upon being absolutely free from the Old-World influence.

The Southern colonies, before the Civil War, however, had a certain style and chivalry all their own. There was a careful regard for dress and for table service. The simplest dinner was served faultlessly. Gallants were ready to draw their swords at a moment's notice to protect (or amuse) the ladies of their fancy. But all of this chivalry and extreme etiquette appears to have gone out when slavery went out.

The Northern colonists, the New Englanders, were of sterner stuff—truer English than their Southern cousins. Braving the rigours of the northern climate, the Puritans determined to live up to their ideals of independence, simplicity, and freedom. The primitive personality is not thrown over so easily. Here, among peoples who had fled oppression and who had founded a new world to serve God each in his own way, the appalling Salem witch craze broke out. Hundreds of innocent men and women were burned or hanged to satisfy the superstitious hysteria of the masses. History simply repeated itself, as usual. In 1515, by the shore of Lake Geneva, more than five hundred people were burnt to death as witches. All through Europe thousands of men and women were burnt as witches, even before the colonies were founded.

The Indians taught our forefathers much in the art of hospitality. It is believed by many that the Indian races are, and always have been, the most hospitable races of the world. It is natural that the early colonists, constantly in contact with the Indians, should have borrowed from them some of their ideas of hospitality. Much that is Indian is woven into our social fabric, as we shall later discover.

The United States which is only three hundred years old as a country of written record, and less than two hundred years old as a nation, has borrowed most of its manners and customs from other, older civilizations. Though there have been in this country many writers on etiquette, the truth is that we have accepted our etiquette ready-made. There are, of course, some customs and fashions that are distinctly American; but the most of the things we do and say show the influence of the Old World.

After all, what customs could we have created here in young America? What code of etiquette could we have developed in the short time that we have been a separate people and a separate nation?

Etiquette is a growth. It began in the earliest times and has been progressing, developing, growing ever since. The history of its development differs in the various countries; sometimes we find a highly developed etiquette as in the time of Marcus Aurelius who, in the Golden Age of Rome, taught politeness and consideration for others, taught courtesy and ease and gentleness. And then we see etiquette sink far below the levels of civilization, as in the time of Nero, who originated so many new ways of torture, who made death a plaything and his savage arena a playground.

Thus etiquette, while it remains always essentially and fundamentally the same, is to a certain extent a reflection of the periods through which it has passed. The age of man and the long ages of antiquity—they blend into one shadowy, beautiful whole, the fabric of human existence.

CHAPTER IV

The Story of Speech

To classify things is to name them, and the name of a thing, or a group of things, is its soul; to know their names is to have power over their soul. Language, that stupendous product of the collective mind, is a duplicate, a shadow-soul, of the whole structure of reality; it is the most effective and comprehensive tool of human power, for nothing, whether human or superhuman, is beyond its reach.

—F. M. Cornford.

MAN'S FIRST LANGUAGE

WHEN we read that "primitive man had at first no means of expression, no way of making known his thoughts and ideas to others," we are tempted to forget, for a moment, the known facts regarding early man, and permit our fancy to wander at will.

Who knows what brutish cave fellows first sat in the sun and talked to a bird near by? Who knows what early cave mother first bent over her child and said strange, crooning things to it? Who knows what savage first shouted his defiance to the stars, daring them to come down and taste his strength?

We can be no more definite concerning the origin of speech than we can concerning the origin of man himself. We are told, and it is reasonable to suppose, that articulate speech originated when men began to clan together and discovered the need for a definite means of expression.

But how can we be certain that savage man did not have an instinctive language regarding which nothing is known? How can we be certain that he did not have a sound, or a series of sounds, which he associated in his own mind with "bear" or "tree" or "sky" or "water"?

The historian and the philosopher have never ceased to speculate upon speech and its origin. Where did it come from? How did it originate? Is it a gift peculiar to man —a "gift of God" as some writers like to express it? Or did primitive man simply imitate the sounds of the animals

Man learned the use of his voice by imitating the cry of the beast, the song of the bird. Imitative sound was the first language of mankind.

around him and of these sounds create the first articulate speech? In other words, is speech a natural human faculty, or is it an art developed by man during his long sojourn on earth?

The problem is still pondered. But most authorities are of the opinion that speech is both divine and human in origin, being a natural gift or faculty developed by man through his own perseverance and ingenuity. And all authorities agree with Charles Hodgin that "it is the power of speech which makes man the highest of all animal beings and which forms the barrier between him and the dumb animals."

Man's first language, however, was not articulate speech. Early man had a means of expressing his thoughts long before he discovered that he could imitate the sounds of the jungle. Before man could speak he could mimic; before he could mimic he could pantomime; before he could pantomime he could gesture.

If you have ever seen any of the Denishawn pantomimes, you know how a beautiful and impressive tale can be told without one spoken word, but solely through dancing, pantomime, and gesture. Not a sound is uttered throughout the performance. Yet when the audience leaves it carries with it a vivid impression of things, places, persons, and happenings.

So it must have been in primitive times before man spoke. If he wished to indicate to the woman sitting before the cave that a huge beast was rushing down upon them, he probably pointed in an excited manner to the direction from which the beast was coming. That gesture warned the woman. It informed her, as definitely as speech, that there was something fearsome and dangerous not very far away.

Or perhaps the man had discovered a spring of clear, sparkling water after a siege of thirst, and he wished to inform someone else of the find. He would probably imitate the action of taking water in his palms and conveying it to his mouth, or the manner in which the water cascaded over the rocks. That would be pantomime—a simple pantomime that any one would understand.

Of course, all this was before man began to reason.

There could not have been very much thinking or reasoning before speech had been developed to some extent. Reason did not produce speech; it was speech that produced reason. In primitive life, words enabled man to record and definitely fix certain facts in his mind; this enabled him to grasp newer and more complex ideas.

THE DISCOVERY OF VOICE

Although it is barely possible that man "spoke" from the first—that is, used his voice to give vent to his feelings, emotions, anger, desires—we know that he did not use his voice in the sense of speech until a certain very definite point in his development.

"Primordial man," says Wells, "before he could talk, probably saw very vividly, mimicked very cleverly, gestured, laughed, danced, and lived, without much speculation about whence he came or why he lived." But when man began to clan with his fellows, and gradually as clan life grew into tribe life, the need for a more satisfactory means of expression made itself felt. Man wanted to interpret his sensations; he wanted to express his purely physical impressions. And doubtless he found his gestures and his pantomime wholly inadequate.

How could he express the fears, the joys, the wonders of his daily life? How could he make that other fellow know of his great strength? How could he tell him of the bear he had killed in the jungle, of the woman he had dragged to his cave?

Groping about for a more definite and tangible way of making his ideas understood, primitive man discovered a power which, until then, he had not used—a natural faculty of which he had not been aware. He discovered—voice.

The ability to produce vocal sounds by means of expired air is not limited to man alone. It is to be noted that all vertebrate animals that perform respiration by means of lungs have this ability also. But the utilizing of this ability for speech, and the development of speech into language, is a triumph which man can claim exclusively.

Man's First Use of Voice.—In civilized life great fear often brings forth an inarticulate cry. You know how violent pain or anguish makes people groan. Anger and impatience cause grumbling.

These strange, unintelligible sounds constituted man's first vocabulary. To express his sensations he made instinctive sounds, like our cry of fear or pain. His earliest use of the power of voice was to utter simple, natural sounds like those we hear in very young children.

It was only through great skill and perseverance that man finally developed language. At this point it is important that the reader know precisely what is meant by "language" as distinguished from voice and speech. Voice, as used here, is meant simply to indicate the power, or ability, of utterance. Speech means the uttered sounds which obtain from voice. Language is used in the sense of words and phrases expressing definite ideas.

"The first rays of language," says Max Müller, "changed the world from night to day, from darkness to light." For the first time man was able to convey definite ideas through definite expression. One must see at a glance what a tremendous impetus this was to thought, to reason. And one must see how man was now completely and forever separated from the lower animals.

But language did not flash upon mankind suddenly. It developed slowly, and through long periods of life—more slowly, as a matter of fact, than most human developments, for reasons which will be pointed out in a moment. Before mankind had a human vocabulary it had what is known as a "monkey" vocabulary. This consisted of sounds and combinations of sounds in imitation of the cries of animals and the sounds of inanimate things of nature.

The Beginning of Words.—Hearing frequently the hoot of the owl, the shriek of the ape, the roar of the thunder, man came at last to recognize these sounds and understand them. With the first triumph of voice discovery he imitated these familiar sounds. Probably they were part of his pantomime, at first. In warning of the beast or telling of the water he may have tried to imitate the sounds he heard. But later, it appears, man actually had a language based upon these imitative sounds. It is frequently referred to as the "monkey" language.

We can easily imagine a frightened cave man rushing to warn his fellows, or his woman, of the approach of some huge beast. The more thoroughly to express the danger he spreads out his arms in wild gesture to indicate the size of the animal, and imitates its cry to tell them precisely what animal it is.

The imitative sound he uses is understood. It is a sound peculiar to the beast that is approaching. There is no mistaking it. The others join him and rush away as though they had actually seen the beast. They did see it in imagination; the sound or sounds made by their fellow created a picture of it in their minds. In other words, the sound conveyed an idea, and by so doing placed itself in the category of language.

Now let us take one sound—the sound used by the savage cave man to imitate a dangerous animal and warn others of its approach. After a certain amount of repetition that sound becomes a word. Let us pretend, for instance, that it had been a bear approaching. The savage may have used a guttural and slow *aahrrr* to imitate the growl of the beast. After a certain period of development he is able to use the word *aahrrr* when he leaves the cave in the morning to convey the idea that he is going to hunt for the bear with others of the tribe. The gesture and pantomime accompanying the sound, as well as the inflection of the voice, help carry the message.

Thus did man begin to speak and form words. We will never know, of course, the first words our ancestors pronounced. We cannot guess the words that were born, lived their brief span of usefulness, and disappeared into eternity.

What we do know, however, is that man emerged from the darkness of prehistory with his gift of voice; that he utilized that voice as a means of expression, to convey his thoughts and his ideas; that in his ingenuity and skill he created a language that has carried its origins to all corners of the earth.

Explanation of the Famous "Bow-wow" Theory.—The first primitive language must have been monosyllabic. But little by little man became skilled and clever in the use of voice and in the art of imitation. He became more agile in the use of sound. And gradually words and even combinations of words multiplied under his tongue.

According to what is known as the "bow-wow" theory, words like cuckoo, crow, peewit, etc., are derived from the sounds made by those birds. At first the words were simply disjointed sounds, like the call of the cuckoo or the crow; but in time these sounds or syllables were elaborated into the words which still exist and are a part of our language.

Similarly words like yelp, roar, neigh, bark, growl, whinny, mew, etc., are derived from the actual sounds produced by the animals suggested. Say the words over slowly. Don't you almost seem to see the animals? Can't you understand how primitive man used sound to convey ideas?

If this theory is correct, we can trace many of the words we use to-day to man's first language—the imitative sound language. Words like bang, crack, purr, hum, whizz, etc., may have had their origin in man's first attempts to imitate these sounds. An arrow shot through the air would whizz; a bit of twig broken underfoot would crack. The collision of hard bodies, jungle sounds, and other familiar daily noises would produce such words as splash, whack, snap, ring, thump, hiss, whistle, pat, murmur.

There is, however, another theory advanced by some

authorities which seems quite as plausible as this "bow-wow" theory. It is that man first gave expression to his ideas and sensations in the form of short syllables, interjections—natural but unintelligible sounds such as an infant might make. They would be interjections like *ah, oh, pooh, um,* etc. Through constant repetition these sounds or syllables would have finally taken upon themselves a certain meaning or significance.

Thus some authorities claim that words like ugly, huge and hug are derived from the deep guttural sound of distaste—*ugh.* From *ah,* which is the natural and instinctive cry of pain and sorrow, we get such words as woe, wail, ache. The natural sound *um,* which one uses instinctively in times of pleasure or satisfaction, would give such words as hum, jump, etc.

It would seem, therefore, that the root words of languages had their origin in the simple, natural sounds of pain, pleasure, tiredness; and in the imitative sounds used by early man to mimic the animals and reproduce the sounds of the inarticulate things of nature, such as the water falling on rocks, the rain pattering on the ground, the thunder rumbling in the heavens.

The gradual transition from guttural sound to articulate language is summed up so perfectly by Xanthes in "Speech" that we quote it verbatim here:

> In the beginning of the world primitive man was contented to imitate the language of the animals. This observation furnished him with a considerable number of imitative words which, in time, were changed into syllables. The needs of existence, then very limited and always the same for everyone, insured the repetition of these syllables which very soon became for men of the same race the distinctive mark of their special affinities.
>
> Later the necessities of existence were increased and the field of imagination was enlarged; man was no longer contented to imitate the sounds which the animals produced. The sound of waters, that of the wind, the murmur of the brooklets, the rumbling of the thunder, in a word, all the impressions which came to them from without, were unconsciously received and imitated by them.
>
> In time these inarticulate cries, these disjointed syllables, were

either united or separated in various ways, so as to form a variety of syllables better adapted to the mentality just coming into existence, and rendered this union or separation absolutely necessary.

Words were thus created.

Philologists claim that our great wealth of words can actually be traced back to no more than five hundred root forms which are based upon the sounds used as words by primitive man.

Why Language Developed Slowly.—In early life there was not, at first, very much need for speech. For narrative purposes our ancestors danced and gestured and pantomimed. In other words, they acted rather than told. To express their emotions they needed, at first, no words. If they were afraid, they cowered in some corner; if they were happy, they danced and jumped; if they were angry they glared and grasped more fiercely their spears or clubs.

The coming of speech, therefore, was retarded; and the growth and development of speech into language was slow indeed. At first different families or clans probably each had their own words which they used and understood. But the women would be carried away by other tribes and the men would be killed in warfare or in the jungle, and thus those first family words would be lost.

But gradually we find families and clans forming themselves into tribes, each tribe talking in common syllables or idioms. Now we begin to notice for the first time a linguistic similarity which enables us to study language, rather than speech, and follow its development through the ages.

THE GROWTH OF LANGUAGE

One day a man went to call on Plato and asked him what was the difference existing between words and languages [says Xanthes]. The philosopher, without replying, pointed with his finger to a plaque hung on the wall representing a goddess with her attributes.

Then, rising, he went toward a large vase filled with coloured stones and picking them up in handfuls, let them fall through his fingers in iridescent cascades.

"These," said he, "are the words or the materials.

"And here is the language," he added, showing the plaque, which was nothing more than a mosaic of a most delicate workmanship.

The languages of mankind are like beautiful mosaics, reflecting the physical and social environment of the speakers. But it took hundreds of centuries of skill and patience to create these mosaics. Some are great and beautiful; others have progressed very little since their first crude beginnings. Thus we find that the language of a people records the social development; and we agree with Max Müller that "there is an historical genuineness in ancient words, if but rightly interpreted, which cannot be rivalled by manuscripts, or coins, or monumental inscriptions."

The Aryan Languages.—Mankind has thousands of different languages. Although scattered fragments of imitative sound in root words can be found in all languages to prove the theory of an original "monkey" vocabulary, the philologists claim that there was never such a thing as one common human language.

It hardly seems probable that there would have been one. Different peoples in different places would have had their "monkey" language; but it is very doubtful whether one tribe would understand the language of the other. Gesture has this great advantage over speech: it is universally understood, and in its simplest forms cannot be mistaken. A gesture of anger, of fear, of impatience is understood the world over.

We are told that it is not possible to trace with any degree of certainty any common features in all the languages of the world. Tribes living in opposite valleys even to-day have different ways of expressing the same thing. For a long time it was impossible to find, among the Caribbean peoples, any two tribes speaking one language. Yet all languages have this common kinship: they grew out of man's first utterances in his early efforts to express his thoughts.

Probably the greatest of all languages are those belonging to the Aryan group or family. This group of languages covers nearly all of Europe and stretches into India. Each language appears to be a variation of the other, and the same fundamental roots are traceable throughout all of them. In this family are included English, Spanish, French, German, Italian, Greek, Persian, Russian, Armenian, Sanskrit, and several minor Indian tongues.

The Aryan languages are by no means primitive. They appear to have become distinct about 4000 B.C.; their earliest speakers were probably past the Neolithic stage.

Latin, the language of the Romans, belongs to the Aryan group. It is of interest to us because it is in a sense a mother language and because many of the fundamental laws of our country are based upon the Roman laws which were written in Latin. Another reason for our interest is that the Bible was translated into Latin before it was translated into any other language. The Latin influence can be very definitely traced in modern English, in French, Spanish, and Italian.

Sanskrit belongs to the Aryan family and is one of its main Asiatic branches. Comparative philology, which means the comparative study of languages, was born when Sanskrit was for the first time made intelligible to the Western world. It was the key that made possible the study of all other languages of the Aryan group.

The Sanskrit language is remarkable in structure. It is more copious than Latin; more exquisitely refined than Greek. It bears in its verb roots and grammatical construction a resemblance to both of these tongues. Indeed, there have been authorities who have claimed that this resemblance is too strong to have been produced by accident and that all three languages must at some time have sprung from a common source which no longer exists.

Old Yaska, of India, was the first of all philologians. He lived about the 5th century B.C. and he was the pioneer in reading and interpreting the ancient sacred writings of India. He and the great grammarian Panini, who wrote about 300 B.C., were the first to teach the scientific division or anaylsis of a word into root, stem, and suffix.

Other Great Language Groups.—A group of languages which appears to have been developed quite apart from those languages that belong to the Aryan group, is known to philology as the Semitic. Aryan-speaking and Semitic-speaking people appear in the same period, and history records them as warring together and having commercial intercourse. The languages, however, remained apart.

Included in the Semitic group are Hebrew, Arabic, Abyssinian, and a number of ancient tongues such as Assyrian and Phœnician. Both the Aryan and Semitic speakers are classed under the common head of Caucasian.

A third group of languages is known as the Hamitic. Some authorities believe that these languages have a common kinship with the Semitic, but others are inclined to disagree. It is generally believed, however, that the Hamitic languages originated along the Mediterranean, on the African coast, and radiated from there into western Europe. At that time there were land connections which would have made it possible for the Hamitic-speaking people to cross into Europe, separate widely, and carry their languages with them into new territories and among strange peoples.

In the Hamitic group are included the ancient Egyptian and Coptic, the Berber language, and the various tongues of eastern Africa. The following comparative words are just a few selected from a great list prepared by Gerald Massey to show the astonishing similarity between Egyptian words and English words actually in use to-day.

English	*Egyptian*
abode (habitation)	abut (abode)
ahoy (sailor's greeting)	ahaui (a salutation)
attack	atakh
autumn (the season)	atum (the red autumnal sun)
bed	pet (a crib)

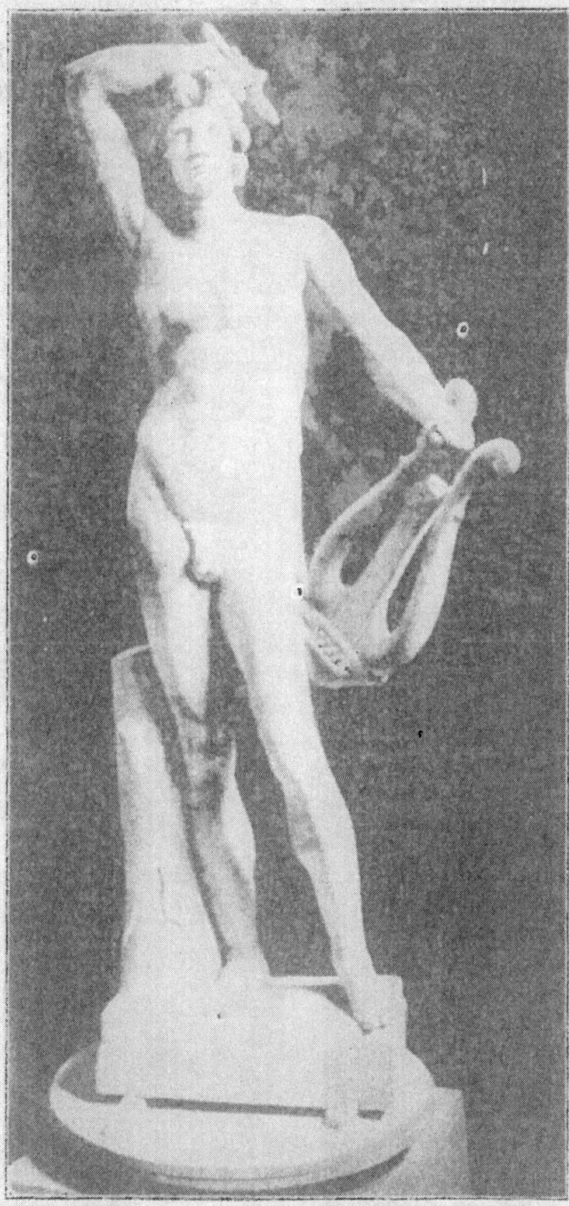

(Courtesy of Metropolitan Museum of Art)

Heroic statue of the god Apollo, with lyre.

(Courtesy of Metropolitan Museum of Art)

Model of the magnificent Pantheon. Roman, 120–124 A. D.

English	*Egyptian*
bib (around child's neck)	beb (a collar)
cackle	kaka (to cackle)
canoe	khenna (a boat)
chase	shas (to follow)
count (a title)	kannt (a title)
cow	kaui (cow)
death	tet (death)
enough	henufi (richess, fulness)
foot	fut (a measure)
gate	khet (to shut)
grape	arpe (grape)
hag (witch)	hek (magic)
ha-ha (laughter)	haa (sign of rejoicing)
hero	ma-haru (the true hero)
honour	han (to adore)
kick	khekh (to sting, to repulse)
look	ukha (to seek)
mamma (the mother)	mama (to bear)
married	mer-t (attached)
mayor	mer (he who rules)
mirror	mher (mirror)
mute	mut (silent)
nabbed (caught)	nabt (tie, noose)
nature	natr (goddess, season)
ought	haut (ought)
peck (a measure)	pekh (to measure or divide)
quick (to be fast)	khi-khi (to move with rapidity)
ray (of sunlight)	ra (the sun)
suit (to satisfy)	suta (to please)
ten (a number)	ten (to reckon or count)
twist	tust (twist)
utter	utau (speak out, give voice to)
waste	ust (waste, ruin)
write	ruit (to engrave or figure)
yacht	iti (a boat)
youth	uth (youth)

Whether this great similarity between English and Egyptian words is coincidence, or whether at some remote time there was a pro-Hamitic language which branched off into the Aryan group, is not definitely known. It is a tempting problem for speculation.

Going northeast of the areas where we find the Aryan

and Semitic tongues, we come upon a group of languages known as the Turanian. This group includes Magyar, Turkish, Manchu, Mongol, Lappish, Finnish, and the Samoyed speech of the Siberians. In the Chinese group we have in addition to the Chinese, the Burmese, the Siamese, and the Tibetan tongues.

Among the American Indians, sign language, which is another way of saying pantomime, was the first mode of expression. The Indians, more than any other people, could act and mimic with great skill. Later, in the age of imitative sound, the Indians became extremely clever in reproducing the cries of birds and beasts. We are told that the Indians imitated the cries of the animals they wished to trap when hunting and actually fooled the animals themselves.

The American-Indian languages are usually gathered into one group or family by the philologist. Among the North American Indians, languages changed with such amazing rapidity that we can find very few Indian tribes speaking the same tongue. When a tribe split up and its members were separated even for only one or two generations, they were scarcely able to understand one another when they came together again.

We have mentioned here only the largest and most important language groups. It would be tiresome to mention all the many other languages which do not come under any one great group, and which could not possibly interest an English-speaking public.

Language and Civilization.—The effect which language had upon the humanizing, or civilizing, of man must be evident to everyone.

Animals can cower in a corner—and actually do when there is a thunderstorm—to show their fear. They can growl and make ready to spring when they are angry. Primitive man, in his animal stage could do these things, and did do them in early life. They represented his only means of expression.

But with voice came speech, and with speech came language. Man was given a tremendous advantage over even the most powerful beasts of the jungle. He was able to convey his ideas definitely and tangibly to his fellows. He was able to seek their assistance, to warn them, to plan and scheme with them, to fix facts in his mind, to record, to *reason.*

Every known people, no matter how savage, has some form of language. It is developed to a greater or lesser extent according to the degree of civilization reached by the people. All languages, like the people who speak them, have passed through many ages of development; and the growth of any one language, therefore, reflects the growth and development of its speakers.

The more a people has reasoned and progressed, the more its language has developed. There are to-day certain savage tribes in Africa and Australia that have no means of counting above two. And there are elaborate languages, like English, which have close to 150,000 separate words.

It is interesting, at this point, to note that the Hebrew Testament, in all it has to say, uses less than 6,000 different words. Milton, in his entire writings, has used only 8,000 words. Shakespeare used 15,000 words, which is believed to be one of the largest vocabularies ever used by an individual. The average person in America uses less than 2,000 words in ordinary speech. And there are certain savage peoples still existing who find a few dozen words sufficient for all their needs.

LANGUAGE IN SOCIAL LIFE

From the very first man was a conceited creature. Let him but feel himself a little above his fellows, a little stronger, a little better, a little cleverer, and he set himself up as a god among them. So it was with the Old Man of the clan who made his personal belongings—and many things not belonging to him—tabu to others. So it was with the hordes of priests and seers and wizards of early life who pretended to be in direct communication with the Unknown. So it was with the kings who gathered untold wealth about them; with the scribes who could write when others could not.

And so it must have been with the first men who mastered speech and language. We can see an imaginative fellow, discovering the powers of persuasion and entertainment which speech gave him, lording it over the others of the clan and pretending to be a favourite of the gods. We can see him combining pantomime and speech as he sits before the clan fire telling strange things that are intended to astonish and impress his hearers. Forerunner of the fiction writer!

It was this capacity for telling things that awakened in early man a social consciousness. After the day's hunt and feasting, it was good to gather around the fire and exchange tales of strange happenings. Men began to find in one another an interest that reached deeper than the mere need for the strength of numbers—the mere joining of forces against common enemies. They found, for the first time, a certain pleasure in one another's company. An instinct which had hitherto been asleep was awakened. And social life was born.

The first tales which early men told one another were probably based upon unusual incidents occurring during daily life, or strange fancies born of dreams. Doubtless each clan had its favourite story-teller—a fellow with a fertile imagination and a goodly supply of incidents who was never at a loss for a tale to entertain and astonish. He would be a sort of wise man, important and privileged. At such an early date did the ability to entertain gain for man social advantage!

Among the Eskimo it was the Old Man who was the teller of tales. It was he who knew all the traditions and creation myths of his people, he who knew all the mysteries and magic of life. He had limitless power among his people. They obeyed him and feared him—and probably loved him for the weird, mysterious tales he told.

The Indians of North America had their "runners"—fleet-footed fellows who ran from tribe to tribe to tell their tales. They belonged to no one tribe, yet to all of them. They were safe in war-time as in peace-time; they were too entertaining, too important a part of social life, to be killed.

The love of attracting attention, of being the centre of interest, made itself felt even among the earliest of our ancestors. Simple, individual fancies were interpreted by their creators as matters of great importance and conveyed to the listening members of the clan with much flourish and pantomime. It is possible that many of the myths and legends that have come down to us through the ages had their origin in early man's love for telling things, for holding the interest of an audience.

The First Great Social Advance.—We should judge that the greatest advance in early social life, as encouraged by language, took place late in the Neolithic age. We might consider earlier man something of an individualist, roaming wherever he liked, caring nothing about clan or kin, finding expression, probably, in dancing, jumping, crying like animals, and, in the case of Palæolithic man, drawing pictures of familiar animals and things.

But Neolithic man was using words, and thinking about them, and groping about for new words to express his new ideas. He was coming under the spell of admiration; speech was beginning to bind him to his clan and his people. He began to invent and tell stories about himself, about the world, about the animals and where they came from, about the tabus of the tribe or clan and why they had to be. In other words, a tribal mind was replacing the individual mind of the earlier ages.

Out of the tribal mind grew tradition. Children, instead of being permitted to grow up wild and free with no more training than was necessary to find food and safety, were now being *told* not to do certain things, not to eat certain things. For the first time, thoughts of the older generation were handed down to the younger. Instead of being obliged to start all over again, man was able to stand on that which had gone before, and in *his* lifetime take another step forward. Man entered definitely upon a social life for the common good. Its progress through the ages we call civilization.

It was the things that impressed Neolithic man most that he spoke about, and that we now find in the mythologies, folklore, and legends of the world. He spoke about serpents because he feared and worshipped them. He spoke about the sun and the moon and the stars because they perplexed and intrigued him. And doubtless, in an effort to increase the wonder of his tales, he dreamed of some day finding out what was beyond the mountains, who was on the other side of the sea, where the sun went to at night and the moon during the day, who lived in the clouds and what demons made the lightning.

All these thoughts appear to have rushed upon early man now that he was able to talk. We can understand how they exchanged ideas and reinforced each other's fears and hopes; how they came to common conclusions and established the tabus and traditions of their tribe; how they were being moulded into a social existence which we must recognize as the foundation upon which later civilization was built.

Words Take On a Social Significance.—As the subtleties of speech developed under man's facile tongue and ready imagination, certain words were created for special, or ceremonious, usage. In the manner that men were gradually divided into castes and classes, words were probably suffixed, prefixed, and elaborated to give them caste or class significance.

Early language consisted very largely of names. If man had one name for an ordinary spear, he doubtless had a way of amplifying or elaborating that name when he wished to indicate that it was the chief's spear of which he spoke. Similarly, if he had one name to indicate "man" in the sense of an ordinary man of the tribe, he doubtless had another to indicate "man" in the sense of head man of the tribe, or wise man, or enemy man.

We can see how customs of politeness in speech, words and titles of deference, expressions of respect, grew out of the early word forms to indicate caste. Men would come to understand the vanities of their tribal leaders and chiefs, and the value to themselves of flattering these vanities.

Thus a kind of carefulness found its way into the speech of these rude, half-savage people, and laid the foundation for our own forms of courteous conversation.

How Language Preserved Unwritten History.—If we were to follow the development of language in its logical sequence, we would come now to a period still shrouded somewhat in uncertainty, during which infant civilizations were probably born in various parts of the world, flourished a short while, and perished; a period during which old languages grew and spread while new ones struggled into being.

But let us skip this period of development which can be of interest only to the historian or the philologist, and let us spend a few minutes instead with those most romantic and fascinating figures of early life—the bards. To them we owe the preservation of some of the world's most beautiful myths and legends; it is because of them that certain important facts of early unwritten history have not been lost to us forever.

All Aryan-speaking peoples have had their bards. They were the natural consequence of language—just as scribes and writers were the natural consequence of writing. In their simple songs and stories these bards of early life made the feats of favourite heroes live again; they brought the battlefield to the fireside; they saw history being made, and they immortalized that history for future generations.

The bards were the guardians of tradition, the preservers of unwritten history. They were, indeed, the first historians, for we are able to glean much that is vital and of importance from their long poetical records, handed down orally from one generation to another.

All this while, you understand, there has been only an oral language—no means of writing down the things that are to be remembered, that are to be handed down to posterity. The bards seized upon every morsel of fact and fancy. They sang their songs of the past and the present; they memorized and chanted the traditions of the people; they invented and related stories based upon the fears and superstitions of the time; they greatly strengthened the development of language, and created much of the stuff that myth and folklore is made of.

The blind bard Homer singing his legends and traditions of Greece to the populace. We are indebted to Homer for the preservation of the Odyssey and the Iliad.

We know from the oral literature that has come down to us that the bards travelled among other peoples and learned of their ways and their traditions. They invented rhymes so that it would be easier to remember the many delightful things they had to tell. They refused to let old battles and old legends die. They recalled forgotten incidents of the past and made them glow with a wholly new significance. They made language live; and in their hands it became a complex, beautiful thing.

The Blind Bard Homer.—One of the greatest bards of whom we have record is Homer. He took the many verbal traditions of Greece, and of them composed the

Iliad and the Odyssey. Word for word the blind bard memorized the exploits of Achilles and Odysseus, weaving exquisite tales based upon old folklore, legends, and traditions.

We marvel at the extraordinary memory of Homer when we glance at the Iliad and the Odyssey and realize that he was able to recite them word for word. The events of these two great epics describe the way of living, the manner of dress, the thoughts of the people, the point which had been reached in social life, during the last centuries of the prehistoric era. Throughout this work there will be quotations from various epics, particularly the Odyssey, to show their influence upon our own social scheme.

Among other records that have been handed down to us by the bards are the old Sanskrit vedas; the sagas of the Teutonic people, which include the famous old English saga, "Beowulf"; and the beautiful legends of the North American Indians made familiar to us by the poet Longfellow.

Bards Flourish after Introduction of Writing.—So great was the spell of the spoken tale, that long after writing was a developed art the bards and story-tellers flourished. They survived, indeed, well into the fifteenth century in the guise of minstrels and travelling songsters. They were to be found all over Europe, in the small towns as in the large cities.

The Troubadours were a class of lyric poets who flourished from the 11th to the 13th century, chiefly in Provence, the south of France, and the north of Italy. Their tales were usually romantic in strain. At the castles of the feudal lords the Troubadour was always welcome, and he was feasted and honoured according to the quality of his tales.

England had its minstrels, more than one of whom lost his head for singing some slurring ditty against the king. And England had also its public criers who made known the news by loud proclamation.

So through the centuries has speech, or language, found a place for itself—in social life as in the life of the individual; in court life as in the life of the people. It has drawn its threads through history; it has determined usage and custom; it has influenced the character of peoples. The truth of this is reflected in the literature, oral and written, of every people.

LANGUAGE AS CONVERSATION

Language concerns us more as a matter of conversation, very naturally, than it does a matter of history. What part does language play in modern social life? And how does it affect us, who are a part of that social life?

All books on etiquette give, as one of the first social requirements, the ability to "converse in a pleasing and agreeable manner." It was Aristotle, standing beneath the porch of the Lyceum, who first taught the world that words bind souls together, that language can illumine like some magic torch the simplest and most unobtrusive environment.

Peering behind the pages of history, we find that conversational ability has played a large part in the making of leaders, of court favourites, of popular idols. The outstanding figures in social life have always been the men and women who knew how to wield language as the general wields his sword.

It is said of Ninon de Lenclos, celebrated beauty of France, that she earned her distinguished place in the brilliant circles of Parisian society almost solely through her great conversational wit. Her words charmed and fascinated. She seemed to know precisely what to say and when to say it. We are told that Louis XIV admired her tremendously for her gift of conversation. He found her always entertaining and clever.

Madame de Maintenon, whom Louis married in 1683 after the death of Maria Theresa, was also a skilled conversationalist and is said to have practised talking before her mirror. She was a master in the art of gesture. During the 17th century when the pendulum swung to the extreme in fashion and etiquette at the French court, and when the court favourite of the moment was the woman who could introduce something novel and unusual, Madame de Maintenon maintained her power entirely through her conversational charm.

Origin of "Drawing Room."—Having firmly established itself in social life, conversation inspired various new customs. Late in the 16th century, for instance, in England, it became the custom for the ladies to withdraw from the dining room to a special room set aside for the purpose of gossip and conversation. The men would remain in the dining room to drink and converse. It is possible that the eloquence of the conversation depended upon the quantity of liquor consumed—which is what Heywood Broun was probably thinking of when he said, recently, "If conversation is to be raised again to its former high estate, drinking is almost essential."

But to return to the withdrawing of the ladies from the dining room—a custom still observed at formal dinners. The room to which the ladies of that period withdrew came to be known as the withdrawing room. This name was used throughout the 16th and 17th centuries, and was then shortened to the more convenient term, drawing room.

And by that name it is known to-day.

The French "Causerie."—The court of Louis XIV was the centre of French social life during the greater part of the 17th century. Whatever was the custom at Versailles, aristocracy obeyed without question. The bourgeoisie (middle classes, properly meaning a freeman of a *bourg* or borough in France) aped as best they could the manners and customs of aristocracy, while the masses—as always—were too vitally concerned with the stern business of living to think in terms of social life.

During Louis XIV's reign, we are told, "The art of conversation was held above all other accomplishments." The court set the keynote, and before long there was a meeting at the Hotel Rambouillet of the great nobles, literary people, and brilliant women of France. They founded what is now known as the French *causerie* (chat). It was merely a gathering of men and women who were to meet at stated intervals at the hotel for the definite purpose of conversation—of "chatting."

Among these people of the *causerie,* people who represented the highest intellectual class in France at that time, there developed a taste for daily talks. The bourgeoisie, instantly following suit, developed an elegant and courteous manner of conversation. All of this great attention to speech could not help influencing, to a certain extent, the manners and the literature of the period.

The French *causerie* had a profound effect upon the manners and customs of France; and it had also a great influence upon English manners. We find, during the time of Charles I, that conversation takes on a certain polish and finesse that it had not before. There is a new brilliancy in repartee; an element of dignity and sense is introduced into social conversation.

In the 18th and 19th centuries special "conversational chairs" were in use in England. These were simply large, comfortable chairs which enabled the dandies to sit and converse for hours in all their glory—without crushing their ruffles or coat tails.

Origin of "Bluestocking."—This derisive name for a literary woman originated about 1750. Mrs. Elizabeth Montagu and her friends made a determined effort to introduce into society a more intellectual tone by replacing cards and gossip with literary conversation and discussions.

Most of the women who attended these meetings were conspicuous because of the plainness of their dress—which was part of their plan—and the men who attended followed the same keynote of simplicity. A certain Mr.

Stillingfleet caused special comment by appearing always in blue worsted stockings instead of the usual black silk.

Because of this last mentioned fact, Mrs. Montagu and her friends became known as the "bluestockings." Some authorities say that at a later date Mrs. Montagu deliberately adopted the blue stocking as the badge of the society. It has since become the custom to speak of literary women as "bluestockings," although the term is rapidly becoming obsolete.

Customs of Courtesy in Conversation.—There is no doubt whatever that France set the pace for courteous and polished conversation. A great deal of French gallantry and politeness which had its origin at the court of Louis XIV still remains; and though having undergone great changes, can be traced in our own courteous customs of to-day.

Titles of respect which we use in our conversation doubtless had their origin in court titles. But there are some which go back even further and had their origin in forms of respect and subservience to some greater power.

Thus "mister" (Mr.) is corrupted from "master," and is an abbreviation of *magister.* The *magister* corresponds with "magistrate" and means one who rules, commands, governs, or sets the law.

Sir was at one time a very dignified title, but through constant application it has now become a meaningless and general form of address. It is derived directly from sieur, the abbreviation of seigneur, which during the feudal system indicated the lordship of land.

Sieur and sire are from the same root source, and originally both signified senior, or elder. The form sire came before that of sieur; therefore the term of respect toward the elder or father preceded the term of respect toward the lord or owner of the land. Consequently, when you address a man as "sir" you are etymologically implying that he is your father.

The general use of sir and madam was most pronounced

in France during the old régime in the 18th century. The lower classes always used these titles when addressing nobility. That we still use these titles, though their original meanings have long since vanished, indicates how potent the French influence has been.

Matters of precedence in conversation still seem to concern the writers on etiquette. "A gentleman waits until the lady has spoken to him," says one recent writer. "Always let your hostess lead the conversation," says another.

In China speech is standardized by age. According to the "Li Ki," no well-bred Chinaman will introduce into the conversation a subject, no matter how important, upon which his senior has not touched.

A simple custom is observed among the Armenians. A young Armenian woman would be horrified at the idea of addressing a woman older than herself unless first spoken to.

On the Fiji Islands a woman does not talk to her mother-in-law. To do so would be considered an insult and a serious breach of etiquette. The Crow Indians, Dr. Lowie tells us, show respect to their sisters by refraining from talking to them. Among the Sioux a young man in the presence of elders does not talk until someone addresses him. Dozens of other instances might be mentioned to show how even savage peoples observe certain courtesies of speech.

Of course, etiquette to-day—true etiquette—does not attempt to varnish life with petty conventionalities. Whether the hostess talks first or the guest is largely a matter of moment and common sense; whether we talk to a stranger or not depends upon circumstances. Etiquette should not lay down definite laws but should aim instead to give poise and ease of manner through knowledge, so that one will have an armour, a protection, against embarrassment.

How to be a good Conversationalist.—In a recent advertising campaign to sell "The Book of Etiquette," a headline was used which read "Are You Ever Tongue-Tied at a Party?" The response was phenomenal. Why? Because thousands of people *are* frequently tongue-tied at parties; because thousands of people often experience keen embarrassment through the inability to express themselves.

It seems to us that the best way to obtain conversational ease is to develop first a complete unself-consciousness. This is not as difficult as it may sound or seem. Any one can, with a little patience and perseverance, develop the kind of poise and self-possession that opens all social doors.

It is said of the famous Hawthorne that he was so shy and self-conscious that he ran out of the house whenever he saw visitors approaching, to avoid having conversation with them. His wife, who was also timid and retiring by nature, was left to entertain the guests as best she could. Instead of trying to overcome his self-consciousness, Hawthorne sought and found forgetfulness in his books. His wife, on the other hand, was forced to overcome her natural timidity and she soon amazed herself by the marvellous poise which she developed.

The first lesson one must learn in overcoming shyness and self-consciousness is to *forget* that shyness. Don't think of it. Don't think of yourself at all. Instead of shrinking from meeting strangers, meet them and talk to them as though they were your brothers and sisters. Forget all about yourself and think of things to say that will interest them.

Courtesy is the very foundation of all good conversation. If you want to be considered a good conversationalist let your proverb be "Talk well, but not too much." Listen politely, talk agreeably, avoid interrupting and express your ideas clearly and simply. Above all, be careful not to give too strong an expression of your likes and dislikes.

We heartily approve of the dictionary habit. A good command of the language gives one a great social advantage. And an excellent way to gain that command is to add one new and useful word each day to one's vocabulary.

As to the matter of slang, which seems to bother most writers, we endorse its use at the risk of inviting criticism. Slang can be colourful and expressive without being discourteous. It is part of the American language and as such must be recognized and accepted. Just one word of caution: use it discriminately and in moderation. To be truly colourful and expressive, the word of slang must be like the uncut diamond in a velvet jewel case—an unpolished word in a setting of beautiful language.

We can think of no better way to conclude this chapter on Speech than to quote this excellent bit of advice from Lord Chesterfield to his son:

> When you are in company, bring the conversation to some useful subject, but *à portée* of that company. Points of history, matters of literature, the customs of particular countries, etc., are surely better subjects of conversation than the weather, dress, or fiddle-daddle stories that carry no information along with them. The characters of kings and great men are only to be learned in conversation, for they are never fairly written during their lives.

(Courtesy of Metropolitan Museum of Art)

Model of the famous Acropolis. Greece, 5th Century B. C.

(Courtesy of American Museum of Natural History, New York)

An Interesting Apache Group.
Notice particularly the type of pottery and the cradle.

CHAPTER V

Concerning Introduction

Human nature is the same all over the world; but its operations are so varied by education and habit that one must see it in all its dresses in order to be intimately acquainted with it. Civility, which is a disposition to accommodate and oblige others, is essentially the same in every country; but good-breeding, as it is called, which is the manner of exerting that disposition, is different in almost every country, and merely local; and every man of sense imitates and conforms to that local good-breeding of the place which he is at.
—L. C.

THE FIRST INTRODUCTION

WE are going to turn back, for a moment, the pages of time. Can you see, with us, the Palæolithic man wandering hungry and alone in a hostile world? He scents food. At the same moment he sees another hungry fellow approaching. They are strangers. Savage, unreasoning, hungry strangers.

Perhaps they fall upon each other and fight then and there. But more likely they stand apart and stare at each other for a moment or two, clubs grasped firmly, muscles tense as the lion's before it springs.

Both hear a young bear approaching, and both at the same moment turn toward the direction from which it is coming. There is food! There are claws and teeth for ornament! There is a soft, warm skin to sleep on!

Without a sound or gesture the two savage men join forces, and quickly, deftly, silently surround and demolish the bear. That was the first introduction.

They are "friends" now, having joined forces against a common enemy. They build a fire and gorge themselves. They sleep off the bear, and wake up to begin their wanderings together, to hunt and eat and live on a friendly and peaceful basis.

Stripped of its ceremonial, what is the introduction? Is it not a social device for placing two or more people on a friendly basis? "The Book of Etiquette" says that the

> purpose of the introduction is to create an immediate friendliness between two people who have met for the first time, to do away with all hesitancy and embarrassment, to create smooth and pleasant conversation, to make the strangers want to continue their acquaintance.

Is there, then, so very much difference between the introduction of primitive life and the introduction of modern life? Is not the difference one of form rather than reason?

So do instincts which once grew out of grim necessity become custom survivals in our social scheme.

The Introduction in Tribal Life.—We turn a few pages in the book of life, and the wandering individual merges into the clan; the clan grows into the tribe.

Can you see one tribe meeting another—perhaps on the desert edges of Africa, perhaps in the jungles of Australia? There are the chiefs, proud in their paint and their bear-claw ornaments. There are the tribesmen, restless and tense like wolves in a pack.

The tribal chiefs are brave, you notice. They advance a little before their fellows and stand a few paces apart examining each other curiously. They notice, perhaps, a certain similarity in appearance. Both have fuzzy hair, both have piercing black eyes, both have huge, powerful arms. A racial sympathy is born.

Now watch carefully. See how one of the tribal chiefs places his club on the ground and by gesture and pantomime indicates his willingness to be friendly. See how the other chief understands the unspoken language, how he rips off his shell ornament and offers it, how he points toward the great ox that has just been killed.

The men of both tribes relax. There is to be no warfare, but a feast instead! They are not strangers. They are friends! The chiefs squat down together while preparations are made for the great ceremonial in honour of their introduction.

Friends or foe? Warfare or feast? All depends upon the manner in which the strange chiefs greet each other. Stripped of its ceremonials, the introduction is simply a social device for placing people on a friendly basis.

That night the ceremony takes place. We see a huge fire cutting through the blackness and silhouetting the jungle against the sky. We see a dozen naked savages dragging the ox for the feast. And we see a grotesque, passionate dance performed around the two chiefs, who finally join the dancers in a weird pantomime around the roasted ox.

And we leave them feasting in friendship while the introduction passes on to its next great stage.

How Fear Encouraged the Introduction.—It is not difficult to see how fear entered into the development of the introduction. We are even to-day instinctively afraid of strangers. We feel somehow so very much more comfortable when we know precisely who everyone is, and when there are no strangers among us.

We can understand how the tribesmen looked with suspicion and distrust upon the woman whom one of their fellows captured and brought into their midst. She was a stranger among them. She might be an evil spirit, she might bring disaster upon them.

To make her one of the tribe so that she could not do any damage, they probably had a solemn tribal ceremony. A fire would be made and meat would be roasted. Perhaps there would be a dance performed by the women of the tribe around the captive woman. And then there would be feasting, and she would be forced to partake of the meat. Is it possible that this is the origin of the wedding feast of civilization?

Having partaken of the tribal food, the captive woman is no longer considered a stranger. Isn't it true in modern life that we consider more of a friend, and less likely to do us damage, the person with whom we have dined?

Just as we regard people who are unknown to us with disquiet, and perhaps with a little distrust, primitive man regarded all strangers with feelings of hostility and suspicion. He would much rather *know* that the other fellow was friendly and had good intentions than worry about having a spear hurled at him when he wasn't looking, or a rock dropped down on his head.

For his own well-being, therefore, he invited the other fellow to eat with him, to share his kill. That would eliminate all doubt and uncertainty. Having eaten together they could not be enemies, for it was one of the beliefs of primitive life that people who ate together were clansmen or kin.

Thus the two savages, eating together, felt safe and comfortable in each other's company. The eating of the food was a symbol of peace and good will. It was their introduction. And like the introduction of to-day, it put things on a comfortable, friendly basis.

We would like to advance here a special theory of our own; we are not sure whether it has ever been advanced before or not. In primitive life whenever people of different clans or tribes were brought together on a friendly basis there was a feast. As a rule one large animal was roasted whole, and all partook of this flesh.

Isn't it possible that these primitive people, in their crude way, believed that the soul or spirit of the animal entered each one of them and bound them together? It would account for the eating of animals in religious ceremonies. It would account for the cannibalistic feasting on the bodies of the dead after warfare, on the principle that the spirits of the dead would strengthen their own spirits instead of roaming about and causing damage. It would account for the feasting at primitive marriages when a member of an enemy tribe became one of their own tribeswomen.

Notice our own custom of touching glasses when drinking together—doesn't it carry the thought of strengthening friendship? And the modern wedding feast—doesn't it carry the significance of binding the two families together?

It is a subject for endless speculation. But while it concerns us somewhat in a social sense, it has little direct bearing upon the introduction, and we leave the fascinating subject with regret.

THE CEREMONY OF EXCHANGING NAMES

To us to-day the introduction means a social ceremony pure and simple—a courteous device for making strangers known to each other and creating a tranquil, harmonious atmosphere. It required, however, long ages of slow development before the introduction became what it is today: the ceremony of exchanging names.

Names, of course, come with speech; and comparatively late in the development of speech. The first names were undoubtedly descriptive. The man who had more bearskins than his tribesmen was probably known by a name equivalent to our "Man of Many Bearskins"; the man who was stronger than his fellows probably had a name equivalent to "Strong Arm"; and the man who could run quickly was probably known as "Fleet Foot."

O'Brien, travelling through the South Sea Islands, encountered many such descriptive names existing among the natives. He tells us of Marquesan personalities answering to such names as Malicious Gossip, She Sleeps with God, Vanquished Often, Hot Tears, Weaver of Mats, Daughter of the Pigeon, and this most gruesome name which suggests a cannibal ancestry—Man Whose Entrails Were Roasted on a Stick! These names belonged to actual people whom O'Brien met and about whom he writes in his "White Shadows in the South Seas." Though they are four and five words long when translated into English, they are just one word in the Marquesan.

To the primitive mind, a man's name is part of his personality. Among many peoples it was believed that to know a person's name was to have a certain power over his soul. To possess a man's name was the equivalent of possessing a portion of his being, and the possessor was able to work mischief on him. Thus it was at one time a widespread custom to keep the name a secret and conceal it from all strangers.

The Arab child, for instance, was taught to conceal his family name and tell it to no one. It was believed that if his name was known to enemies he would probably fall victim to an intertribal blood feud.

It is contrary to Corean etiquette, even to-day, to utter the name of a parent or of an uncle. A Massim would not think of pronouncing these names himself; and for others to do so in his presence he regards as insulting.

Out of the custom of concealing the name grew the later custom, among some peoples, of exchanging names to show that they trusted one another and were inclined toward friendliness. Thus among the Shoshones, "To bestow his name upon a friend is the highest compliment that one man can offer another." And in certain sections of Australia the exchange of names with a European is considered the greatest and most profound mark of brotherly feeling.

Exchange of Names in Modern Introductions.—Fundamentally, the introduction of to-day is an exchange of names. We feel more friendly toward the stranger who knows our name, and whose name we know. We no longer consider that we are entirely strange, or apart.

Problems of precedence entered the introduction at an early period. Just as it was the custom in primitive life to show deference to the most important and powerful person—the Old Man of the clan, the chief of the tribe—so it became the custom in introducing to show deference to the person of most importance. The logical way to show that deference, of course, would be to introduce people *to* him. In other words, his name would be mentioned first.

It was very possible during the age of chivalry, when the women of the court were made to feel that they were the "flower of the land"—when customs of chivalry and courtesy were created for their pleasure—that the custom of mentioning the woman's name first was definitely established. We can understand how the gallantry of the period entered the introduction and made it a thing of ceremony rather than empty form.

The etiquette books tell us that to-day the man must always be presented to the woman, which means that the woman's name is mentioned first, in this manner: "Miss Blank, may I present Mr. Jones?" But, we are informed, if the man is a prince, or a duke, or an important member of the clergy, or the President of the United States, his name is mentioned first. In other words, the courtesy established in the age of chivalry remains so long as there is an equality between the persons introduced. But let there be any great inequality between these two persons, and chivalry is forgotten while we revert to the earlier and safer rule of mankind:—deference to the person of most importance.

Concerning the Acknowledgment.—The "acknowledgment" in primitive life probably involved the life and death of the individuals. If one fellow showed signs of friendliness and the other either misinterpreted him or decided to be disagreeable and refused the proffered friendship, there would be a terrific fight then and there. You know how, even to-day, we grow warm and uncomfortable at the merest suggestion of a slight, even though it may be unintentional.

But the acknowledgment is of particular interest in modern life because it is the doorstep to friendship. We are sometimes attracted to a person by his nod or handshake. We are sometimes prejudiced against him from the start, for the same reason.

In early life there were many forms of acknowledgment. Some of them still survive. The Kingsmill Islanders, for instance, when they exchange names rub noses as a mark of greeting and friendship. The Fuegians express friendship by jumping up and down. They also have the custom of hugging and patting the newcomer, so that a European travelling among these people sometimes finds himself embraced by a friendly native. It is not a pleasant sensation to a people accustomed to shake hands on greeting.

The Andamans welcome strangers by blowing into the

hand. The Brahman to whom you have been polite enough to tell your name will salute you with the phrase, "Mayst thou be long-lived, O gentle one!" According to Spencer the Snake Indian says, "I am much pleased, I am rejoiced." With us the customary phrase is, "I am glad to meet you."

Origin of the Handshake.—With the passing of the ages, manners and customs become abbreviated and simplified. Among the New Caledonians crouching is to-day a sign of respect, as it was among most primitive peoples. Early in life prostration of the whole body was a form of inferiority. During feudal times the knee was bent in salutation. To-day a slight inclination of the head, a nod, is all that remains.

Similarly, kissing the ground on which the king had walked was once a form of obeisance. The Coast Negroes are still accustomed to fall on their knees before a superior and kiss the earth three times. Later, kissing the feet became a general form of obeisance and greeting. To-day kissing the hand still exists among some people.

The handshake itself has passed through many stages of development. In primitive life the hand must have symbolized strength and power, for it was with the hand that enemies were subdued, animals killed, spears and implements made. It would have been a sign of good will to extend the right hand, or weapon hand, and show that it was not armed, not prepared for fight. But as to this we can only conjecture; we have no way of proving it definitely.

The hand found its way into early religions possibly for the same reason,—that it signified power. In Egyptian hieroglyphics the glove is the symbol of the hand. The hieroglyphic hand is TUT, and the word signifies "to give." It means also that which is distinguished and ceremonious. Among the early Greeks the Olympian gods were prayed to in an upright position with raised hands. This presentation of the hands, joined palm to palm, was at one time required throughout Europe from an inferior when professing obedience to a superior. The feudal vassal, doing homage, placed his joined hands between the hands of his superior. This, we can readily see, was symbolic of placing himself under the power of the suzerain or lord. It is interesting to note that the attitude of prayer as taught to children to-day is like that employed by the early Greeks—hands upstretched and joined palm to palm.

Among the Arabs it was customary for a long time to kiss the hand of a superior. Later, among polite Arabs, the offer of an inferior to kiss the hand of a superior was resisted. Probably the two persons each wished to make obeisance to the other by kissing the hand, and each out of compliment refused to have his own hand kissed. Can you see what would happen? There would be a clasping of the hands and a scuffle while each tried to raise to his lips the hand of the other and "though at first such an action would be irregular, yet later it becomes a regular and rythmical motion."

The early Greeks extended the right hand of fellowship to a stranger. Salt was presented to him as a symbol of hospitality and to indicate that he would be safe under the entertainer's roof.

So through the centuries did the use of hands descend into social intercourse. To-day we extend our hand in greeting instinctively, impulsively, without stopping to think about it. Yet it is an ancient custom that has belonged to mankind for ages and that has been handed down to us through many generations.

Of course, there have been many variations of the handshake. The Ainu simply rubs his palms together and strokes his beard. Negro chiefs on the coast of Africa snap the middle finger three times when greeting. In the Banks Islands a man locks the middle finger of his right hand with the corresponding finger of the man he wishes to greet, and pulls it away with a crack.

The correct acknowledgment of to-day is a firm, cordial

handclasp or the friendly smile and inclination of the head. The flourish, finger-tipping, and high handshaking of the last generation have passed out with other affectations.

Custom of Raising the Hat.—Like the extending of the hand, the raising of the hat passed through many stages of development. We must seek its true origin, doubtless, in the stripping of captives in early life to prove their entire subjugation.

Thus among the Assyrians it was the custom to strip completely the men captured by them in warfare. Their nakedness indicated their inferiority, their subjugation to the Assyrians.

Nakedness, partial or complete, was a form of obeisance in early life. The uncovering of the upper part of the body was, and still is, a particularly widespread custom among uncivilized peoples. The Tahitians, for instance, uncover the body as low as the waist in the presence of a king. It is very possible that the uncovering of the head was suggested by the uncovering of the upper part of the body.

Asiatics have made familiar to us the custom of baring the feet. The Japanese have the custom of removing a slipper when they salute ceremoniously. In Persia everyone who approaches the royal presence bares his feet. Similarly in ancient Greece and Rome worshippers at certain shrines were compelled to remove their sandals. And among the people of Arakan it is still the custom to remove the sandals in the street and the stockings in the house as a sign of greeting.

On the African continent there exist many variations of disrobing for the purpose of showing respect or subservience. An Ethiopian, for instance, takes the corner of a stranger's robe and ties it about himself, so as to leave the other almost naked. In some sections baring the shoulder is like unhatting among us, and is a custom frequently observed. Incidentally, among some Africans as among the natives of Tasmania, it is considered natural politeness for a man to turn away when he sees a woman. Does this have any bearing upon our own custom of waiting for a woman to make first sign of recognition?

During the age of chivalry it was customary for knights to wear full armour in public. In accosting each other friendly knights raised the visor as a sign of mutual recognition. And upon entering an assembly of friends, the knight removed his helmet entirely. This was symbolic of the fact that he believed himself safe among friends and had no need for his protecting helmet.

This raising of the helmet in days of chivalry was doubtless an impetus to the already established custom of raising the hat as a mark of courtesy. And as a mark of courtesy we still retain the little ceremony of raising the hat and of removing it entirely in the presence of friends. That the custom in modern life concerns the raising of the hat to women more than men is simply due to the fact that ceremonial customs of any sort tend to become less pronounced among the members of one sex, even while they become intensified between the sexes.

Some Curious Customs of Greetings.—With us the raising of the hat and the extending of the hand are merely a polite part of our social scheme and do not carry with them any very great significance. But they happen to be much modified survivals of primitive forms of obeisance and salutation; and while they have become mere forms in civilized life, they still exist as parts of important ceremonial among certain peoples who have not followed the march of civilization.

On the Sandwich Islands, for instance, complete prostration is the sign of respect and politeness. The form has not been abbreviated to a simple inclination of the head, as among us. However, these people have one custom in common with us. They believe that to sit or recline while superiors are standing is a mark of disrespect.

Every one knows of the minute politeness of the East.

Among certain peoples the formalities of meeting and greeting occupy at least a quarter of an hour.

The Chinese, who have a kind of ritual by which they regulate the number of words and bows to be used, not only depreciate their own status in greeting, but attempt to exaggerate that of the other person. The result is a verbose salutation which is somewhat tedious to the traveller.

If a Chinese man meets another after a long separation, he falls on his knees, bends his face to the earth, and employs other affected modes of greeting. But the common salutation amongst the lower orders is simply an inclination of the body and the phrase, "*Ya fan?*"—meaning, "Have you eaten your rice?" With the influx of the Europeans into China many of the old and picturesque customs are falling into disuse. A good many are already obsolete, except in the smaller provinces.

The Japanese do not kiss or clasp hands. But they have an exquisite courtesy and kindness which never fails to impress the stranger.

Kissing as a form of greeting and affection did not come until comparatively late. The habit of kissing is unknown to the Polynesians who greet by pressing noses. The Laplanders also apply their noses against the person they wish to salute. In Otaheite, we are told, they rub their noses together, and of course we all know this is the favourite form of greeting and affection among the Eskimos.

The Greenlanders have no forms of introduction and no forms of greeting based upon precedence or superiority. They laugh at the idea of one person being inferior to another.

The North American Indians, though of extreme politeness and noted for their hospitality, do not have many conventional forms of salutation. Their etiquette is to meet in silence and generally to smoke before speaking. Smoking together among the Indians is symbolic of peace and friendliness, just as eating together symbolizes friendliness among other peoples.

We are told that islanders near the Philippines take a person's hand or foot and rub it over their face. In the Straits of the Sound it is customary to raise the left foot of the person greeted, pass it gently over the right leg, and then over the face—a rather complicated and awkward ceremony. Natives of the Philippines bend very low, raising one foot in the air with the knee bent. They also place their hands on their cheeks in saluting a friend.

The inhabitants of Carmene, when they wish to indicate particular attachment, break a vein and present the blood to the friend or acquaintance as a beverage. To refuse to drink the beverage is as much an insult as to refuse to acknowledge an introduction in modern life.

Lefevre tells us of the early Romans that

> if any one entered whilst they were sitting, they rose up to do him honour, and did not meet in the streets without saluting each other, in the morning with the word *"Ave"* and in the evening with *"Salve."* It was the custom to cover the head with a corner of the robe to defend it from the injuries of the weather; but when any acquaintance accosted them, they immediately uncovered.

In New Ireland when one man says to another "I am glad to see you" he pats him on the head. With us he slaps him on the back.

In following any custom through its periods of development we must remember that man has always been influenced by his environment. The Europeans with their mountains and their clear, cool air, and their lakes and seas, very naturally were of a different type than the people of Central Africa, who lived and bred in the heat of the jungle. They developed more rapidly because natural conditions were more favourable to development. To-day they have civilization and culture; but civilization has not yet penetrated to the heart of the jungle in Central Africa.

We can see, even from the customs of salutation and

greeting in the various countries, how natural conditions affect the manners and customs of the people. The Dutch, for instance, who are known to be great eaters, have a morning salutation which is common to all ranks and classes. People say to one another, *"Smaakel yk eeten!"* (May you eat a hearty dinner!) as frequently as we say, "Good morning."

In Cairo, where a dry skin is a sure indication of a destructive fever, the usual salutation is the equivalent for our "How do you sweat?"

The proud gait of the Spaniard and his haughty, inflexible solemnity are expressed in his mode of salutation. He says simply, *"¿Cómo está?"* (How do you stand?) The French carries a more frivolous tone, a certain light gaiety characteristic of the Frenchman: *"Comment vous portez-vous?"* (How do you carry yourself?)

Leave-taking has always been ceremonious. One Arab, when leaving another to whom he has been introduced, usually says, "May your day be white!" The answer is, "May your day be like milk."

The Papuans have a curious mode of leave-taking. They smear themselves with river mud and wail piteously. It sounds sincere enough until the stranger is out of sight. Then they wash off the mud and begin singing, laughing, and enjoying themselves again.

Before leaving, a group of Abipones will say, *"Ma chik kla leyá?"* (Have we not talked enough?) No attention is paid to the first person who quotes this customary phrase. But the next person takes it up, repeats it, and it travels around the circle. The last person says, *"Kla leyá"* (We have talked enough), and they all rise together and depart in their various ways.

CHAPTER VI

Débutantes of Yesterday

When human beings began to come together in social relations there developed among them customs, or methods of action, sanctioned by usage. If a person lives by himself he becomes a law unto himself, but if he lives with his fellows, his habits must harmonize with theirs for the sake of the common welfare. Hence, in early civilization whatever conduced to group safety was enforced by public opinion. Conversely what was inimical to public safety was frowned on, and became tabu, or prohibited.

—J. Q. Dealey.

THE GIRL IN PRIMITIVE LIFE

NOTHING very definite is known about woman in early life. She seems to be the background against which man emerged from the darkness and made himself known.

The little information which has been culled from various corners of the world seems to indicate that among some early peoples the woman was worshipped and feared; among others she was subjugated and made to feel her inferiority. We know, however, that primitive man feared whatever he did not understand; and it is very possible that the miracle of birth so filled him with awe and amazement that he regarded all of womankind with a superstitious respect.

Nevertheless, the position of the young girl in primitive life must have been precarious. For a while, undoubtedly, she romped and played as any young child does to-day—with pebbles and knuckle-bones as playthings instead of kiddie cars and clever mechanical toys. But as she approached marriageable age, she was either stolen by some wandering tribe or bartered by her own people.

Woman is of the "weaker sex" not only because biology

(Courtesy of Metropolitan Museum of Art)

The Obelisk in Alexandria, before removal to the United States. Now in New York.

(Courtesy of Metropolitan Museum of Art)

A 19th Century interpretation of the primitive chant. By MacNeil.

makes her so, but because ages of social unfairness have accentuated her weakness through the centuries. In the dawn of life, while her brothers were being taught to fight and kill and protect themselves, while they hunted and fished and learned to make spears and arrows, she was confined to one little spot where she was assured protection. We have many instances of her actually being forced to live in a cage for many years, until her people were ready to sell or exchange her in marriage.

Under conditions such as these, the primitive "débutante" must have found life wretched in the extreme. She dared not wander far from the camp, lest she be captured by a wandering beast or man. Yet certain writers tell us that conditions within the tribe or clan were so difficult for the girl, so many hardships were forced upon her, that frequently she wandered from her people purposely, permitting herself to be captured and carried away as a bride.

But barbarous though they may have been, devoid of love and gentleness, primitive peoples seem to have had a very pronounced moral sense. They recognized as dangerous that which we, of a later age and advanced civilization, consider sinful. There are to be found, among most savage peoples, curious customs which were intended primarily for the protection of the young girl.

Separation of the Sexes.—Whether for purposes of protection, religious tabu, or personal gain, savage man kept his young women apart from the rest of the tribe. Perhaps a little of all three elements entered into the separation. That we do not know. But it has been definitely established that the separation of the sexes was one of man's earliest institutions.

Among certain animals, when the young are in a helpless state they are carried about by their parents—the males by the father and the females by the mother. Nature seems to have arranged for this by instinct. In savage life it was quite the natural thing for young boys to go with their father and for girls to remain with their mother.

In Australia, New Caledonia, and various other countries, brothers and sisters were not even permitted to talk to each other. We are told by some authorities that in primitive life it was the custom among certain Australian tribes to kill the young girl who permitted herself to be seen by her brothers. To-day a boy does not enter his sister's room without trepidation. How much of it is due to courtesy and custom and how much to inherent fear of "sin" is a matter for speculation.

Among the Nairs of Malabar it is considered a great dishonour for a man to remain in the same room with his sister. Similarly, in Tonga men are most reserved in their behaviour toward their sisters. A chief in Tonga never enters the house of his eldest sister. It would be considered an insult for him to do so.

Mr. Pritchard, who lived among the Samoans and studied their manners and customs, says:

> Of all their customs, the most strictly observed, perhaps, was that which forbade the remotest reference to anything, even by way of a joke, that conveyed the slightest indelicacy in thought or word or gesture, when brothers and sisters were together. In the presence of his sister, the wildest rake was always modest and moral. In presence of her brother, the most accommodating coquette was always chaste and reserved. This custom remains intact to the present day.

The sexual tabu, forbidding marriage within the same totem or among kin, probably induced the separation of children in the home in a religious sense among many savage peoples. These sexual tabus seem to account also for the seclusion of girls in primitive life, of which our own début dance, our own "coming out" party, is a survival. survival.

Seclusion of the "Débutante."—Among early peoples, each sex was made tabu to the other. But while the men were permitted to roam freely where they pleased, while they were allowed to join in the hunt with their elders, the young women were carefully secluded and in many instances actually imprisoned. We are told of many savages who imprisoned their girls in "cages" from puberty to marriage, and that during the imprisonment they were not seen by any men—not even the men of their own family. Thus Kaffir girls at puberty are even to-day placed in separate huts where none but females are permitted to visit them.

Loango girls at puberty are secluded in huts which are built for that purpose in the forest, and no man may venture near them under pain of death. From the very

Among many savage peoples the girl is tabu and she is confined to a little hut until married. The coming out of the hut is accompanied by much celebration—a custom paralleled in modern life by the "coming out" party of the debutante.

first day of their seclusion they are instructed in the duties of married life and motherhood, and this instruction continues until they are given in marriage. During the period of her seclusion, the Loango girl is called *nkumbi* (hymen).

The Cambodians speak of this custom of seclusion as "entering the shade." The Cambodian girl who "enters the shade" must promise not to let herself be seen by a man; not to look at men herself; not to bathe until night; not to eat certain forbidden foods.

It appears that in many instances certain foods were

forbidden young people. A Wagogo child was not permitted to eat the liver, kidneys, or heart of any animal until reaching a specified age. The Yaunde was strictly forbidden the flesh of sheep or goat until after initiation. In New South Wales only married men were permitted to eat duck. Young Fijians even to this day do not eat river fish or eels until they reach a certain age.

You know how modern parents exact the promise from young people not to smoke or take after-dinner coffee until they reach the age of twenty-one. You know how young girls are told that they may not have such and such a thing, or may not do such and such a thing, until after their "coming out." It is an interesting parallel.

But to return to the custom of seclusion. We are told that in New Ireland girls were at one time confined for four or five years in small cages. They were kept in the dark and were not allowed to set foot on the ground. The girls were placed in the cages when quite young and were forced to remain there until they were young women. Then they were taken out, given a great feast, and permitted to marry. Don't you see in this a prophecy of the début dance of later civilizations?

The natives of Vancouver Island place their girls in a sort of gallery in the house, surrounding them completely with mats so that they cannot be seen by men.

Amongst the Zulus, as amongst most South African tribes, the girl is secluded in a hut for some time after the first appearance of puberty. Many of these peoples have elaborate ceremonies when the girls "come out." It is remarkable that the term "coming out" should have survived even to our own polished 20th-century civilization, in connection with the débutante who "comes out" of social seclusion and is introduced to society.

In China and Japan young girls are kept carefully separated from the other sex even to this day. And we are told that it was a custom until recently for the Hindu girl to be kept in a dark room for four days, upon reaching maturity, and she was forbidden to see the sun or receive visits even from the men of her own family. The sun probably has a religious significance. Its fertilizing powers were well known to early peoples, and they probably connected it in some way with birth and procreation.

High Degree of Morality Among Primitives.—As has already been indicated, early peoples had a sense of morality despite their barbarism. We find an astonishing morality even among the savage races still existing.

The Kaffir woman, for instance, is extremely chaste and modest.

Among the inhabitants of Lob-nor, a people whose social scheme is wretched in the extreme, immorality is severely punished.

In New Guinea chastity is strictly maintained and immorality is punished.

Mr. Winwood Reade tells us that among the Equatorial Africans, the girl who disgraces her family by wantonness is banished from her clan. He adds that in cases of seduction the man is flogged—sometimes killed. Nevertheless, it must be mentioned that some African tribes have no morality whatever and live even to-day in a state of promiscuity.

Among various Northern Indians girls were from early age prohibited by custom from joining in the most innocent amusements with boys. Even the girl of seven or eight was guarded rigidly and forbidden to play with children of the opposite sex.

Tribes of the East Coast in Madagascar have a high morality. The sexes are separated in early life and the girls are carefully guarded.

The Corean girl is taught that it is disgraceful to permit herself to be seen or spoken to by a man outside of her family circle. Perhaps this accounts for her great modesty. After the age of eight she is forbidden to enter the men's quarters of her own home. She is scrupulously kept from any sort of intercourse with the male sex until marriage. No modern débutante receives more protection than the young Corean miss.

The Original "Coming-Out" Party.—The "coming-out" party of modern life seems to be a vestige or relic of the time when girls "came out" of the huts where they had been imprisoned—and were offered in marriage to the highest bidder, the best hunter, or the man betrothed in infancy, according to the custom of the people.

Coming out of the hut symbolized to early peoples the putting away of the old life of childhood and sexlessness—the taking up of the new life of young womanhood and its responsibilities. Like all changes in life, it was dramatized. We can see these early "debuts"—the girls half glad and half sad, thrilled with their new freedom, proud of their momentary importance, afraid of their new duties, for all the world as excited as the debutante of to-day! And we can see the men dancing around them, painted and decorated for the occasion, shouting and feasting and dancing in weird pantomime—making a ceremony of the business of selecting a bride.

In modern American society the proper age for the début is eighteen. There are usually a dance and a dinner—and, if the truth be known, a set of young men and a set of young women studying one another with an eye for matrimonial possibilities!

Of course, the débutante of to-day is far removed from the débutante of yesterday who was imprisoned in a hut and who, more frequently than not, had her husband selected for her. Each new generation does things which the generation before would have considered "impossible"; and each fading generation laments the boldness and self-assertiveness of the new. But human nature is essentially the same as it was ages ago, and life goes on in the same old groove, scarcely changing its course despite the automobile and the freedom it has brought, despite the rolled stockings and the cigarette case of the girl who breaks down traditions, despite the new generations that are constantly treading upon the toes of the old.

The débutante of to-day is taken to Europe, as a rule, to get a glimpse of foreign social life. She is instructed at home, if she is not fortunate enough to be given the European trip; but by no means may she "come out" until she knows precisely what to do and say, precisely what is expected of her as a member of society.

In primitive life, we find that it was the custom to prepare youth for their mutual relations in later life. The Swahili girls at puberty were, and still are to some extent, instructed in matters relating to sex and motherhood. The Apache girls on arriving at the marrigeable age were instructed by the chief in the duties and responsibilities of married life. Among various African tribes, and among certain Australian peoples, the girls were entrusted with such feminine lore as the woman possessed, and were instructed in matters of importance concerning marriage and motherhood. The boys were instructed in all the secrets of tribal history and religion, and the cherished tribal myths and legends were related to them.

The girls alone did not suffer in primitive life. They were imprisoned and they were obliged to accept in matrimony men they had never seen before, but the boys had to undergo cruel and barbarous initiation customs. Tests of endurance were imposed upon them. Among certain peoples they were beaten; among others they were obliged to fast for long periods. Among many savage peoples it was the custom for a finger to be cut off, or a tooth or two knocked out. It was a curious belief among savages that to remove or sacrifice one part of the body was to purify the whole.

These ceremonies of initiation form an important part of savage life. In Australia there is a universal law which forbids a youth to marry until after the ceremonies of initiation have been concluded. At these ceremonies the boy is sometimes given instruction in his future duties.

No boy is considered a man until he has gone through the initiation ceremonies prescribed by his particular tribe.

Incidentally, it is very possible that our custom of initiation among young people seeking admission to clubs or fraternities had its origin in the customs of initiation among primitive peoples—customs which changed the status of boy to man.

A "Début" Dance among the Indians.—If you have ever witnessed a true Indian dance you know that you can never forget the thrill of it, the almost uncanny eloquence of it. It is almost like a language. The weird steps and pantomimic gestures of the dancers seem to speak.

Secretary of the Interior Work recently received a report from the superintendent of the Reno Indian reservation in Nevada, telling of the unique "début" dance which is still a prominent part of the social life of the Washoe Indians. We quote the following from a New York newspaper:

> The dance or ceremony is called "the girl's dance," and the girl who is the central figure eats nothing for a period of four days. On the fourth night the dance is held, beginning at eight o'clock in the evening and continuing until sunrise the following morning. It consists of the Indians joining hands in a circle and moving by short dance-steps sideways around the ring, humming a sort of chant without words or meaning. The girl, accompanied by some older woman, evidently a chaperon, carries a long staff to support her because of her weakness through loss of food during her fast, weaves in and out of the dance, and joins in the steps.
>
> As the dance proceeds late into the night, the family of the girl give money and other possessions to the dancers to keep them moving and to induce others to join in the dance, the greatest number of dancers signifying the popularity of the family. Shortly after midnight a big feast is given by the girl's relatives, all present participating.
>
> The ceremony closes at sunrise, when the girl is taken inside of her tepee and attired in bunches of sagebrush, in which money is concealed. She appears later before the assembled dancers outside and throws the money to them amid a wild scramble. A can of

water is then dashed over her head, concluding the ceremony, after which she is ready to receive a proposal of marriage.

Many Indians, like those of the Reno reservation, have preserved their age-old customs and ceremonials. We see in all of them an inclination to celebrate with dance and pantomime the important periods of life. And there are few celebrations as elaborate and impressive as those that, in various tribes, mark the change from girlhood to young womanhood—the period during which the young woman "comes out" and is ready for marriage.

The Chaperon in Antiquity.—In an early social scheme where girls were kept secluded and sexual tabus were made and enforced, one can see the importance of the "chaperon." She was the guardian of the tribal chastity; she was the protector of the unmarried girls; she saw that the tribal tabus were obeyed.

We to-day consider sinful what primitive man considered dangerous and contrary to the natural laws. That eliminates, to a certain extent, the need for a "chaperon." But a few examples will show how absolutely essential she was in early life.

Among many African, Australian, and early Asiatic peoples, the girl who was betrothed in infancy to some important person was kept secluded in a small cage until she was ready for marriage. The man of importance would see that she was carefully guarded and kept from all intercourse with the other sex. He would select a woman whom he trusted, and place the girl in her care. This woman was the original chaperon.

After betrothal in Nias, Borneo, and the Watubella Islands no communication between the pair is permitted until the day of the wedding. To enforce this custom the girl is carefully guarded by a woman retained for the purpose. This woman, like the chaperon of more recent times, accompanies the betrothed girl wherever she goes.

Similarly, in Buru, Ceram, and Luang Sermata a youth,

when engaged, may not venture near his fiancée. She is not permitted to look at him or speak to him. Here again we find the girl guarded by a woman to see that the betrothal law is obeyed.

Among the Loango Negroes, the mother is the girl's "chaperon." No Loango youth would dare to speak to a girl if she were not with her mother. In her mother's presence, however, it is perfectly good etiquette for him to do so.

Wives of the chiefs in Tonga are not permitted to walk abroad without women attendants. We are told that in early Rome the same sort of custom prevailed. No woman of importance would venture forth without her "lady." Indeed, no matter in what country we search, and no matter among what people, we find someone who seems to parallel the chaperon of a later day—someone who serves in the capacity of protector, advisor, guardian, or companion.

Perhaps it was for selfish reasons that the young girl was protected in early life. A marriageable daughter was an asset to the family, a valuable and marketable possession. As such she had to be protected. She might run away and deprive the family of her bride-price. She might be stolen by some other people, her tribe might attempt to recapture her, and warfare would result. All things considered, the wisest and safest thing was to keep her carefully secluded and carefully guarded. Hence—the chaperon.

As interpreted in a later civilization, chaperon means companion more than guardian. Where there is no seclusion of the sexes, no chaperon to guard the secluded is needed. Where there are no tribal tabus to be enforced, no chaperon to enforce the tabus is needed. Thus the original chaperon gradually lost her position of power and importance and merged into the companion and associate of a later day.

As is the case with most customs that grew out of the

necessities of early life, the custom of the chaperon is fast falling into disuse; indeed, in the United States it is practically obsolete. But so difficult is it for custom to die that we find the chaperon still firmly entrenched in the social life of various European countries—a social figurehead, as kings are fast becoming royal figureheads.

CHAPTER VII

A Short History of Courtship

Because of her motherhood, woman's sexual nature gradually became purer than man's. The child became more and more the centre of her thoughts and her deeds. Thus the strength of her erotic instincts diminished. The tenderness awakened in her by her children also benefited the father. Out of this tenderness—as also out of the admiration for the manly qualities which the father developed in defence of herself and her children—gradually arose the erotic feeling directed to this man alone. Thus love began.

—Ellen Key.

THE FIRST KIND OF COURTSHIP

FROM the very first men have wooed and won the women of their choice. Whether the wooing took the form of brutal capture, of purchase, or of actual courtship depended entirely upon the period or stage of development and upon existing conditions.

Some authorities believe that the very first form of courtship was a system of pairing off, such as is found among the lower animals. They tell us that it is very probable that in the earliest times a human pairing system existed. They place this season at about the time that would correspond to our June, which seems to account, to some extent, for the age-old desire for marriage in that month.

This first pairing off of men and women would scarcely be in the nature of courtship. We cannot conceive of the element of love entering into it at all. The male undoubtedly played the more active part, as is true in the courtship of almost all animal species. So deeply ingrained is this instinct in human nature that it is even to-day considered immodest and indelicate for the woman to take any active part whatever in the courting.

We can understand, however, how even at this early period women tried to make themselves attractive to the men. What chance had they, alone and unprotected, in a hostile world? It was good to have a man to hunt and bring in food, to fight off dangerous animals, to bring in queer shells and soft skins.

And so, in the pairing season the woman would be as eager to find a mate as the man was to find a woman. But very probably the courtship was entirely a one-sided affair, the woman having very little to do in the matter. While the man might select at will, she was obliged to go with whatever man to whose fancy she appealed. Thus was inequality between the sexes born in the very earliest period of life, and its influence has permeated through the social fabric of all ages.

Yet it is very possible that in this early pairing season woman had various ways, of which we know nothing, of making herself attractive to man. Necessity has always been the mother of invention, and despite the unfair conditions against which she had to contend, we feel certain that early woman had some means of winning the man she wanted.

But on the whole, courtship would have been brief, rude, with little or no preliminaries. Perhaps he would come upon her as she bathed in the stream, a little distance from her people, and would carry her off without further ado. One authority tells us that women actually wandered away from safety and protection for the purpose of being carried off by a man. It was better to be the property of one man than the property of the whole tribe.

Or perhaps she would come upon him while he battled with a bear or some other beast, and she would squat down nearby until the beast had been demolished. Then by gesture and expression she would indicate her admiration. We can see the fellow puffing out in pride, beating his chest and crying out in defiance of the whole world. Perhaps he rips off the claws of the animal and gives them to the woman as ornaments. And we can see them going off together—a woman and her mate—after this brief, simple courtship.

The Dawn of Love.—No one knows precisely when love began, or how it began, or even whether it is a natural or developed instinct. Many have written on the subject. Many have expressed their opinions. But the true origin of love must for ever be lost in the dim ages of the beginning of mankind.

We are inclined to believe that mankind always had the capacity to love but that for ages love was a dormant instinct, asleep, while man struggled for his foothold on life. During the first difficult ages of development there could have been no awakening of love, no definite consciousness of the finer instincts.

But let us skip a few pages in the book of life and come to that period when man is chiefly carnivorous, and when he is established in a cave home with his woman and his children. We see now the importance of the male in supplying food for the subsistence of the children; and we can see the woman, in an awakening love for the children, drawn in a deeper attachment toward the father. It is he who supplies them with food. It is he who rolls the rock down upon enemies and keeps his family safe. Thus, as Ellen Key points out, the need for protecting the child and supplying it with food was the spark that fanned the tiny flame of love into glowing; and it has been glowing with greater and greater intensity ever since.

Of course, love as we interpret it to-day belongs to a highly advanced civilization. The love that gives without thought of gain, the love that is self-sacrificing and self-effacing, is an entirely different kind of love from that which we find among primitive men and women who continue to live together solely because of benefits to be derived for the young. But this is a book of origins, and if we are to go back to the true and original source of love, we must find its first spark centred around the child and the home.

The blossoming and developing of love into one of the most exquisite and inspiring instincts of civilized life is a vast subject in itself, and a proper study of it would require a volume.

EARLY BETROTHALS

The courtship we have been considering thus far is the courtship that in primitive life precipitated almost instant marriage. Now let us consider courtship in the sense of the betrothal or engagement. This form of courtship came when men were already established in clans and tribes, and when savage peoples were in various ways endeavouring to make themselves attractive to the opposite sex—by ornamenting, mutilating, painting, and tattooing themselves.

There were diverse ways for obtaining a wife. Of course, there was marriage by capture, which we will forget for the moment. But in early life betrothals were frequently arranged by parents between infants, sometimes even before they were born. Relatives frequently selected a bride for the youth, usually one who would be profitable to their own ends. True courtship did not exist to any very great extent, and love, if it entered into the matter at all, was a rare and uncommon thing.

It is interesting to note the betrothal customs of early savage peoples. We are told that among the Javanese courtship was carried on entirely through the medium of the parents. On the Sandwich Islands the father had the power of life and death over his children, and could promise them in marriage to suit his own whims and fancies. The Mandingo girl was obliged to marry the suitor selected for her by her people, or remain for ever after unmarried.

Wrestling and fighting appear to have been a primitive method of courtship. This was among people who did not practise infant betrothal and among whom children were permitted to select their own mates. If a young woman had two suitors they fought together, and the stronger won the bride. This corresponds with the custom, among various peoples, of forcing young men to undergo tests of endurance before granting them permission to marry. The underlying principle, of course, is that no man may have a wife until he can prove that he is able to protect her.

The beautiful Atalanta, we are told, gave herself to the best runner. The hero suitors of the Finnish myths had to undergo difficult trials to prove their courage. The Dyak was obliged to show himself a hero before he could marry. You know how, even to-day, women worship feats of strength; if a modern woman has two suitors she will invariably select the one she believes to be the stronger and the more courageous. It is the old, old instinct of self-preservation.

In Wales, a ceremonious betrothal usually came first, after which a sham fight was staged. The betrothal was usually arranged by the parents. But among the Muscovites an actual invasion came first, as a rule, and the bridegroom's party carried off the lady. Later, the consent of the parents was sought, and if obtained there was great feasting and celebrating in the form of a betrothal or before-the-wedding party.

Whenever an alliance was desired among the North American Indians, the young man himself presented to the parents of the young woman he sought to marry a belt of wampum, a bracelet, or some such gift. If she received it, it was a sign that he was accepted and preparations for the wedding feast were started at once. Courtship among the Indians was always simple and brief.

The Custom of Infant Betrothal.—One of the most widespread customs of betrothal in primitive life was that of promising a child in infancy. And among most peoples this betrothal was considered as binding as marriage. Among the Yorubas a child betrothed by her parents is considered practically a wife.

In New Caledonia it was the custom to betroth a girl

(Courtesy of Metropolitan Museum of Art)

Bust of Herodotus, Roman, probably 2nd Century, B. C.

(Courtesy of Metropolitan Museum of Art)

"The Wandering Minstrel."
A water colour by A. L. Leloir (1873).

as soon as she was born. This custom still exists to a very great extent among the New Caledonians.

The Bushmen generally betroth their daughters as children without consulting them. But if a girl grows up without having been betrothed in childhood, she may select her husband and marry without the consent of her parents.

In the Fijis children are married by their parents when they are three or four years old. This marriage is merely a ceremony, but it is a binding ceremony, and when the children grow up they are man and wife.

Among the Tasmanians wives are as a rule betrothed to their husbands from infancy. The parents usually arrange marriages for their own selfish gain.

The Yorubas, Mandingoes, and Koosa Kaffirs follow the custom of infant betrothal. Among these peoples infant betrothal has been a custom for many long ages, and they know no other form.

Among certain Eskimo tribes as soon as a girl is born a young man who wants her for a wife, or the father of that young man, goes to the father of the child and makes the offer of marriage. If he is accepted, a betrothal promise is given which is considered as binding as our own marriage ceremony. The girl is delivered at the proper age. Sometimes she does not see her husband until the day of the marriage.

Infant-marriage as a form of betrothal is common in British India, in the Malay Archipelago, among the Samoyedes. This type of betrothal is found also in New Guinea, New Zealand, Tahiti, and many other islands of the South Seas.

The custom of promising brides in childhood existed among some European countries during the early periods of civilization. Spain knew the custom; it existed at one time in Russia. And we know from our history how frequently brides were promised to infant royalty in both France and England.

The Bullroarer in Courtship.—Among the Australians

of the Arunta and other neighbouring peoples, among many African tribes and among the Apache, Navajo, and various other Indians, traces have been found of a remarkable instrument which has been given the English name of "bullroarer." We mention it here because at one time it played an important part in courtship.

The bullroarer is simply a small, flat slip of wood through one end of which a hole is made. A string is passed through this hole, and by means of this string the instrument is swung around rapidly. It makes a peculiar booming, humming noise.

This instrument was treated with the utmost respect among primitive peoples. The Blackfellows particularly feared and worshipped it, using it to a great extent in their initiation ceremonies. Among many African peoples it was used, and is still used to-day, in festivities and dances.

It was at one time a common belief among various peoples that a man could charm a woman to love him by making the peculiar humming sound with the bullroarer. The sound or humming was considered a sort of spiritual invitation. Instances have been recorded of women using the bullroarer to charm the men they sought as husbands.

In the Yaroinga tribe, and among neighbouring tribes, each boy at puberty was given a bullroarer. It was symbolic of the fact that he was now ready to woo and win a wife. The instrument had the highest mystic significance and the boy valued it as one of his most important possessions. To-day it is no longer held in superstitious dread, although it is still to be found in actual use in religious ceremonies among various savage peoples.

Did the serenade of later life grow out of the bullroarer and its reputation for charming the ladies? One wonders.

ROMANCE ENTERS COURTSHIP

It seems to us that romance must have entered courtship when the struggle for mere existence became less pronounced—and mankind began to day-dream.

It would have been a crude and elementary sort of romance at first. A girl stealing away from her tribe at night to join a youth with whom she had been forbidden marriage. A savage fellow forgetting the chase and watching at the stream for hours for another glimpse of the girl he had seen there. A necklace of claws, made with painstaking care and offered without a word, accepted without acknowledgment. We suspect that many such instances of tenderness and of simple romance lie hidden beneath the known facts of early man.

But as we follow the customs of betrothal and courtship through many centuries of development, we find that romance and civilization mark time together. Where infant civilizations flame out of the long darkness that is prehistory, cutting through the blackness like tiny shafts of light to show us the way, there we find for the first time actual recorded instances of romances.

In Greece, for instance, we find names being inscribed by lovers on trees—a custom which still survives. We find flowers telling their eloquent tale of love. The doors of beautiful maidens were decked, we are told, from morning to night with flowers placed there by their lovers.

A solemn betrothal almost invariably preceded the actual marriage in Greece. At this betrothal the dowry of the bride was settled, and it is interesting to note that her position as a married woman depended largely upon the value of this dowry. Records have come down to us of the daughters of poor but worthy citizens being presented with dowries by the state or by a number of private citizens.

Exchange of Gifts.—We are told that in Homer's time the bridegroom wooed the bride with rich gifts. Iphidamas, for instance, offered a hundred heifers and a thousand goats as a nuptial present.

The exchange of gifts would naturally have come into courtship at a very early time. The presenting of gifts is one of the simplest and surest methods of winning favour.

In primitive culture the gift meant a great deal more than it does to us to-day. The primitive man or woman felt that part of himself or herself was being presented.

Among the Khakyens even now there seems to be little more of a marriage ceremony than the interchange of presents. And in Japan, the sending of presents to the bride by the groom is one of the most important parts of the marriage ceremony. When the gifts have been received and accepted, the contract is considered complete and neither party can draw back.

As we follow the development of gift-making in courtship, we find that a certain romance centres around the flower. A Timorese woman, even to-day, bestows the highest mark of attachment upon her lover when she gives him the flower garland from her hair. Among the Polynesians, men and women alike wear flowers behind their ears when they are in love. The flower is, as a rule, the gift of the lover.

It was an ancient betrothal custom among various peoples, conspicuously among them the Greeks, to wear a flower as an external and conspicuous mark of the engagement. The full-blown flower suggested love awakened, and it was with the flower that lovers in early days exchanged their engagement vows. A short-lived emblem indeed with which to plight a life-long love!

But there have been many other favourite courtship gifts beside flowers. The custom of giving a bit of jewellery or something decorative to wear probably originated in the myth that whoever wore the magic girdle of Aphrodite became the object of great love. And the custom of the young woman making something for her betrothed to wear probably had its origin in the old Scandinavian tradition that for a wedding to be happy, the bride must make with her own hands the groom's bridal shirt.

Everyone knows that the teacup is "quite the thing" to give to an engaged girl. But why?

Tradition tells us that a lover, who was on one occasion

obliged to go away on an extended sea journey, gave to his betrothed a delicate china cup, asking her to drink tea from it every afternoon at a certain hour. He said, "If I am unfaithful, the cup will fill to overbrimming and the tea pouring over the sides will crack the thin china. Then you will know I have broken faith."

Origin and Development of the Kiss.—Kissing as a form of affection did not develop until comparatively late. But we know that kissing as a form of obeisance existed in the most primitive times. In many African tribes the natives kiss the ground over which a chief has trod. In Australia kissing the ground, or rather breathing upon it, is a form of greeting among various peoples. Kissing the hand and the foot has been a mark of respect and homage from the earliest times.

Havelock Ellis, in his "Psychology of Sex," says:

> Manifestations resembling the kiss are found among various animals lower than man. Snails caress antennæ. Birds use their bills for a kind of caress. The dog who "licks" his master is really kissing him.

As primitive man paralleled the lower animals in so many things, it is very possible that the primitive mother kissed her child, in the sense of fondling it. But we cannot trace the kiss as a form of affection in antiquity in any sort of pronounced manner.

Lombroso tells us that kissing is a Caucasian habit and that Orientals are strangers to it. He says its origin is to be found undoubtedly in the maternal caresses. Out of these maternal caresses grew the kiss of feeling and reverence as we know it to-day.

The Samoan kiss is a sniff. The Polynesians show affection by rubbing noses together—as do the Laplanders and the Eskimo. Neither the Chinese nor the Japanese kiss. It is only in America and Europe that the kiss is practised to any great degree—although in time the moving pictures will probably introduce the custom to many other people!

Following the development of the kiss—and it developed very rapidly among Aryan and Semitic people—

Though the kiss in love and courtship is more modern than most of us suspect, the affectionate caress traces its origin back to the earliest times when the primitive mother fondled her infant as any mother does to-day.

we find that "kissing the mouth or the eyes as a form of dignified greeting was practised among the early Romans."

Mention of the kiss is found also in the memoirs of Pomponius, who suffered his lips to be kissed by worthy and deserving nobles, his hands by less worthy nobles, his feet by the least worthy nobles.

We learn from Erasmus that when he visited England he found kissing in use as a form of greeting everywhere. When a visitor entered a house he kissed his host and hostess, all their children, and even the dog and cat!

One of the first definite instances of kissing as a form of love and affection is noted by Leybard, the famous saint of Tours in the 6th century, who gave his betrothed "a ring, a kiss and a pair of shoes"—the latter being a sign of his great subjection to her. The ring was to bind them both together. The kiss, evidently, was the seal of affection.

Of course, the kiss as a form of affection may have existed very much earlier than the 6th century. We don't like to believe, somehow, that Cleopatra knew nothing at all about it. Yet we have no definite records other than those that are quoted here.

In France the kiss developed very rapidly and quickly found a permanent place for itself in courtship and love. Montaigne tells us that in France any Jack with three lackeys was privileged to kiss almost any woman he pleased. When dancing become popular, almost every dance figure ended with a kiss. According to one writer, Louis XII is credited with having kissed every woman in Normandy.

From France the kiss spread quickly all over Europe. In Russia we are told it reached the proportions of an epidemic. A kiss from the Tsar became one of the highest forms of official recognition.

The development of the kiss as a form of homage in royal circles and among the nobility of various countries is fascinating. But the subject has no place here. We are concerned solely with the kiss as it relates to courtship.

Like the flower of an earlier civilization, the kiss in courtship became the "seal with which lovers plight their troth." It became also an important feature of the marriage ceremonial and is now firmly established as a symbol of hope and love and tenderness. As such we interpret it in courtship and in marriage.

THE ENGAGEMENT RING

"It is the custom to seal the engagement pact with a ring," says "The Book of Etiquette."

What a world of romance and tradition lurks behind that simple sentence! We could not possibly tell all the fascinating tales that concern the engagement ring and its development through long ages of courtship and marriage, but we shall try to give you the most important and outstanding facts.

The ring as a pledge can be traced back to great antiquity.

> And Pharaoh said unto Joseph, See I have set thee over all the land of Egypt. And Pharaoh took off his ring from his hand, and put it upon Joseph's hand. (Genesis XLI, 41, 42.)

Similar use of signet rings as symbols of respect and authority is mentioned in several parts of the sacred narrative. It would appear that rings were commonly worn by persons of rank at that period, and that they were bestowed upon others either as gifts or for the purpose of transferring authority.

Of course, we know that rings as ornaments were worn in early Egypt, in Greece, and even among savage peoples. But whether or not they served any definite purpose other than ornamentation, we do not know and cannot say.

A wealth of folklore and mythology surrounds the ring. Nizami, the famous Persian poet who died in 1209, tells this story: A hot vapour once rent the ground and in the chasm was discovered a horse of tin and copper. There was a large fissure in its side. Passing by the place, a shepherd saw the horse and discovered in the fissure the body of an old man, fast asleep, with a gold ring on his

finger. He took it and went the following morning to his master to learn its value. During the visit he discovered that when he turned the seal toward the palm of his hand he became invisible. Determining to make use of this great power, he proceeded to the palace, secretly entered the council chamber, and remained unseen during a long council. When the nobles left, he revealed himself to the king and proclaimed himself a prophet. The king at once took him as his minister, and eventually the shepherd succeeded him on the throne.

But let us forget the fascinating folklore that surrounds the ring and study the development of the engagement ring as we know it to-day.

Development of the Engagement Ring.—It was anciently the custom among people of the lower classes to break a piece of gold or silver to seal the marriage pact. One half of the token was kept by the man, the other half by the woman. This custom came before the exchange of rings.

The custom of "breaking gold" is mentioned in an old play called "The Widow," an extract from which is to be found in Strutt's "Manners and Customs." In this play the widow complains that Ricardo has artfully drawn her into a verbal contract. One of her suitors says:

"Stay, stay—you broke no gold between you?"

"We broke nothing, sir," she answered.

"Nor drank to each other?"

"Not a drop."

Upon which the young man declares that "the contract cannot stand good in law."

Even prior to the breaking of gold, we can understand how lovers must have exchanged tokens of some sort. It would have seemed to them the logical way to prove their love. The man particularly would be eager to present the woman with a gift of some sort, because in primitive culture the gift is part of the person and by accepting it the woman acknowledged her acceptance of the man.

In ancient Ireland, for instance, it was the custom for the man to give the woman he wanted to marry a bracelet woven of human hair. Her acceptance of it was symbolic of accepting the man, of linking herself to him for life. In Halmahera and Borneo the proposal is made by offering betel to the girl. She shows her acceptance of the proposal by accepting the betel. (See p. 323.)

It appears that the ring as a love pledge existed at a very early period. We find many references to it in literature and in history.

Philip de Comines relates in his "Memoirs" that a diamond ring of great value was sent as a pledge or token by the Princess of Burgundy to the Duke of Austria (1477). This ring signified her consent to the alliance, arranged by her father. We see here two old customs: the first, betrothal by the father; the second, sealing of the engagement pact by exchange of rings.

It was quite a customary thing, in the early Middle Ages, for solemn betrothal by means of ring to precede matrimony. In England "rings were exchanged to seal the verbal contract of betrothal." In Italy the use of the ring was widespread, and the diamond was the favourite gem.

In an old play called "The Dutche Courtezan" a pair of lovers are introduced plighting their troth. Beatrice says to Freeville, "I give you faith; wear this slight favour in my remembrance." The "slight favour" is a rich and costly ring.

Codrington, in "Youth's Behaviour" (1664), says: "Rings and ribbands are but trifles, but believe me, they are not trifles that are aimed at in such exchanges; let them therefore be counselled that they neither give nor receive anything that afterwards may procure their shame." He is referring, of course, to young women who accept gifts of "rings and ribbands" from men.

The joint ring seems to have been a common token of love between betrothed people. We gather, from the following passage in Dryden's play, "Don Sebastian" (1690), that rings of this sort were by no means confined to the lower classes, but were exquisitely and expensively made for the wealthy classes:

> A curious artist wrought 'em
> With joynts so close as not to be perceiv'd;
> Yet are they both each other's counterpart.
> (Her part had *Juan* inscribed, and his had *Zayda*.
> You know whose names were their's) and in the midst,
> A heart divided in two halves was placed.
> Now if the rivets of those two rings, inclos'd,
> Fit into each other, I have forged this lye;
> But if they join, you must forever part.

The famous Jummal ring (known also as the gemmel-ring) is mentioned by Herrick in his "Hesperides." The Jummal ring was curiously made in two parts linked together, a sort of joint ring like that mentioned above.

> Thou sent'st me a true-love knot; but I
> Returned a ring of jummals to imply
> Thy love had one knot, mine a triple-tye.

This quotation seems to indicate that the Jummal ring sometimes had more than two links and was more of a "true-love token" than an engagement ring.

A curious old custom still prevails in Guernsey, although it is no longer as widespread and common as it was in the 18th and 19th centuries. When a young man offers himself to a young lady and is accepted, the parents of both parties give what is termed a "flouncing." All their friends are invited and a great feast is prepared. The young lady is led around the room by her future father-in-law, the young man by his future father-in-law, and they are introduced to all the friends and relatives of the opposite families. Rings are then exchanged publicly and the couple is considered betrothed. This ceremony is almost as binding as actual marriage, and once the rings are exchanged, the thing is done! They are as good as man and wife.

The "Hand-fest."—Among the early Danes there existed a curious kind of marriage-contract known as *hand-festing.* Strong traces of it still remain.

According to this *hand-fest* it was customary and entirely correct for unmarried persons of both sexes to choose a companion and live together for one year. If they were pleased with one another at the end of the year, they remained together for life; if not, they separated and were free to make another choice.

We find traces of a custom very similar to this in England in the 17th century and in Scotland in the 17th and 18th centuries. It is known as "hand-fasting" or hand-in-fist. At the beginning of the period there is a "mutual interchangement of rings," and at the end the period, if they do not wish to remain together they return the rings, separate, and seek another companion. This custom appears to have been quite common during the reign of Queen Elizabeth. It was also a widespread custom, during her reign, for women to give their lovers tiny lace handkerchiefs (about three inches square) which they wore in their cuffs or hats.

The Custom of the Diamond.—In modern times the diamond is the favourite gem for the engagement ring. Indeed, one thinks only of the diamond in connection with rings of betrothal. There is a reason for this.

According to an old superstition, the origin of which is unknown, the sparkle of the diamond is supposed to have originated in the fires of love. Therefore the diamond engagement ring is considered by superstitious persons the only *true* engagement ring, portending love and happiness throughout life.

The diamond was particularly esteemed in Italy in mediæval times and was the favourite stone for setting in engagement rings. It was called *pietra della reconciliazione* because of its supposed power to maintain concord between man and wife.

To-day the etiquette books say, "The convention is that the ring be a diamond solitaire set in gold or platinum, or, if it is preferred, a diamond set with other stones." As always, custom prevails.

HOPE CHESTS AND BRIDAL SHOWERS

The "hope chest" must certainly have grown out of the old, old custom of the dowry.

The dowry itself grew out of the custom of marriage by purchase, which shall be discussed later in detail. It represents an indirect way of compensating the bridegroom. The dowry in early life was intended entirely as a reward or return for the bride-price paid to the parents.

Of course, the nearer we come to the touch of higher civilization, the more the original purpose of customs such as these fades into the background. To-day the hope chest is simply a relic of other days, retained because it is a pretty and convenient custom and because of the ages of tradition that lurk in its depth.

There is, for instance, the tradition that to make every bit of finery and household linen that goes into the hope chest is to earn everlasting happiness for one's self. We can see how a superstition such as this would have been born among thrifty mothers who told the tale to their daughters, who in turn handed it down to their own daughters, and they to their daughters after them, so that the superstition has survived and still can be found among various European peoples. In Roumania, to give one instance, even the tiniest girls, some of them as young as five years, are to be seen working on their bridal finery, each one striving to outdo the other in beauty and elaboration of work. Each finished article is laid carefully away in a huge chest until such time as a suitor appears.

Wardrobes in which to hang clothes came at a comparatively late period. Chests were used to store away household linens and wearing apparel, and each household had its collection of chests. In most homes there would be one chest set aside for the daughter, and into this chest would be placed the bits of finery and the hand-made linens which were to go into "the home of her hopes." Can't you see the origin of the name "hope chest"?

Origin of the Bridal Shower.—The bridal shower is one of the prettiest customs that has been brought down to us through the centuries. It is a charming way for friends and acquaintances to present gifts that would seem too trifling if they were presented individually.

Many, many years ago in Holland a beautiful girl gave her heart to a miller—a young fellow who hadn't much in worldly goods but whom everyone loved because of his kindness. He was poor because he gave his bread and his flour to the needy.

The girl's father forbade the marriage and told his daughter that she could not have the dowry he had placed aside for her if she married the poor miller. He had selected what he considered a satisfactory husband for her—a man who owned a farm and a hundred pigs!

The people to whom the miller had given bread heard the story and were sorry. They got together and talked the matter over. Too bad the beautiful girl would lose her dowry. Couldn't they do something about it? They didn't have much money, but each one thought of a gift he or she could contribute so that the miller and the beautiful girl could marry and have their own home.

And they came to the girl in a gay procession: one with an old Dutch vase; one with plates for the kitchen shelves; one with linens made on the hand loom at home; one with a shiny new pot. They showered her with their gifts and gave her a finer dowry than her father ever could! Many brides-to-be to-day must be grateful to the little Dutch maiden whose "shower" set such a happy precedent.

A good many years later, an Englishwoman heard of a friend who was about to be married and decided that the only gift she could afford was too slight an offering to express the good wishes that she felt. Remembering the story of the Dutch "shower," and knowing that there were other friends who felt the same way as she did, she called them together and suggested that they present their gifts at the same time. The "shower" which they gave was so successful and caused so much comment in fashionable circles that it became definitely established as a social custom, and has remained ever since.

Kinds of Showers.—There was a time, not so very long ago, when the linen shower was considered the most correct and appropriate type of shower to give the engaged girl. Young people who planned to "shower" their

Origin of the bridal shower—Holland.

bride-to-be friend contributed each an article of linen for the new home. But to-day there is a great variety of showers, and the clever hostess always selects one that is novel and interesting.

The book shower is quite new, and a great favorite of the moment. Everything may be included, from the Bible to the best-seller. The hostess of the shower may supply the book case, if she likes, or a pretty little book rack. The guests supply the books. It is a wise thing to compare notes beforehand, so that no books are duplicated.

The kitchen shower is always good. Gifts may consist of chinaware, kitchen tableware or woodenware. The aluminum shower appears to be very popular, but one should ascertain first whether or not the bride-to-be wants aluminum in her kitchen.

The radio shower is the "last word," of course; but one should not give a radio shower unless one is quite positive that both bride and groom are radio "fans." In this case the shower guests as a rule pool their money and purchase the complete radio set which they present *en masse.*

The shower can be made a delightful social function. Only intimate friends of the bride should be invited, and the affair should be informal in character. Of course, it is always more interesting if the shower is a complete surprise to the bride.

THE PERIOD OF THE ENGAGEMENT

All writers on etiquette seem to be agreed that "there is no time when the rules of etiquette need to be so strictly observed as during the period of courtship." This thought is clearly paralleled in primitive culture.

Among the Afghan tribes, the greatest reserve is maintained between men and women who are to be married. No man may even see or speak to his promised wife from the time of betrothal until marriage. Strangely enough this same custom exists among the warlike Eusofyzes.

In Russia, it was at one time considered a great disgrace for a man to propose directly to a lady. Between the day of settling the dowry with the parents and the exact day of marriage, he was strictly forbidden to see his betrothed or even venture near the house.

To parallel this in modern life, right here in the United States, you know that it is still considered good form for a young man to obtain the formal consent of the young lady's parents before asking her hand in marriage. It isn't always done, of course, but the custom exists, never-

(Courtesy of Metropolitan Museum of Art)

Proof of a Greek gravestone, 4th Century, B. C. Notice the handclasp —a symbol of farewell.

(Courtesy of Metropolitan Museum of Art)

An ancient vase, red figured. A warrior bidding farewell to his family. About 450 B. C. Attributed to the "Lykaon Painter."

theless. And you know that it is an old, old custom for the bridegroom to be forbidden the house of the bride on the day of the wedding. A superstition exists to the effect that if the bride permits herself to be seen by the groom on the day of the wedding, before the actual time of ceremony, the wedding will not be quite as happy as she had hoped.

Etiquette is harsh in Greece. Rings for betrothal are exchanged in the priest's presence, and the engagement may then not be broken without the consent of the priest. Following the betrothal, the engaged couple may not see each other or talk to each other until the day of the wedding.

We find traces of similar customs in various countries and among various peoples. It would appear that customs such as these grew out of the fear of the bride's parents or people of being cheated of her bride-price if she decided to elope with her betrothed before the day set for the wedding, although in many instances it was necessary to pay the bride-price even before the wedding day was set. It is curious that even courtship, and customs concerning courtship, should still be linked in so many ways to the primitive level.

Announcing the Engagement.—When a suitor is accepted there follows the necessity of announcing the betrothal to the friends and acquaintances of both families. Customs of announcing the betrothal have varied among different peoples and in different periods.

In primitive life the occasion was one of great festivity and celebration. The families came together and ate and drank, which was the universal way of indicating kinship. The very act of eating together appears to have been symbolic of the binding together of both families. Thus, among certain peoples, the contract was not considered binding until a feast had been given and both families had eaten together.

In modern life, it is customary to celebrate the engagement with a dinner party or an engagement supper.

The original purpose is forgotten, but the custom remains.

We are told that in early Rome the contract of marriage was sealed with an iron ring, and the contracting parties drank together. Drinking together appears to have been a common and widespread custom in Europe. We find frequent allusion to it in literature. For instance, in Middleton's play, "No Wit Like a Woman's" we discover this line:

> Ev'n when my lips touch'd the *contracting* cup.

Reference has already been made to the play called "The Widow" (See p. 189),in which the suitor asks:"Nor drank to each other?" Because there was no drinking together and no exchange of rings he holds that the contract will not stand good in law and that she is therefore free to marry him.

Park, in his "Travels in the Interior of Africa," tells us of the following betrothal custom:

> At Baniseribe, a Slatee having seated himself upon a mat at the threshold of his door, a young woman (his intended bride) brought a little water in a calabash, and kneeling down before him, desired him to wash his hands. When he had done this, the girl, with a tear of joy sparkling in her eye, drank the water; this being considered as the greatest proof of her fidelity and love.

This custom is simply a primitive method of publicly announcing a betrothal. It existed among various North American Indian tribes, as well as among many tribes in Central Africa. The washing of the hands in the water was, in early days, symbolic of placing the taste of the man's strength in the water, since his strength was believed to be in his hands. The woman, drinking the water, *tasted the strength* of the man she was to marry. Variations of this custom are found among many widely separated peoples.

A curious custom existed in England in the 18th and early 19th centuries. During that period it was a popular thing to cry out "Halves!" on seeing a person pick up anything he had found. This exclamation entitled the person to one-half of the find. The custom still exists to a certain extent, and is particularly prevalent in England among young boys.

Out of this grew the custom of publicly announcing a betrothal to which the parents of the young people objected. A youth would drop a ring before the girl he wished to marry. She, conspirator that she was, would cry "Halves!" and be given one-half of the ring. This, you remember, was an ancient custom practised before the exchange of engagement rings. A bit of gold was broken and the man kept one part while the woman kept the other.

Now, each holding half of the ring, the young man and woman would attract the attention of passers-by and call upon them to witness the fact that they were now betrothed and that the token sealed their betrothal vows. They would then parade to the home of the young woman, the gay crowd behind them, and announce what had happened. Under the circumstances the families usually acquiesced, and the marriage followed.

As a popular fad, the custom existed for more than a century but gradually fell into disuse and is to-day entirely obsolete.

It is a modern custom to give the news of the engagement as nearly the appearance of "leaking out" as possible. This may be a survival of the custom, among early peoples, of keeping the engagement or betrothal quiet as long as possible, so as still to receive offers from other suitors and select at last the offer of the highest bidder, Thus news of a betrothal was not made known until all details concerning bride-price and date of marriage were finally settled and agreed upon.

To-day the betrothal is very rarely announced until the young people are at least approximately aware of the time when the marriage will take place. The accepted way of announcing the engagement is to invite a small number of intimate friends to a dinner party and have the news imparted to them for the first time during the course of conversation. The announcement is usually made by one or other of the young woman's parents, or by her nearest relative.

There are other accepted modes of announcing the engagement. Cards may be sent to friends and acquaintances; informal letters may be sent to the family friends by the bride's parents; public announcements may be made in the columns of the local newspapers; the word may be whispered to a gossipy friend who can be trusted to carry the news.

COURTSHIP IN YOUNG AMERICA

One of the most romantic pages in the history of courtship belongs to that period when the young colonies in the New World were struggling with life and gaining their first foothold on freedom. The courtship among the men and women who had left their native lands, who had crossed an ocean to found new homes and a new mode of life, must have been a beautiful and inspiring courtship indeed.

In a land of unbroken forests, in a strange new country with just a handful of white people among hosts of Indians, what safety had an unmarried woman? And what chance for comfort had an unmarried man? We can understand why they married young, and why their marriages were tinged with a certain solemn significance. They not only joined their lives in love, but also in the pledge to find freedom, happiness, and prosperity in the infant civilization they were founding. "The Courtship of Miles Standish" gives us an excellent picture of life and love and courtship in the days of our country's beginning.

Many Old-World customs came across the ocean in the *Mayflower*. The Puritans were able to cut themselves adrift from the motherland, but they were not able to cut loose the age-old moorings that bound them to the customs and traditions of their ancestors.

In the first years of the colonies, there existed a formal ceremony of betrothal very similar to that which we find in England at the corresponding period. In Plymouth this ceremony was known as the "pre-contract." There was no merrymaking—the business of living was too vital for that—but banns or bulletins were published and the betrothal made known to all. The young people were presented with gifts and a home was built for them. After the marriage—and it usually followed quickly upon the heels of the betrothal—the governor allotted a certain amount of grain and corn to the couple.

The old custom of seizing a girl's gloves and demanding a kiss as a forfeit appears to have been practised in early New England. Alice Morse Earle, in her delightful book, "Customs and Fashions in Old New England," gives an account of the amusing love affair between Sarah Tuttle and Jacob Murline. She tells us that "Jacob Murline entered and, seizing Sarah's gloves, demanded the centuries-old forfeit of a kiss."

From the pages of Judge Sewell's diary we learn many amusing and interesting things concerning courtship in those early days. In his early widowhood, the Judge courted the widow Winthrop. On one occasion he succeeded in removing her gloves and holding her hand, which he conceives as a great triumph. His entry in his diary follows:

> I asked her to Acquit me of Rudeness if I drew off her Glove. Enquiring the reason I told her 'twas great odds between handling a dead Goat and a Living Lady. Got it off. . . .

Later we learn that the Judge's interest in the widow Winthrop lagged and he

> fluctuated to a new widow, Madam Harris, who gave him a "nutmeg as it grew," ever a true lover's gift in Shakespeare's day.

Most amusing are these sidelights on courtship! Yet even as they amuse they give us a clear and definite insight into the manners and customs of the people of that time.

The "matrimonial" advertisement appeared for the first time in the New World in 1759. We can imagine what a fluttering of hearts this notice must have caused among the eligible young ladies—and among those not so young and not so eligible! It appeared in the Boston *Evening Post* of February 23, the forerunner of many more of its kind:

To the Ladies: Any young Lady between the Age of Eighteen and Twenty-three, of a Midling Stature; brown Hair, regular Features and a Lively Brisk Eye; of Good Morals and not Tinctured with anything that may Sully so Distinguishable a Form; possessed of three or four hundred pounds entirely her own Disposal, and where there will be no necesity of Going Through the tiresome Talk of addressing Parents or Guardians for their Consent: Such a one by leaving a Line directed for A. W. at the British Coffee House in King Street appointing where an Interview may be had will meet a Person who flatters himself he shall not be thought Disagreeable by any Lady answering the above description. N. B. Profound Secrecy will be observed. No Trifling Answers will be regarded.

We have no record of the success of this early advertising writer; but we know that vast numbers of matrimonial advertisements promptly made their appearance after this one. But though the manner of courtship took on many strange new twists, the age-old customs and traditions were never forgotten, and are not forgotten to-day.

A groom in ancient England, breaking a bit of gold; peasantry in Holland planning a dowry for their favourite daughter; lovers plighting their troth with a flower—these are the age-old traditions and customs that have been handed down to us from one generation to another and that blend with the modern order of things, adding a touch of old romance to the new.

CHAPTER VIII

Marriage Customs

Life to-day, no less than in the past, is made brighter for the Caveman by examples of symbolization that we scarcely recognize as such. These acts satisfy our unconscious desires for primitive expression, often without the least conscious inkling of their real underlying significances. For instance, we throw rice and old shoes at newlyweds without comprehending the true meaning of the act Consciously we are following an established custom, but unconsciously we are doing something more important. We are giving expression in a symbolical way to a wish that is quite appropriate for the occasion, but which our conventional ethics would not permit us to express in a more direct way.

—William J. Fielding.

THE ANTIQUITY OF HUMAN MARRIAGE

MARRIAGE is one of the oldest and most sacred of human institutions. It emerges from the long shadow of prehistory and silhouettes itself against the blackness of savage life like a sun in a cloud-shrouded sky.

Writers of authority, such as Bachofen, Morgan, Lubbock, McLennan, Bastian, Wilken, and others, are of the opinion that man lived at first in a state of promiscuity. That is, the earliest men and women had no bond to unite them except the fact that they lived together. They had no higher marriage sense than the animals.

On the other hand, Westermarck, whose "History of Human Marriage" is one of the finest discussions ever written on this subject, declares that there is not a shred of genuine evidence to prove that simple promiscuity ever prevailed. There was, of course, a time when there was no man-made marriage ceremony; but in the actual union of man and woman in early life there was latent the idea of marriage.

We are inclined to believe that men, from the very first,

were on a higher plane than the animals, and that marriage in its truer sense has existed since the very beginning of time. Its origin seems to us coeval with the origin of man, and its development follows in the footsteps of man's development.

But marriage in the sense of binding together by man-made law or ceremony is another thing. This marriage grew out of external conditions, and was precipitated by certain very definite circumstances influencing the daily life of man.

Early Sexual Relations.—We cannot attempt to discuss at any great length the sexual relations of mankind at the remote period of life's beginning. Nothing very definite is known; we can only theorize and conjecture, as so many have done before us. Yet the earliest relations of men and women had so tremendous an influence upon the later habits and customs of life that we dare not leave the subject untouched.

In the very earliest times, if promiscuity existed at all, it probably did not exist for any very great length of time. We know that it never formed a general stage in the social history of mankind. It could not have been a common or general state, for reasons which will presently be set forth.

From what is known of the jealousy of all male quadrupeds in matters relating to sex, it is very unlikely that early man would have been satisfied to share his woman with other men. He would have preferred to live with one woman who belonged to him alone, than to live promiscuously and share his women.

According to the famous old Thlinket myth, the jealousy of man is older than the world itself. This myth tells us that there was an age when men groped in the dark searching for the world. They knew it existed, but they did not know where it was or how to find it. During this age a Thlinket lived with his wife and sister; and he was so insanely jealous of his wife that he killed all his sister's children because they dared to look at her.

But even jealousy could not have played so large a part in sexual relations as the natural attraction of one certain woman for one man. As Westermarck says, "I am strongly of opinion that the tie which joins male and female is an instinct developed through the powerful influence of natural selection." This influence undoubtedly played a large part in establishing monogamy.

At this point it may be useful to define certain terms that will be used constantly throughout this chapter.

Monogamy means the marriage of one man to one woman, marriage as it exists in modern civilized life.

Polygamy means one man but several women in the marriage union—in other words, more than one wife.

Polyandry is the exact opposite—several men but only one woman.

Exogamy relates to the law prohibiting marriage between persons of the same blood or stock as incest.

Endogamy is the opposite law, prohibiting marriage with any persons except those of the same blood or stock.

It is interesting to note how various existing conditions in widely separated parts of the globe induced habits of life. For instance, where there was a scarcity of women, polyandry flourished. Where there were many more women than men, polygamy was the custom.

Why Man Became Monogamous.—Man appears originally to have practised polygamy. If he saw a woman he wanted, he took her. Possibly three or four women lived with one man at one time. The woman was a captive before she was a wife.

But while this may have been the state of existence among various wandering tribes or even among a great body of people, it is easy to see why polygamy could not have survived as a universal and general thing. In the first place, conditions all over the world—the world of that time—were not the same. Some peoples practised infanticide, killing chiefly the female infants. This resulted in a scarcity of women. Among other savage peoples, constantly at war with each other, there would be a scarcity of men in proportion to the women.

This disproportion between sexes would lead at first to polygamy or polyandry, according to the direction in which the pendulum swung. But later it would tend to turn man toward monogamy. The woman would try to hold the affections of one man so as to be assured of his protection and a constant supply of food. This would give her an advantage in a community where men were scarce. Taking the opposite angle, the man would want to be assured of at least one woman whom he would not have to share, in a community where women were scarce. Thus would evolve the idea of one woman for one man, one man for one woman.

However, there seems to be no doubt that the child was the greatest impetus toward monogamy. As Andrew Lang indicates, "The family is the most sacred of human institutions." Among many savage peoples even to-day the marriage is not solemnized until the first child is born, and if no child is born the man is at perfect liberty to leave the woman.

Even among the lower animals the natural instinct to protect the young and supply food for the subsistence of the young is strong. In primitive life it must have been the tie which bound man to one cave, one woman, one home.

In the first flush of passion, let us suppose, man found a home for himself where he would be safe with his woman —where no stronger fellow would be able to steal her from him. He probably discovered a cave for himself, advantageously situated on a hill or in a grotto; and here he would bring his bride. He would roll a stone against the entrance at night to keep out wild beasts. He would contrive in various crude ways to make his little home a stronghold, entirely protected from invasion by either man or beast.

To this home the man would return after the hunt, knowing that he would find his woman safe, and that he himself would be in safety. Here, probably, a child or two would be born, and the man would begin to find pleasure in coming home to those who waited for him eagerly. He would bring queer shells for the young to play with, food for the woman to cook, ornaments for himself. And he would be happy.

So potent is habit, that the man would not think of wandering off in search of another woman—would not dream of leaving the little stronghold he had built, the home he had come to know and depend upon. Thus the family would become an important factor in his life—and monogamy would enter the social life of even the most primitive peoples.

Morality enters into a discussion of the sexual relations, although in a minor sense. We have already discovered the high morality that existed among primitive men (see p. 169). There are numerous people to-day, whom we would consider otherwise savage and barbarous, among whom intercourse out of wedlock is rare and unchastity on the part of either man or woman looked upon as a disgrace and even a crime.

Morality may have had a little to do with the ultimate establishing of monogamy; but we doubt whether it actually helped induce it. Selfishness and jealousy; the fear of being forced to fight to keep three or four wives when another fellow hadn't any; disproportion between the sexes; perhaps even scarcity of food; most certainly the powerful influence of natural selection; and finally the child and the family—these are the outstanding causes that led to monogamy.

As we proceed with the study of marriage in all its many phases you will recognize certain other factors which helped to strengthen monogamy in the march through time.

The Ceremonious Aspect of Marriage.—We can understand why man came to celebrate marriage and make of it a ceremony. It was a change from one mode of life to another. It was the throwing aside of childhood and of sexlessness. To the primitive mind it was one of the most important changes in life, and it was dramatized accordingly. Later, in tribal life, marriage was the breaking down of the sexual tabu (see p. 166), and grave, solemn rites were considered essential to appease the tribal deities.

Few peoples are known to us who are without marriage ceremonies of some sort. Ever eager to pantomime, to play at make-believe, to express the hopes and joys and passions that surged through him, primitive man made of marriage a ceremony and a celebration. There grew up in various places, among widely separated peoples, customs of celebrating marriage, some strangely similar, some exactly opposite, in nature, some weird and barbarous. Nevertheless, they were ceremonies, and many of them have contributed, as we shall see, to our own 20th-century marriage customs.

As marriage ceremonies arose by degrees in various ways, it was inevitable that an element of religion should enter into them. The linking together of two lives, the mating of a man and a woman, was undoubtedly regarded as a matter of importance; and it was natural that a religious character should be given to the ceremonies in the sense of invoking help for the future union.

Among many savage peoples, the marriage was not considered solemnized until certain ceremonial tribal rites had been performed. We are told that among primitive Aryans certain religious ceremonies were required before the marriage was considered valid. The Greek and Catholic churches made marriage a sacrament. And through the ages, marriage has never lost its religious, ceremonious aspect.

The Three Great Stages of Marriage.—Marriage seems to have passed through three great stages of development. Each of these stages has contributed its share to the customs of modern marriage; therefore a glance at them will be helpful.

The first great stage, of course, was marriage through force. Some writers refer to it as a form of "glorified rape," but it was really a form of marriage. When primitive man stole a woman, he stole her, more often than not, because he wanted a wife.

Marriage through contract or purchase followed marriage by capture. The transition from the first stage to the second was probably brought about in this way: The tribe felt it was a duty to avenge the woman stolen from them. They marched against the tribe which held the woman captive, and that tribe, to avoid too great damage, offered compensation. Out of this grew the idea of offering compensation beforehand—in other words, buying the bride.

The next great stage is marriage through mutual love. That love entered marriage at an early stage we know, because of the wealth of tradition and lovelore that has come down to us. But it did not come until both marriage by capture and marriage by purchase had run their course. And even then, traces of both these two great stages lingered—and linger to-day—in the customs of those who marry through love.

"Giving the bride away" in the modern marriage ceremony is a relic of the time when the bride was really sold. The bride's veil is a reminder of days when she was actually shrouded from head to foot. The "best man" suggests the strong-armed warrior who assisted the would-be bridegroom to carry off his bride. The honeymoon itself symbolizes the period during which the bridegroom was forced to hide with his prize until her kinsmen grew tired of searching for her.

So do customs manifest themselves even after they have been thrown aside. Once a custom has been definitely established it will never, as Keats would say "pass into nothingness."

Marriage by Capture.—In primitive culture, groups of people were almost habitually hostile. Herbert Spencer, in his "Principles of Sociology," tells us that in all times and places, victory in warfare was followed by pillage. The conquerors took whatever portable things they could find, and women were taken along with other booty.

We can understand why the women were taken. Primitive man undoubtedly preferred a captured wife because she had the added value of being a trophy. She attested to his prowess in warfare, to his strength and courage in carrying her off. Throughout primitive life we find that members of the tribe who are married to captive women are considered more honourably married than those who have taken wives from within the tribe.

But no system of marriage as widespread as that of capture could have grown out of the simple desire to possess that which belonged to someone else. Many conditions induced marriage by capture as a system for obtaining wives.

In the first place, there are the rules or laws of exogamy which are found everywhere among primitive peoples. We find the horror of incest even among the most savage and barbarous tribes. Somehow, even the earliest people, who reasoned no more than was necessary in daily life, had the feeling that to intermarry with kin, between persons of the same blood or stock, was indecent and shameful.

Thus men sought their wives outside the tribe. The system of marriage by capture was actually forced upon them. Since marriage with the woman of the clan or the tribe was prohibited, they were obliged to seek wives elsewhere.

Nor was this arrangement entirely unsatisfactory to the women. In early tribal life, the man who captured a woman belonging to another tribe assumed individual and exclusive right to her. She was his property. He provided her with food, shelter, and protection, and no one else in the tribe—with the possible exception of the chief—had any right to her. The women who belonged to the tribe, however, were in many cases subject to the attentions of all their tribesmen. Their position was therefore comparatively insecure. Envying the individual attentions bestowed upon the captured women, the women of the tribe often allowed themselves to stray away from the protection of their tribesmen and be captured by a man of some other tribe.

Disproportion of sexes also led to marriage by capture. Even before laws of exogamy existed, men belonging to tribes that practised female infanticide would be induced—through lack of women within the tribe—to seek wives elsewhere, steal them from neighbouring hordes.

"The men of a group, since women were in the minority, must either have quarreled about their women and separated, splitting the horde into hostile sections, or indulged in savage promiscuity." Many primitive battles must have been fought among peoples who had a scarcity of women. That divisions of tribes into two or more hostile sections occured frequently cannot be doubted. And it cannot be doubted, either, that conditions such as this led to the habits that firmly established exogamy.

Another reason for the widespread system of marriage by capture is the innate desire to display courage on part of man. We can imagine a savage fellow dragging in his captive bride and displaying her with pride and boastfulness to his fellows. *He* captured her. *He* stole to the outskirts of the sleeping horde on the other side of the valley and stunned her with his club before she could make outcry. *He* dragged her home and she belonged to him. Naturally, the others admired and envied him, which was precisely what he wanted.

Marriage by capture existed almost everywhere in early life, and it still prevails in certain parts of the world. Among the Ahts, for instance, a man occasionally steals a wife from within his own tribe. Similar practice occurs, although no longer to any great extent, among the Maoris, on the islands of the Fiji group, in Samoa, New Guinea, the Indian Archipelago and among the Tartars of Central Asia.

All Carib tribes at one time captured their wives from other tribes. The Uaupes have never had any particular marriage ceremony—except that of always carrying away the girl by force—even though she and the parents are willing. In Tasmania the capture of women for wives was widely prevalent. Traces of marriage by capture are found among the Laplanders, the Esthonians, and the Finns. In Tierra del Fuego it was at one time the custom for the young Fuegians to carry off women for wives as soon as they were able to procure or construct a canoe for the purpose. The Indians on the Amazon and the Orinoco sometimes captured their brides. Wherever we go we find traces of this once universal system of obtaining wives.

Several cases of marriage by capture are cited in the Bible. The tribe of Benjamin, for instance, procured wives for themselves by massacring the inhabitants of Jabez-Gilead and capturing four hundred of their virgins. At another time the Benjamites carried off women during a feast near Bethel. And of course everyone knows the story of the vanquishing of the Midianites by the Israelites and the carrying off of all the cattle, children, and women. (See Numbers XXXI, 7-9. Also See Deuteronomy XXI for full description of marriage by capture as practised among the Israelites.)

An old Irish poem, "Duan Eiranash," speaks of 300 women being carried off by the Picts from the Gaels. The latter, finding themselves thus deprived of their women, finally decided to ally themselves with the Irish.

Traces of marriage by capture remained among almost all peoples, even after the necessity for this form of marriage disappeared. Sometimes we find a form of symbolized marriage by capture in instances where the bride and her family are entirely satisfied to have the marriage take place.

Thus among the Araucanians, for instance, carrying off the bride by pretended violence is absolutely essential before the marriage is solemnized. Among the Mosquito Indians, after a wedding is arranged and the bride-price paid, the bridegroom carries off the bride and is followed by female relatives who stage a mock battle and pretend to rescue her. The couple finally escape to "go in hiding," which is merely another way of saying that they go on their honeymoon.

(Courtesy of Metropolitan Museum of Art)

"The Porch of the Maidens."
Erechtheion; Greece, 5th Century.

(Courtesy of Metropolitan Museum of Art)

"The Rendezvous."
By Attilio Simonetti.

Among the Wakamba, marriage is entirely an affair of barter or purchase, but the bridegroom must pretend to carry off the bride. The same sort of custom prevails among various African and Australian tribes, and distinct traces of capture remain in their marriage ceremonials. Plutarch informs us ("Dionysius of Halicarnassus") that marriage by capture was once customary throughout ancient Greece and that the form was retained by the Spartans as an important symbol in the marriage ceremony. And we are told that even after Christianity had abolished marriage by capture, the Anglo-Saxons persisted in simulating the capture of the bride.

The symbol of capture as retained in later systems of marriage appears to be due to a primitive conception of modesty and delicacy. The screams, tears, and struggles of the bride among various peoples are known to be merely a part of the marriage routine; yet they are considered absolutely essential to show her bashfulness and modesty. In other words it is a prudish way of indicating that the marriage was forced upon the girl and that she is not entering it willingly.

We know, however, that in early times marriage was usually a change for the worse; and perhaps the girl, realizing this, resisted all the more.

Among the Arabs of Sinai, a girl until recently acquired permanent repute in proportion to her tears and her struggles of resistance on her marriage day. Among the Irish mountaineers, a marriage is considered quite a tame affair, and scarcely legal, unless the bride attempts to escape and the bridegroom overtakes and "captures" her. A custom in Cardiganshire, Wales, is for the relatives of the bride to seize her as she reaches the church door and ride off with her. The bridegroom and his party must follow in pursuit. Upon being overtaken, the bride is at once handed over to the groom and his party, and a very popular superstition is that whoever caught her is certain to be married within the year.

McLennan, in his "Primitive Marriage," gives many instances of symbolized capture existing among savage peoples to-day. He reports that on one occasion Major-General Campbell related that he

> heard loud cries proceeding from a village close at hand. Fearing some quarrel, I rode to the spot and there I saw a man bearing away upon his back something enveloped in an ample covering of scarlet cloth; he was surrounded by twenty or thirty young fellows, and by them protected from the desperate attacks made upon them by a party of young women. On seeking an explanation of this novel scene, I was told that the man had just married, and his precious burden was his blooming bride, whom he was conveying to his own village. Her youthful friends (as it appears is the custom) were seeking to regain possession of her and hurled stones and bamboos at the head of the devoted bridegroom until he reached the confines of his own village.

As we shall presently see, marriage by capture has left some very definite traces in our own marriage customs. They have assumed, of course, an entirely playful character.

Marriage by Purchase.—There is scarcely a race which has not passed, at some time or other in its development, through a stage of marriage by purchase. A handsome daughter has always been a distinctly marketable product; and the primitive father appears to have been nothing loath to sell her to the highest bidder.

At first marriage by capture merged into marriage by purchase, and the two represented one system of marriage. In other words, the bride was first stolen and restitution was made later to escape the vengeance of her people. Thus among the Ahts when a man steals a wife, as he still occasionally does, a purchase arrangement usually follows. Among various other savage peoples the bride is stolen first and the bride-price paid later. It would appear, from this, that the custom of wife purchase originated in the desire to placate the enraged parents, and also to prevent warfare between tribes as has already been indicated (see p. 209).

Perhaps in the earliest stage of wife purchase an exchange was made instead of a bride-price being paid.

For instance, let us pretend that the bridegroom is overtaken by the enraged father. He is taken to the tribe of his captive bride and ordered to pay the bride-price. Unable to do so, he possibly offers to give his own sister, or horses, cattle, or land in exchange. In this way he is able, not only to regain his freedom and perhaps save his life, but to keep his bride as well. This kind of marriage by exchange is still prevalent among barbarous peoples. Some writers tell us it exists to some extent even among the Chinese and various Mohammedan tribes. And we know that it is an almost universal form of marriage contract in Australia.

But even more common than exchange is the custom of obtaining a wife by services rendered the father. This appears to have been one of the most prevalent of the elementary stages of marriage by purchase.

The custom of obtaining a wife by working for the father for a certain period was practised among uncivilized races of America, Africa, Asia, and the Indian Archipelago. The men who were unable to pay the bride-price served in the house or on the grounds of the father-in-law, and thus ultimately earned the bride.

Among many early peoples, brides were not bought, but valuable presents were given to the parents. In Japan it is, or was until recently, the custom of the man who wished to marry a certain young woman to send presents to her and to her parents. The type of gifts and their value is not left to the good will of the would-be groom, but is definitely stipulated, and often long negotiations take place before an agreement is reached. The sending of these presents forms an important part of the marriage ceremony. Once they have been received and accepted, the contract is considered complete and neither party may withdraw. Native books do not explain this custom, and the only way we can account for it is that it is a survival of the primitive custom of marriage by purchase.

But the most common compensation for a bride, in primitive life, was property paid for her to her owner or owners. Her price varied according to her charms, her health, her rank, her condition as a virgin, a widow, etc. We are told that among certain peoples a widow brought only one-half the sum which the father or guardian of a maid usually demanded.

One of the most perfect systems of wife purchase existed among the Babylonians. Twice a year all girls of marriageable age were assembled in a space before the temple and offered for sale to the highest bidders, very much in the manner of our modern auction. (Herodotus, Book I, 196.) The handsomest girls brought large prices, and this money was turned over to the homely girls who had appeared at several "auctions" and could not be disposed of. The money was an attraction, of course, and thus every girl ultimately won a husband. So were human souls bartered while civilization was young!

The ancient Scandinavians believed that even the gods bought their wives. We find this thought prevalent throughout their mythology. Abduction without payment seems to have been prevalent, however. But the young people were obliged to remain in hiding until they were able to pay to the guardian or parent the customary bride-price or compensation.

In his "Curiosities of Popular Customs" William S. Walsh says:

> Marriage by purchase was prevalent among the Anglo-Saxons at the time when Christianity first reached them. Every woman was under the care of some man who was termed her *mundbora*, or guardian; and no one could marry her without having paid a sum of money as a compensation to him. The father was the guardian of his unmarried daughters; the brother, if the father died, and the next to him, the nearest male relative. If, however, the female was friendless and alone, she found in the king her legal guardian.
>
> The maid was estimated according to her rank in life. The first step in courtship, therefore, was to buy the consent of the *mundbora;* the lover was then admitted into the society of his mistress and allowed to claim her in due course as his wife. If, however, her personal charms or her disposition proved, on better acquaintance,

unsatisfactory to her suitor, and he failed to complete his bargain, he immediately became amenable to the law.

If a man ventured to marry without first having bought and paid for his wife, he was guilty of the crime of *mundbreach*, the consequences of which were both vexatious and disastrous. The husband in such a case possessed no legal authority over his wife; he was a husband, in fact, without a wife; he had no right to her property. By the same law a maiden and a widow were of separate value; the latter could be purchased for one half the sum that the guardian of a maid was entitled to demand; the man, therefore, who could not afford to purchase a maid might perhaps be able to purchase a widow.

We quote this bit of discussion concerning the Anglo-Saxon laws of wife purchase to show you how close to a trade marriage was at one time in our development. A trade in human lives, in human souls. Yet if the truth be known, a modified form of wife purchase exists even in modern society. As Westermarck says, "wife purchase and husband purchase still persist in modern society, though in a disguised form."

In the earliest written laws concerning marriage by purchase we find that the marriage consists of two separate transactions. First there is the agreement between the bridegroom and the bride's father or guardian, each formally binding himself to perform his part of the marriage contract. Secondly there is the delivery of the bride, the payment of the price agreed upon, or payment of part of the price and security that the remainder will be paid to the widow in case of death. We see here the beginning of the dower (from *dos*, Italian) in the later and more advanced sense—a provision for widowhood. In other words, instead of the price being paid to the father or guardian, it is paid to the bride.

It is interesting to glance at the wife-purchasing customs of various peoples and see what they considered a "good price" for a bride. The Navajos of New Mexico considered twelve horses an exorbitant price for a wife, and paid it only on rare occasions when the rank and personal charms of the woman warranted it.

The Patagonians exchanged mares, horses, silver ornaments, and trifles of various sorts for brides. One bride, we are told, brought "three horses, a silver cup, several rich skins, and a collection of inexpensive bracelets."

In Africa, we notice, horses are not considered "proper to exchange for wives," but it is perfectly fine to exchange cattle for women. Certain savage tribes hold an ox and a woman at about the same value.

Among the Kaffirs, ten cows is considered a fairly good price. But some brides bring as many as thirty. In Uganda, the usual price is four bullocks.

Origin of the Word "Wedding."—We who use the word "wedding" so casually and promiscuously do not realize that the very word betrays the great stage of wife purchase through which marriage passed. The *wed* was the money, horses, or cattle which the groom gave as security and as a pledge to prove his purchase of the bride from her father.

To quote from Walsh once again:

> Often they (the Anglo-Saxons) were betrothed when children, the bridegroom's pledge of marriage being accompanied by a security or *wed*.

From this *wed* we derive the idea of *wedding* or *pledging* the bride to the man who pays the security for her.

We are told that as late as the middle of the 16th century the English in their marriage customs preserved traces of the ancient legal procedure connected with wife purchase. And in France it was, until the marriage of Louis XVI, the custom to pay down thirteen *deniers* upon the conclusion of a marriage contract.

A CONTEMPLATION OF EXOGAMY

One of the chief characteristics of primitive marriage systems is exogamy. No study of human marriage, brief as it may be, could be considered complete without a brief contemplation of this widespread custom.

What is exogamy? How did it begin and how develop? How does it affect our own marriage customs?

Exogamy, as we have seen, (p. 205), is the law of a tribe or a race prohibiting marriage between persons of the same blood or stock. It has existed since the earliest times. The horror of incest appears to have been an almost universal characteristic of mankind; although there are a few striking cases which indicate not only an absolute absence of this feeling, but an inclination to adopt the opposite view.

Many theories have been advanced by writers who have attempted to account for the widespread prohibitions of marriage between near kin in primitive life. Some ascribe these laws of exogamy to the fear of concentrating affection within too narrow a circle. Others believe such laws were created for the purpose of preventing marriages from taking place at too early an age. Still others declare that primitive man was afraid of making relationship within the tribe too involved. In modern times the reason given is that incestuous marriages prove injurious to offspring.

But there dosen't seem to be a shred of actual evidence to prove that any of these theories are true. We know only that mankind, as a general rule, has had a horror of incest from the very first; and that laws of exogamy were created for the purpose of preventing such marriages.

In New Britain it was believed that marriage within the totem (clan) would bring instant destruction to the woman. If she did not die, her parents or relatives usually killed her, so great did they consider her shame. The man's life was usually insecure also.

The Greenlanders refrain from marrying near kin even to the third degree. The reason they give is that such matches are unnatural and contrary to the wishes of the gods.

The Eskimo disapprove marriages between cousins, as do also the Chippewas, the Mahlemuts, and many other peoples, both savage and civilized.

Countless tribes have laws of exogamy, prohibiting men and women of the same clan or the same totem from intermarrying. The Algonquins put to death those who broke this rule. In Samoa such marriages were carefully guarded against, and even to-day incest is looked upon with dread. In China, incestuous marriages are not only prohibited but severely punished. Among the Dyaks a man is strictly prohibited from marrying a cousin, aunt, or niece. In Polynesia marriage with blood relations is avoided and rarely occurs. The Andamanese do not permit marriage with people even distantly related.

There is an old Greenland Eskimo tale which suggests our own belief that incestuous marriages result in poor offspring. The father of Kakamak is made very unhappy because all his grandchildren have died before reaching the age of puberty. Drawing his son-in-law aside, he says, "Perhaps we are too near akin." (Rink, "Tales and Traditions of the Eskimo.")

The same thought is found in Hadith, the collection of Mohammedan traditions. We read: "Marry among strangers; thus you will not have feeble posterity."

Two Mohammedan travellers of the 9th century relate that the Hindus never married relations because they firmly believed that such marriages would prove harmful to the children. They thought that alliances with unrelated persons improved the offspring—a belief which many of us have to-day but which has never been definitely or adequately proved.

Out of the laws of exogamy in primitive life grew queer rites and ceremonies which have left their influence upon the marriage customs of the world. We will touch upon these ceremonies as we study the marriage customs of modern society.

It is notable, however, that one of the most outstanding effects of exogamy upon modern life is that relations fear to marry; and it is rare indeed that cousins, or persons similarly close in relationship, marry each other.

THE MOTHER-IN-LAW "TABU"

A custom which has survived with astonishing obviousness is that which concerns the common tabu between a man and his mother-in-law. Although we treat the matter in a jocose manner to-day, and it has no significance other than that of supplying gaiety to poor wits, it formed at one time a real and important part of the marriage system.

The mother-in-law tabu began, in many cases, with betrothal. In the tribes of New South Wales, for instance, there is a tabu between a man and the mother of his promised wife. They may not see or speak to each other. In some Victorian tribes the girl's mother may not look at the suitor nor speak to him from the moment of betrothal until death. He is forbidden to pronounce her name.

Most authorities are agreed that the mother-in-law tabu either evolved from the laws of exogamy, or was a part of those laws. In other words, the avoidance of the mother-in-law probably was due to fear of unlawful intercourse—exogamy. The Gaboon natives have certain laws concerning the groom and the mother-in-law which, they say, were founded to "prevent incest." There are, indeed, a few recorded cases in which a man has married mother and daughter at once, and we can readily understand how primitive men evolved mother-in-law tabus to prevent just such a thing.

Professor Tylor has another explanation of the tabu. He says that the groom was regarded as an outsider and a stranger. Tracing this back to a system of "*cutting*" which existed in early life, he reaches the conclusion that the groom was not recognized in the family. This would cause a breach between him and the bride's mother, and they would try to avoid each other.

Sir John Lubbock traces back the mother-in-law tabu to the days of marriage by capture. "When the capture was a reality, indignation of parents would also be real; when it became a mere symbol, parental anger would be symbolized also and would be continued even after its origin was forgotten."

Among the Zulus, the mother-in-law tabu is just one little detail in an intricate system of social and sexual tabus. The Zulu groom is placed under certain very definite restrictions. Among other things, he is not permitted to enjoy his mother-in-law's company, he may not remain in the same hut with her, nor may he pronounce her name.

The prohibition against uttering each others' names is found in the Torres Straits, among the Sioux and Omahas, the Kåffirs, in Baru, the Aru Islands, the Kei Islands, Wetar, and other widely separated places. From what we know of primitive reasoning, the uttering of the name was supposed to give the groom power over the mother-in-law, whose name he uttered. Therefore he was prohibited from doing so. This, according to the primitive mind, would prevent him from weakening the mother-in-law and perhaps inducing her to break the sexual tabu.

Among the Sarae and Barea the mother-in-law conceals herself when she sees her son-in-law approaching. Among the Arawaks, the son-in-law may not see the face of his wife's mother; if they live in the same house they are obliged to occupy opposite sides.

In Australia, a man scrupulously avoids his mother-in-law and does not exchange words with her, unless it is absolutely necessary. This prohibition of speech with the mother-in-law is practically universal throughout Australia.

A Congo proverb says, "My mother-in-law is angry with me, but what do I care? We do not eat from the same dish." (*Jour. Anthrop. Inst.*, vol. XXIV, p. 296.) This indicates the separation of the mother-in-law and the son-in-law, their avoidance of each other.

This amusing story is told of a Maori Christian wedding. It shows us that, though occupation or invasion of an area by civilized whites quickly breaks down aboriginal manners and habits of life, it cannot entirely destroy the age-old traditions of the natives.

A Maori woman, mother of the bride, came to the missionary, a certain Mr. Yate, and told him she was pleased that her daughter was going to be married but that, according to the custom of her forefathers, "she must be angry about it with her mouth." Returning from the church, the bride and bridegroom were met by the mother.

"She began to assail us all furiously. She threw her garments about, tore her hair, and said, 'Ah, you white missionary, you are worse than the devil. You first make a slave lad your son by redeeming him from his master and then marry him to my daughter. I will tear your eyes out.' The old woman, suiting the action to the word, feigned to snatch at my face, at the same time saying in an undertone that it was 'all mouth' and that she did not mean what she said."

So does the fiction of the custom remain after the fact has vanished. The Maori mother felt it her duty to show her dislike of her son-in-law, even though she was really delighted with the marriage. Old tribal customs like these, merging with the newer Christian marriage rites which are being introduced to our semi-barbarous brothers, add a certain touch of humour. It is not surprising that we have borrowed the mother-in-law tabu and have made it a frequent subject of humorous anecdote.

LOVE ENTERS MARRIAGE

It was not until the 9th century that women obtained the privilege of choosing or refusing their husbands according to their own judgment. Of course, rare cases occur not only earlier than the 9th century, but even in primitive life, where women have the sole right to select their husbands at will; but it was not until well into the 9th and 10th centuries that the custom became at all widespread.

That love entered into marriage at a fairly early period we know from the love tales that abound in mythology and in the many beautiful legends that have been bequeathed to us.

The Tongans, for instance, have a delightful tale of a chief who loved a maiden already promised to a superior. It seems that she was caught with other relations of a rebel and all of them were condemned to death. The young chief stole among the enemies, rescued her, and carried her to a cave which he had located. After many difficulties they escaped to the Fijis where they lived "happily ever after," in the manner of our modern fairy tales.

Another legend concerns Hinemoa and Tutanekai. Strangers, they met one moonlit evening near the bank of a river and love was born between them. At first this love began with stolen glances; then, we are told, they laughed boldly into each other's eyes; and finally Hinemoa stole away from her people and swam across to Tutanekai's island, guided in her course by his music.

Such legends and traditions as these prove without a vestige of a doubt that love actually entered into marriage, perhaps even earlier than we suspect. But what chance had the tiny flame of love to flare in many hearts when marriage by capture and marriage by purchase tore apart the souls of women? It was left to a higher and more advanced civilization to raise marriage from its primitive levels and give love the chance to blossom.

It is the position of the woman that gives us our surest index to the point of civilization which any people, or any race, has reached. Where we find marriage by purchase falling into decay, there we find the beginning of a civilization. Where we find marriage by capture still prevailing, we find a people in the lowest stages of barbarism. In modern civilized life marriage by capture occurs as a symbol; marriage by purchase is a rarity; marriage based upon love and mutual respect is the customary marriage.

Egypt, one of the earliest civilizations, honoured and respected its women. The Egyptians were ruled at different times by several queens. We are told that Amenophis IV (Akhnaton) was passionately fond of his wife and admired her as a noble and intelligent woman. He was sculptured in one instance with his wife on his knees; in another, in the act of kissing her in a chariot.

Among the Greeks of the Homeric age, another early civilization, the father did not always keep the wedding presents for his own use, as was customary among other peoples, but bestowed them on his daughter as her marriage portion. The same process of development occurred among the Teutons. Originally the purchase sum, bride gifts, or bride-price went to the father or guardian. Gradually it came to be considered her own property and was given her upon the day of her marriage. Thus purchase became more or less a symbol, and elevated ideas regarding women followed in natural sequence.

Love Makes Elopement Necessary.—Elopement could not have flourished very greatly in primitive life. The women were guarded too closely (see pp. 166-167). Parents or guardians arranged marriages to suit their own greedy ends, consulting neither the wishes nor happiness of the girl.

But we hasten to correct the impression left by certain recent writers on the subject to the effect that elopement is a remnant of marriage by capture. All the facts we are able to gather indicate that precisely the opposite is true. In all ages elopements took place, rarely at first, a little less rarely later on, and finally as a general thing. And always love, or at least a great mutual attraction, induced the elopement.

We can easily understand why young people eloped in days when marriage by capture had hardly been forgotten and marriage by purchase was still a grim reality. To avoid marrying a man she disliked but who was able to pay the bride-price her parents demanded, a young woman would elope with the man of her choice. Or to avoid waiting until he was able to pay for his bride, to escape being forced to work for her under the service contract (see p. 215) the man would induce the girl he loved to elope with him.

It was decidedly a more difficult feat to elope in those days than it is to-day. In a social scheme which counts a daughter a salable possession, a source of profit, it was not possible to "come home and be forgiven." The young people had to burn all bridges behind them, escape into a strange world, probably without means of livelihood, and begin life all over again far away from their people.

In Afghanistan, elopement without paying the bride-price to the family is considered an outrage. It is held very much in the same light as we would hold the murder of one of the members of the family. Such elopements are the cause of feuds among clans and tribes; frequently they cause long and bloody wars.

In Sumatra, on the other hand. the defeat of parental matrimonial plans by elopement is so common that it is now sanctioned and regulated by law. It is regarded as a special system of marriage and is called *telari gadis*.

To-day elopement is common among civilized peoples and is even looked upon with approval where parental objection seems to be unfounded. The pendulum of life swings sometimes in wide arcs across the ages.

THE DEVELOPMENT OF MODERN MARRIAGE

In the period just preceding Christianity, marriage was sometimes a solemn religious ordinance, sometimes a purely civil contract. But with the coming of Christianity, marriage was given a distinctly religious character.

At first it was the custom for Christian couples, seeking marriage, to ask simply for the blessing of their pastor. There were few other ceremonials connected with the marriage. But gradually the religious aspect of marriage became more and more significant, and in mediæval times the priest was even called in to bless the marriage bed. The custom of religious marriage, performed in the church or by a clergyman in the home, became general. In 1563 it was made binding at the Council of Trent.

Some of the tales concerning the origin of marriage in various countries are interesting enough to quote. The Chinese annals recount that "in the beginning, men differed in nothing from other animals in their way of life. As they wandered up and down in the woods, and women were common, it happened that children never knew their fathers but only their mothers." The Emperor Fou-hi abolished this indiscriminate intercourse of the sexes and instituted marriage. (Gouget, "Origin of Laws, Arts and Sciences," vol. III, p. 311.)

The remote Laplanders have a tradition concerning the origin of marriage. They sing of Njavvis and Attjis who were the first to institute marriage and to bind their wives by sacred oath.

Cecrops is credited with having introduced marriage to the Greeks. He is said to have raised himself from obscurity to be king of the people later known as the Athenians, and during his sway he introduced many useful institutions.

The ancient Egyptians are indebted to Menes for the institution of marriage. At first they had no idea of conjugal union and gratified their desires more or less promiscuously. But Menes established definite laws and rules of marriage.

Possibly Christianity found its inspiration for a religious and binding marriage in the examples of these earlier peoples. We know, of course, that Christianity dealt a death blow to marriage by purchase; its advent was the advent also of a new, more wholesome and more civilized attitude toward women and toward marriage. But customs change slowly, and it required several generations before the civilized world was emancipated from the evils of wife purchase and woman barter.

The modern marriage, of whatever sect, is given a more solemn and religious aspect because of the background of Christianity. Yet despite this religious character, shreds of old traditions and customs still cling, blending the old with the new, making our marriage of to-day as colourful and romantic as any of the early or middle ages.

WEDDING-RING TRADITIONS

The true origin of the wedding ring will never be known. Many facts have been recorded concerning the ring and the part it has played in various marriage systems. But what of the facts that have not been recorded? What about wedding rings, and wedding-ring secrets, that have never been unearthed and that are buried forever in the dim and dusty past?

We know, for instance, that primitive man believed in magic. We know also, from what authorities tell us, that primitive man wove a cord with his own fingers and bound it around the waist of a woman he wanted. He believed—and she believed—that her spirit entered his body when this little ceremony was performed, and she was bound to him for ever.

Is it not barely possible that the idea of the wedding ring grew out of this ancient custom? The primitive mind conceived the cord around the woman's waist to be the magic vehicle through which her spirit passed into his body. Could not other people have conceived the same thing to be true of the ring?

Glancing a bit later, but still in the lowest primitive scale, we find a woman with fetters bound around the wrists and ankles to indicate that she has been captured and is the property of one man in the tribe. Couldn't the ring be the wristlet or the anklet in miniature? We do not know. There are no records. We can only contemplate, imagine, and accept the facts that are known.

The First Wedding Rings.—From the records that are available, it would seem that the Egyptians were the first to use the wedding ring in making marriage vows. Mention of such rings appears in ancient Egyptian literature. In hieroglyphics a circle represents eternity. It is not surprising that the circular form should have been adopted as being symbolic of the marriage ties, implying a marriage that will be binding throughout eternity.

Tradition likes to tell us that the first wedding ring was

(Courtesy of Metropolitan Museum of Art)

An old Athenian toilet box of the school of the "Meidias Painter." About 450 B. C. Scene portrays maid bringing gifts to a bride.

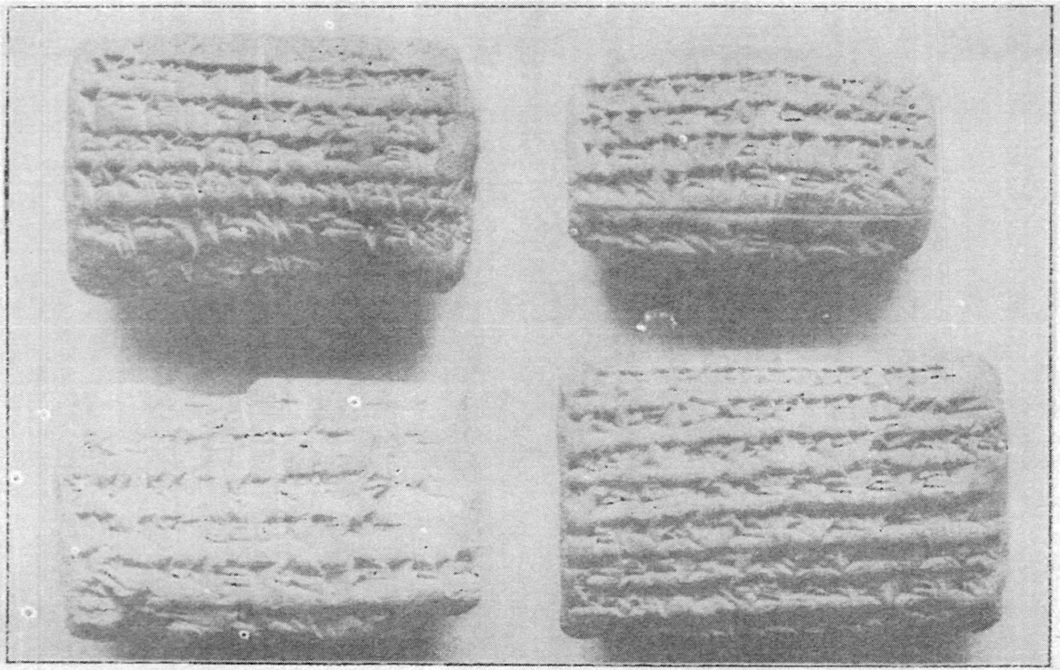

(Courtesy of Metropolitan Museum of Art)

Tablets of baked clay discovered in Babylon.

made of iron and adamant by Tubal Cain for a man named Prometheus. Perhaps it was. We cannot be certain. But it is quite likely that wedding rings were known and used long before that time.

The early Romans used a plain iron ring. The early Assyrians, Hebrews, and Greeks used rings as seals for signing orders and for transferring authority. But whether they used these rings in their marriage ceremonies or not we cannot be certain, except in the case of the Hebrews.

Among the Hebrews, the finger of God denoted his power. According to the Hebrew manner of marrying in early times, before the bride's dowry is produced and read, the

> bridegroom putteth a ring upon the finger, in the presence of two witnesses, which commonly used to be the Rabbis, saying, withal, unto her, "Behold, thou art my espoused wife, according to the custom of Moses and of Israel."

The early Anglo-Saxon groom gave a pledge or *wed* to the bride at the betrothal ceremony (see p. 218). Included in this *wed* was a ring which was placed on her right hand, where it remained until the marriage ceremony, at which time it was transferred to the left hand.

The ring was used in marriage among Christians as early as 860. We are told that when a marriage settlement had been properly sealed, rings bearing the names of the newly married couple were handed around to the guests and examined by them.

Wedding-Ring Materials.—Rings have been made of every conceivable material. Besides the various metals, such as gold, silver, iron, steel, and brass, wedding rings have been made of rush, leather, wood. There is an instance on record of a ring being cut out of the bride's kid glove. There is still another record of a wedding ring being made, on the spur of the moment, of a piece of old leather.

One writer tells the story of a clergyman who used a brass curtain ring to marry a duke. Another tells of a church key being used in an emergency. Horace Walpole in a letter to Mr. Mann (later Sir Robert Mann), dated July 27, 1752, includes this little incident:

"The event which has made most noise since my last is the extensive wedding of the youngest of the two Gunnings." He proceeds to describe an assembly at the home of Lord Chesterfield, with the Duke of Hamilton making love to Mrs. Gunning. Two nights later, it appears the Duke sent for a parson to perform the marriage ceremony. The parson refused to act without a license and a ring. The Duke declared in irritation that he would send at once for the Archbishop. At last they were married with the ring from the bed-curtain "at half-an-hour past twelve at night, at May Fair Chapel."

Long after the Norman Conquest peasants used circlets of rush because they could afford no better. Wedding rings in early times were fashioned to suit the means, rather than the tastes, of lovers. Some were large and heavy; others small and threadlike. They differed as much in shape and size as they did in the materials of which they were made. .

The rings of the Hebrews were generally of large size and elaborate workmanship, as were the rings of the Greeks. The Romans used plain, heavy iron rings. It was, incidentally, a custom of the Romans to give the keys of the house with the bridal ring. One such ring with the key attached is illustrated. (See p. —)

Mr. Wood tells us that in Iceland a large ring was used, variously formed of bone, jet, gold, silver, stone.

> Sometimes [he says], it was so large as to allow the palm of the hand to be passed through it. In the solemnization of a betrothal contract the bridegroom passed four fingers and his palm through one of these rings, and in this manner he received the hand of his bride. Sometimes these rings for confirming mutual contracts were placed upon the altar before their use. We may, perhaps, trace this custom to an old form of marriage in the Orkneys where the contracting parties join their hands through a perforation, or ring, in a stone pillar.

A writer of the early 17th century says, "Howbeit, it skilleth not at this dae what metal the ringe be." And in the 18th century, we are told, parsons always carried a supply of brass curtain rings with them—to be ready for an emergency!

Significance of the Circle.—"The form of the ring being circular, that is round, and without end, importeth thus much: that mutual love and hearty affection should roundly flow from one to the other, as in a circle, and that continually and for ever."

By its very form the wedding ring is a symbol of the intention of both parties to keep for ever the vows they have made, to recognize as eternally binding the ties which join them in marriage. Herrick has expressed it beautifully in this bit of simple verse:

Julia, I bring
To thee this ring,
  Made for thy finger fit;
To show by this
That our love is
  Or should be, like to it.

Close though it be,
The joint is free;
  So, when love's yoke is on,
It must not gall,
Nor fret at all,
  With hard oppression.

But it must play,
Still either way,
  And be, too, such a yoke
As not, too wide
To overslide,
  Or be so straight to choke.

So we who bear
This beam, must rear
  Ourselves to such a height
As that the stay
Of either may
  Create the burthen light.

And as this round
Is nowhere found
To flaw, or else to sever,
So let our love
As endless prove,
And pure as gold forever.

Some authorities connect the circular form of the ring with the rounding out of the life of the man or the woman. To the primitive mind, a man without a wife is half a man; a woman without a husband is half a woman. When they are married the unit is complete. This is represented by the circle which symbolizes the linking or joining together of the two.

Others claim that the wedding ring in the form of a circle simply grew out of the circular fetters or bracelets placed upon the captive woman of primitive times. According to this belief, the idea of eternity as implied by the circle came later.

Changing Fashions.—The wedding ring has not always been the simple gold band we know. As has already been indicated, almost every conceivable material has been used for wedding rings, and many sizes and forms were used also. The first rings were heavy, awkward, clumsy. The Greeks made rich and elaborate rings, many of them with seals engraved upon them. Some wedding rings were adorned with precious stones; others were just ugly bands of iron.

In Shakespeare's time it was the custom to make engravings on the wedding ring. Sometimes as many as three or four lines of verse were engraved inside the ring in letters so minute as to be scarcely readable. This was an attempt to provide enduring record of the marriage. Many mottoes were created for bridal rings. Some of them which have been brought to our attention are, "I will be yours while life endures"; "In thee my choice do I rejoice" and this bit of verse—

Love in the small but perfect circle trace,
And duty in its soft but strict embrace.

At about the same period, bits of religious wisdom began appearing on the wedding rings used in Jewish marriages. This practice continued into the 17th century when almost every ring was inscribed with a motto or quotation of some sort. Only in those days the word was not "motto." The sentiments were known as "poesy verses" or "chantons."

We are told that the ring with which James, Duke of York (afterward King James II), married Mary of Modena was of plain gold set simply with a ruby. During her exile, the Queen showed this ring to the nuns of Chaillot. She had given up all her jewels, but this ring she prized above everything and would not give up.

Louis IX of France was married, in his youth, to Marguerite of Provence. Marguerite, you remember, was the victim of a cruel jealousy on the part of the King's mother, Blanche of Castile. Louis, who loved Marguerite dearly, wore throughout life a ring ornamented with a garland of lilies and daisies. An enormous sapphire bore the image of a crucifix, and the inscription, *"hors cet annel pourrions nous trouver amour."*

Mary, Queen of Scots, was married in the privacy of Rizzio's chamber to Darnley with a diamond ring enamelled red. Later, when the nuptials were solemnized in the Chapel Royal of Holyrood, three rings of magnificent richness were used; but Mary always valued most the red enamelled ring with which "she was espoused."

Jones, in his "Finger-Ring Lore," tells us of one of the smallest wedding rings of which there is record. He says:

> Perhaps one of the smallest wedding rings on record is that which is mentioned in the *fiancailles* of the Princess Mary, daughter of Henry VIII, to the Dauphin of France, son of King Francis I. The fiancé was represented on that occasion by Admiral Bonnivet, the French Ambassador. The Dauphin was born February 28th, 1518, and the event of his birth was made a matter of state policy for more intimate alliance with France. On October 5th, in the same year, the bridal ceremonies took place at Greenwich with great pomp. King Henry took his station in front of the throne; on one side stood Marie of France and Queen Katherine; in front of her

mother was the Princess Marie, just two years old, dressed in cloth of gold, with a cap of black velvet on her head, blazing with jewels. On the other side stood the two legates, Wolsey and Campeggio. After a speech by Dr. Tunstal, the Princess was taken in arms; the consent of the King and Queen was demanded, and Wolsey approached with a diminutive ring of gold, fitted to the young lady's finger, in which was a valuable diamond. Admiral Bonnivet, as proxy for the baby bridegroom, passed it over the second joint. The bride was blessed, and mass performed by Wolsey, the King and the whole court attending it.

This admirable description gives us an excellent picture of court infant betrothal as it was practised by powerful nations to make themselves more powerful. And it gives us also an idea of the importance attached to the ring at that period.

It would appear that the English people, after Queen Mary's time, favoured the plain gold band. There seems to have been a reaction against the elaborate and richly embellished wedding rings that were being used until that period. The plain gold band became popular among all English-speaking peoples. Finally, the custom spread over Europe, and to-day the gold band is considered the correct form for the wedding ring.

Tradition tells us that at the marriage of Queen Mary with Philip of Spain in 1554 some controversy took place as to the nature of the ring. The Queen herself ended the dispute by saying finally that she would use a simple ring unadorned with gems, for "she chose to be wedded with a plain hoop of gold, like other maidens."

The Ring Finger.—It is said that the ring is worn on the left hand to signify the subjection of the wife to the husband. This may be mere superstition; we do not know. But it is certain that in early times the right hand signified power and authority, the left, subjection. Thus there may be some truth in it.

The wedding ring is worn to-day on the fourth finger of the left hand. A pretty bit of anatomical fiction, which has come down to us from the ancient Greeks, is that a certain vein of blood, passing directly from this finger, flows on to the heart. Probably the true reason for wearing the ring on this finger is that it is the least used of all the fingers, and therefore ornaments worn upon it are not inconvenient.

There was a period in England during which the wedding ring was worn on the thumb. In Southerne's "Maid's Last Prayer" (Act IV, p. 67) we find:

> Marry him I must, and wear my wedding ring upon my thumb, too, that I'm resolved.

At Stanford Court, Worcestershire, may be seen portraits of the ladies of the famous old Salway family, in the days of Queen Elizabeth. It is significant that all of them wear their wedding rings upon their thumbs. But it is possible that this was only a passing fad, like the "Orange Blossom" rings and "Venus" rings advertised by jewellers at the present moment. According to the "British Apollo" the rings were placed on the proper finger at the time of the marriage ceremony, but later the ring was removed by the fashionable bride and placed upon the thumb. This custom refers to the time of George I, but the same state of affairs undoubtedly prevailed at the earlier period.

A great deal of sentiment has always surrounded the wedding ring. It is related that when Baron Rosen was sent a captive to Siberia, in consequence of political tumults, his family trinkets were taken from him. He was required to give up a gold ring which he wore on his finger. He refused. "It is my wedding-ring," he said, "and you can have it only by taking the finger also." We are told that the ring was spared—evidently because the guards had as much respect and sentimental regard for the wedding ring as the Baron. Surely they would not have spared him on the strength of his pretty speech.

Dean Comber and Wheatley sum up the whole tale, or symbolism, of the wedding ring in this manner:

> The matter of which this ring is made is gold, signifying how noble and durable our affection is; the form is round, to imply that our respect (or regards) shall never have an end; the place of it is on the fourth finger of the left hand, where the ancients thought

there was a vein that came directly from the heart, and where it may be always in view; and, being a finger least used, where it may be least subject to be worn out; but the main end is to be the visible and lasting token of the covenant which must never be forgotten.

WEDDING CUSTOMS AND THEIR ORIGINS

There are many customs that are so natural and obvious a part of our marriage ceremonials that we do not even stop to think about them. Yet each custom has a little story of its own. Each custom stretches back across the centuries and links us a little closer to our forefathers.

Bancroft says:

> To things we do not understand we give names, with which by frequent use we become familiar; and then we fancy that we know all about the things themselves.

Apply this to wedding customs. Don't we do things and say things because it is the custom to do and say those things? And because we are accustomed to doing and saying these things by frequent popular use, don't we think that we know all about them?

Yet how many people really know why rice is thrown after the bride, what the old shoe signifies, how the honeymoon originated, when the bachelor's dinner originated? We accept these things because they are custom. Now you are going to find out precisely why they are custom.

The Wedding Ceremony.—Before considering the various customs attendant upon the ceremony, let us glance at the ceremony as a whole. We know that, from the earliest days, all marriages have had a religious character; Christianity emphasized this religious aspect of marriage and made of the ceremony a sacrament.

Among the Anglo-Saxons, during the first centuries of Christianity, certain marriage vows were repeated and certain rites performed out of which have grown the rites and ceremonies now prevailing. Walsh and Thrupp, both authorities, tell us that the bride was taken "for fairer or fouler, for better or worse, for richer or poorer." Among other things, she promised to be "buxom and bonny" to her future husband. It was the custom at the ceremony for the bridegroom to put the ring on each of the bride's fingers, on the left hand, in turn. At the first he would say, "In the name of the Father," at the second, "In the name of the Son," at the third, "In the name of the Holy Ghost." Reaching the fourth and final ring finger he said simply, "Amen" and the wedding ceremony was completed.

Some of our marriage customs are borrowed from the ancient Hebrews. The Hebrew marriage ceremony is picturesque and colourful. Like the Christian ceremony it is tradition-bound, and many of the customs observed in the service reach back to the days of long ago.

> The bride dresses in pure white satin, and faces the bridegroom under the *chuppah*. [This is simply a canopy, like the Anglo-Saxon care-cloth.] The ritual is read, and a cup of consecrated wine is presented to the bride and groom to be sipped. Then comes the address from the officiating rabbi, who closes by taking a glass of wine in his hands and pronouncing the seven prescribed benedictions. Again bridegroom and bride taste the cup, after which the groom places it on the floor and crushes it to atoms under his feet, as a symbol that the marriage must last until the fragments can be united. The first kiss under the new relation is given, and the newly wedded man escorts his wife from *chuppah* to entrance, and then home to the marriage feast. (*William S. Walsh, "Curiosities of Popular Customs."*)

The "something blue" which brides are advised to wear at wedding ceremonies is borrowed from the ancient Israelites. They were "bidden to put upon the borders of their fringed garments a ribband of blue—blue being the colour of purity, love, and fidelity." Brides are still advised to include a bit of blue in the bridal costume, according to this old bridal saying:

> Something old and something new,
> Something borrowed and something blue.

Obvious survivals are found in our modern marriage service. The "bridal escort" goes way back to antiquity.

The very phrase, "Who giveth this woman to this man?" is a relic of marriage by purchase. The custom of decorating the church with flowers and of carrying flowers in the bridal procession is many generations old. The very wording of the marriage service is similar to that of our forefathers, a few obsolete words only being changed.

The Bridal Escort.—"The Book of Etiquette" gives the accepted method of conducting a modern church wedding. Among other important features of the ceremony, it gives space to "The Wedding Procession" which is considered an important feature even of the simplest marriage.

> The ushers enter first, walking slowly down the aisle, two by two. The bridesmaids follow in the same manner, the maid of honour, who is unattended, comes next, followed by the bride, who leans on the arm of her father. Flower girls may precede the procession or they may walk just in front of the bride, and a page or pages may be added to the group to bear the train of the bride's gown. The bride is always the last to enter, and she comes alone or with whoever is to give her away at the altar.

Why this impressive escort for the bride? How did the custom originate?

The "best man" is undoubtedly a relic of marriage by capture. When the ancient bridegroom set out to capture a bride, he was usually accompanied by a strong-armed friend who covered the pursuit of the girl's protector. (See p. 209.)

In early Anglo-Saxon marriages, men were no less primitive in their courtships than their forefathers. We are told, for instance, that

> the heathen Anglo-Saxon stole into the girl's home, bluntly announced his purpose, and had a horse brought to the door for her. She didn't have the opportunity even to say "This is so sudden." If willing, she was treated gently. If not, her wrists were bound and she was tied to the saddle. Of course, her father pursued out of the kindness of his heart, but the wise groom always had one or more friends ready to cover his retreat. These fighting friends are believed by some antiquarians to be the original groomsmen.

Seldon, in his "Uxor Ebraica" (1646), tells us that in

mediæval times the groomsmen were known as *bride knights.* It would appear that the original purpose of the groomsmen disappeared, but the custom of having them remained. The pendulum swung to the other extreme, and instead of serving the groom these *bride knights* served the bride. They led her to the church, accompanied her to the altar, and after the ceremony relinquished her to the groom.

The origin of the custom of bridesmaids is to be found, according to all the known facts, in the old custom of pretending to struggle. You remember that after marriage by capture fell into decay, it became the custom for the bride to pretend that she was captured, and that she was unwilling to go with the groom. It was considered the modest and maidenly thing to do. Her friends would attack the bridegroom and his party and attempt to rescue the bride (see p. 212). As the bridegroom's fighting friends developed into the groomsmen, the bride's fighting friends possibly developed into the bridesmaids.

But some authorities take a different view of the origin of the bridesmaid. It was anciently the custom in Rome to have ten witnesses at the solemn marriage ceremony. These witnesses were usually friends of the bride's family. There are antiquarians who firmly believe that the custom of having bridesmaids developed from the old Roman custom of having witnesses.

The flower girl of to-day is based upon a picturesque mediæval custom. Two little girls, usually sisters, dressed precisely alike and carrying garlands of wheat, walked before the bride in the marriage procession. This symbolized the wish that the union would prove fruitful, and that the bride and groom would have "an abundance of happiness."

Later ornamental baskets replaced the garlands of wheat, and flowers were strewn from these baskets in the path of the bride. It is not known definitely how old this custom of strewing flowers before the bride actually is, but we find mention of it in Herrick's "Hesperides" (1648). We quote the following:

> The showers of roses, lucky foure-leav'd grasse,
> The while the cloud of younglings sing,
> And drown ye with a flowrie spring.

The custom of pages originated in England at an early date. We find pages playing a conspicuous part in court processions in Italy during the Renaissance, but we have no record of the page in the wedding ceremony. It was during mediæval times in England that the page, probably for the first time, took his place in the marriage group, where he has remained even to this day.

Usually the groomsmen wear at the marriage a bit of jewellery presented by the bridegroom. This is a curious survival of primitive marriage customs, when the groom was obliged to capture the bride with the help of his friends. Because she was fleet-footed (or perhaps because he was lazy), we can imagine him bribing his friends, or possibly even her own kinsmen, to lure her to the place where he was waiting.

During the time of the *bride knights* the bride presented the gifts instead of the groom. The glove was considered an acceptable gift for the services rendered by the *bride knights.* But to-day it is the bridegroom who makes the gifts, while the bride remembers her bridesmaids with some slight token.

Origin of the Bridal Veil.—There are various contradictory tales concerning the bridal veil and its origin. Some writers believe that the veil originated in the covering of the bride in ancient times to show her submission. Others claim that the exact opposite is true—that the veil was originally an emblem of freedom and that it succeeded the custom of wearing the hair flying free at the marriage ceremony.

We know that among various ancient peoples it was customary to keep the bride hidden from her future husband until the day of the wedding. In Egypt, for instance, the groom was not permitted to see the face of his bride until the marriage day. On this occasion he went through the solemn ceremony of uncovering the face. The same sort of custom prevailed among the Arabs, among the Hindus, and among various other European and Asiatic peoples. Perhaps the custom of wearing a veil grew out these earlier customs of concealing the bride entirely.

At Druse marriages, for instance, it was at one time the custom to keep the bride hidden from her future husband. Later it became the custom to hide her in a long red veil on the day of marriage. A veil is used to conceal the face entirely in China, Burma, Corea, Russia, Bulgaria, Manchuria, and Persia. Among the Bedouins the bride is completely concealed under a canopy carried by several girls. Among the Chinese, we are told, a sacred umbrella is held over the head to prevent evil from coming down upon that sensitive part of the body.

It is barely possible that the custom of the bridal veil originated with the Hebrews. At Hebrew weddings it is customary to erect a square vestment with pendants about it over the heads of the bride and groom. This is a sort of canopy, and it is held over the heads of the bride and groom by four intimate friends. Although the theory has never been advanced to our knowledge before, it would seem to us this custom of holding a canopy (a care-cloth among the Anglo-Saxons) over the two people who are to be married grew out of the religious desire to recognize a higher power—that is, to symbolize the fear of this higher power by protecting the bride and groom with the canopy.

In primitive marriages the rites and ceremonials were given a religious character. The purpose of this religious aspect, as has previously been mentioned, was to invoke the help of the gods in making the marriage happy and prosperous (see p. 208). Does it not seem possible that the canopy was erected for the purpose of protecting the bride and groom if the gods proved dissatisfied with the marriage? The sacred umbrella of the Chinese seems to bear out this belief.

The veil could have developed from the canopy or care-cloth. It would have evolved in a period when man considered himself above the universe, and woman entirely subjugated to him. The veil would be her mark of submission—to him as to the higher beings.

But this is merely conjecture. As is also the belief that the veil originated in sexual shyness in women and the attempt to hide themselves from view. But we know that, following quickly upon the canopy, the veil found a place for itself in the marriage ceremonies of the early Romans and Hebrews. We are told that these veils were of a yellow stuff—possibly linen—and that they were all-enveloping, like a shroud. Among some early peoples the veil was indeed a shroud. It was worn at the marriage ceremony, placed away, and taken out again only when the woman was ready to be buried. Among sentimental European peasantry it is still the custom to place the bridal finery in a chest and take it out again only for the purpose of "burying the bride" in it.

The early Anglo-Saxon bride went to the wedding with her hair hanging loosely—as a sign of her freedom, we are told. After the marriage ceremony, the hair was bound up as a sign of submission. According to this, it would appear that the veil was a sign of freedom rather than one of submission. It became popular in England in the days of Shakespeare and took the place of the flowing tresses.

Although we cannot be definite concerning the origin of the bridal veil, we know that no matter what its original significance may have been, it is to-day merely one of the pretty customs which the bride borrows from the pages of yesterday to make her own marriage more romantic and picturesque. It has no real significance; it serves simply the purpose of making the bride more lovely and "veiling her modesty from the world."

Bride Favours and Flowers.—Among ancient peoples, the knot seems to have been the symbol of faith. The "true love knot" was used to symbolize the indissoluble tie of love and duty in marriage.

The early Anglo-Saxon bride gave to her friends small knots or ribbands to wear or carry. This custom survives in the buttonhole bouquets of the groomsmen, and the ribbon-tied Bibles or bouquets of the bridesmaids.

The custom of bride favours possibly grew out of the custom of the "true love knot." The custom of wearing fragments cut from the bride's ribbons was introduced into England from Spain when Charles II brought Catharine of Portugal to be England's Queen. Later, instead of destroying the bride's ribbons it became the custom to present the groomsmen with huge white satin rosettes, which were called bride's favours, and which they wore throughout the ceremony.

During the reign of Queen Elizabeth it was the custom for the bridegroom to present the guests with gloves, garters, scarfs, and other "favours." Later this custom was discarded, and to-day "favours" or slight tokens of appreciation are presented to the groomsmen only.

Orange blossoms have been worn or carried by brides since earliest times. The blossoms are believed to portend good luck and happiness. Both Spenser and Milton were of the opinion that the orange was the "golden apple" presented to Jupiter by Juno on their marriage day, and it is very probably because of this belief that the orange blossom came to be associated, in later times, with happiness in the marriage tie.

Myrtle was a favourite of the ancients. They believed that its perpetual freshness was a token of the fact that it was a favourite of the gods; therefore it was used by them to symbolize constancy in duty and affection.

Lilies-of-the-valley and roses have always been favourite wedding flowers, but because of their prettiness rather than of any significance. However, we are told that the ancient Greeks regarded the rose as queen of flowers and considered it an emblem of beauty and happiness. And young Romans were in the habit of sending baskets of roses to the ladies they admired.

At one time a garland of flowers was absolutely essential in the marriage ceremony. It was placed on the bride's head and was known as the "coronet of the good girl." Rare old books tell us that it was the privilege only of the virtuous bride to wear a garland of flowers, and that to prove her inalienable attribute of virtue the bride should wear "a ring on her finger, a brooch on her breast, and a garland on her head."

Cutting the Bride's Hair.—In early life it was a widespread practice to deprive women of their ornaments as soon as they were married. Some peoples actually mutilated their brides so that they would not be attractive to other men.

In early Japan, for instance, the eyebrows were shaved off. The Japanese considered heavy eyebrows one of woman's greatest charms. Other people blackened the teeth of brides. Still others tattooed the face. Many cut off the hair.

This cutting of the hair had two possible meanings. The first was to make the woman unattractive. The second was to symbolize her submission and subjugation to the man.

Thus in Egypt the bride's hair was tied up upon the conclusion of the wedding ceremony. This was for the purpose of symbolizing the giving up of her freedom. The custom prevailed also in ancient Britain and among various other peoples.

One authority says that the custom of shaving off the bride's hair was to protect her from danger. This may have an element of truth, although we doubt that it was the sole reason for cutting off the hair. We know that in primitive life one part of the body was sacrificed to protect the rest. Mandan boys, for instance, have the little finger cut off at puberty "as a sacrifice to their patron deity." When a Japanese boy reached puberty a "godfather" cut off his forelock and gave him a new name. It is very possible that some peoples cut off the bride's hair at marriage to insure her safety and protection.

(Courtesy of Metropolitan Museum of Art)

An Egyptian mummy label of wood.

(Courtesy of Metropolitan Museum of Art)

Egyptian script writing on papyrus.

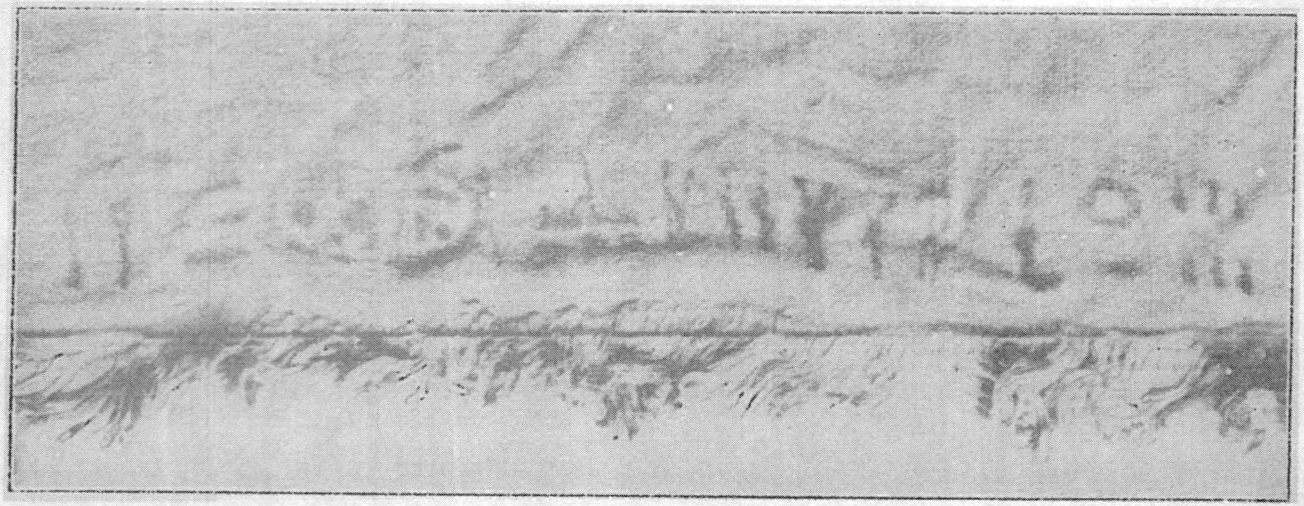

(Courtesy of Metropolitan Museum of Art)

Mummy cloth, 18th Dynasty, Egypt.

The custom of cutting the bride's hair is now obsolete except among remnants of savage tribes. But some authorities still connect this ancient custom with the bridal veil. (See p. 242.)

Casting the Shoe.—Many and various are the tales concerning the bridal shoe or slipper. No two authorities seem to be entirely agreed as to its origin.

William J. Fielding says:

> During all ages and in the folklore of all races shoes have been a symbol of the female genitals and rice (or wheat or other common cereal) the symbol of the male fructifying seed. Hence, we unconsciously indicate the sexual character of the new relationship with the normal outcome of fruitfulness or prolificacy, which the conventions of modern society would not permit us openly to mention.

That the casting of a shoe after the bride signifies a fruitful marriage seems to be implied in the old Mother Goose rhyme:

> There was an old woman who lived in a shoe;
> She had so many children she didn't know what to do.

But as a general rule, authorities are inclined to believe that the true significance of the shoe is an exchange of authority.

Among the Assyrians and the Hebrews, for instance, when a bargain had been made, a man usually gave his sandal as a token of good faith and to symbolize the transfer of property. The Egyptians had the custom of exchanging sandals to show that property had been exchanged or authority granted. For instance, there are in existence actual paintings of Egyptian slaves showing them carrying their masters' sandals in token of submission.

The flinging down of a sandal upon a territory was a symbol of possession.

> Upon the land of Edom do I cast my shoe. (9th Psalm.)

Among the ancient Israelites, when property was bought and passed into another's hands, it was customary for the seller to pull off his sandal as a sign that he surrendered all claim to it.

Thus hurling the shoe after the bride was meant originally, it would seem, to indicate the transfer of authority over her from her father to her husband. We are told that the Anglo-Saxon bridegroom always hung a slipper in a prominent place in the new house, for the sentiment of that period seems to have been:

> A spaniel, a woman and a walnut tree,
> The more they are beaten the better they be.

In describing a solemn marriage ceremony, William S. Walsh says:

> The father gave to his new son one of his daughter's shoes, in token of the transfer of authority which he effected, and the bride was at once made to feel the change by a tap or blow on the head given with the shoe. The husband on his part took an oath to use his wife well. If he failed to do so, she might leave him, but by the law he was allowed considerable license.
>
> He was bound in honour "to bestow on his wife and apprentices moderate castigation." An old Welsh law decides that three blows with a broomstick on "any part of the person except the head" is a fair allowance, and another provides that the stick shall be no longer than the husband's arm nor thicker than his middle finger.

In Arabia it was once customary for a man to have first right to marry his cousin. He was not obliged to marry her, but any one seeking to do so, had first to gain his permission. If he gave up his right to the hand of his cousin he said, "She was my slipper, I have cast her off." It meant, of course, "I had first right to her as my cousin, but I have given up that right."

Some authorities believe that the wedding shoe is a relic of marriage by capture, and that it grew out of the custom of hurling missiles after the robber bridegroom by the father or guardian of the girl. But while they differ on this point, they are inclined to agree that the shoe having always been a symbol of authority, is connected in the marriage ceremony with the transfer of possession and authority.

In connection with the shoe, it is interesting to note that the foot has been regarded as a sacred symbol as far back as the Bronze Age. Pottery, breast-plates and other relics of that period show decorations in the form of human feet. Ancient Greeks and Romans, we are told, approaching a certain shrine were compelled to remove their sandals and approach in their bare feet. It was a form of worship.

Another curious thing is that the throwing of the shoe has always been accounted lucky. In Scotland, for instance, the custom was not confined solely to marriages, but old shoes were thrown after a sailor going on his first trading voyage, a man starting out on a new enterprise, etc. The Irish appear to have had the same custom. Old shoes were thrown after a person when his friends wished him to succeed in whatever it was he was starting.

In his "Lyrical Monologue" Tennyson mentions the custom of casting the shoe for luck. He says:

> For this thou shalt from all things seek,
> Marrow of mirth and laughter,
> And wheresoe'er thou move, good luck
> Shall throw her old shoe after.

In her Journal Queen Victoria relates that when she first entered Balmoral Castle (September 7, 1855) old shoes were thrown after her for good luck. And in Germany, we are told, it was until recently the custom for the bride to be attended to her chamber, where she took off her shoe and threw it to all present—as we to-day throw the bridal bouquet. The one who caught the shoe was considered lucky. He or she would not only be the next to marry, but would have good fortune throughout life. A similar custom prevailed in Kent, except that the groomsman selected by the bride cast the shoe among the bridesmaids, and they alone were privileged to jump for it.

"The Book of Etiquette," sanctioning the age-old custom of casting the shoe after the bride, says:

> It would not be objectionable at all if some over-enthusiastic individuals did not overdo it to the extent that it becomes almost

riotous. After a solemn, dignified, well-ordered wedding ceremony, and a charming reception, it is nothing short of ridiculous to spoil it all by boisterously overdoing an old tradition.

The Handful of Rice.—The practice of throwing rice after a departing bride and groom originated in primitive times. Among early peoples rice and grain were emblems of productiveness, and grain of some sort was used in the marriage rites to symbolize fruitfulness for the union.

Rice was not always the grain used. We are told that an old Greek custom was to pour flour and sweetmeats over the bride and groom, to symbolize an abundance of all that is sweet and good and desirable. There are records of wheat having been used among the early Anglo-Saxons, and certain peoples used corn.

According to records that have come down to us it was customary in Greece to place a piece of raw cotton on the mule which carried away the bride's dowry. When the mule, bearing the dowry, reached the bridegroom's house, his mother repeated the little ceremony and placed another bit of cotton on the load. The purpose was to insure a future abundance of good things for the bride and groom.

Rice has always played an important part in the Persian marriage ceremony. Among these people rice is regarded as an emblem of fruitfulness. We are told that the bride and groom, after marriage, were required to meet at midnight and go through this ceremony: The sponsor for the man would touch the forehead of the woman and ask her if she would have the man. Replying in the affirmative, she gave her hand to him. Then the same ceremony was gone through by the sponsor for the woman, and the hands of the contracting parties were joined. After this ceremony rice was scattered over them and prayers were offered for their fruitfulness.

Some authorities tell us that the practice of throwing rice originated in an entirely different manner. They say that rice was thrown after the bride and groom for the purpose of giving food to the evil influences that surrounded them. It was a primitive belief that evil spirits were always present at a marriage, and it was for the purpose of appeasing these spirits and keeping them from doing injury to the bridal pair that, according to some writers, the custom of rice-throwing was originated.

Still another theory is that the rice is an inducement to the soul of the bridegroom to stay. In Celebes, for instance, there is a widespread belief that the soul of the bridegroom, unless bribed, is likely to fly away at marriage and never return. To prevent this, rice is scattered over him. Thus the soul is induced to remain.

Among various peoples the act of eating rice constitutes marriage. How customs such as these originated is not known; unless eating together symbolized living together and eating out of the same dish, and rice was used possibly because it happened to be the food of the locality. We know that primitive peoples always ate together to symbolize friendship, peace, and kinship.

The Batta groom is obliged to sit next to the bride publicly and to eat rice with her from the same dish. At Dyak marriages, the bride and groom first eat together and are then sprinkled with rice. At the Malay wedding, friends put into the hands of the bride and groom uncooked rice, and with this they feed each other simultaneously.

From all the records concerning rice that have been preserved, it would seem that the use of rice as a symbol of productiveness or fruitfulness is the most plausible explanation of our custom. Thus, when you cast your handful of rice after the bride and groom what you are really doing is indicating to them your wishes for their fruitfulness—a sentiment which modern society does not permit you to express in the ordinary way.

The Marriage Feast.—The simplest and most universal of all marriage ceremonies is that of eating and drinking together. At the risk of being monotonous, we wish to repeat that eating together in early life symbolized kinship. The mutual partaking of food appears to have been one of the strongest ties of early life. One of the most important of sexual tabus was that of eating together.

To the primitive mind, eating together produced indentity of substance, of flesh. Therefore those who ate together were kin. The savages had "female food" and "male food" and there were food tabus as there were sexual tabus. We can scarcely conceive of the importance held by food in primitive culture.

Eating together, among many primitive peoples, constituted marriage. There was little or no other ceremony. In the Fijis, for instance, the marriage ceremony was considered complete as soon as the pair had eaten out of the same dish. In Madagascar to become man and wife it is necessary to eat out of the same dish. In Ceram the bride eats a male opossum and the bridegroom eats a female opossum. In Barbar the bride and groom were required to eat together out of one dish. This same custom in Rae is a "token of friendship."

In ancient Rome, at the dignified and solemn marriage by *confarreatio,* the bride and groom ate together. Drinking together, we are told, was also a common method of solemnizing the marriage.

The Navajo bride and groom ate maize pudding together. Among Nufi people it was the custom to celebrate the payment of the bride-price and the solemnizing of the marriage by feasting. Eating and drinking together formed, and to some extent still forms, part of the marriage ceremony in Japan, in Russia, in Scandinavia, among various Brazilian tribes. Until recently the Servian bride ate only once in her life with a man, and that was on her marriage day, when she ate with her husband.

At marriages among the Hebrews the rabbi hands to the couple a glass of wine which has been blessed. After both drink from it, the glass is smashed under the heel of the groom. The breaking of the glass symbolizes eternity; the meaning behind it is that the bride and groom will be joined in happiness and love until the glass is made whole again, which is another way of saying for ever. Isn't it possible that this custom goes back even farther? Perhaps the glass is broken to prevent magic use of the vessel, by enemies, to bring harm upon the bride and groom. Many such fears and superstitions existed among early peoples.

From all these customs it is easy to see why the marriage feast came to be accepted, at last, as a customary part of marriage festivities. "At marriage, the friends of both feel somewhat bound together by the union of the pair, and expression is given to this by eating and drinking together."

Sir John Sinclair tells the following in his "Statistical Account of Scotland" (1792):

> When a young man wishes to pay his addresses to his sweetheart, instead of going to her father and professing his passion, he goes to the public house and, having let the landlady into the secret of his attachment, the object of his wishes is immediately sent for, who almost never refuses to come. She is entertained with ale and brandy, and the marriage is concluded upon. The second day after the wedding, a *creel,* as it is called, takes place. It is very similar to our [English] wedding breakfast.

The Wedding Cake.—The wedding cake is a direct survival of a particular kind of cake used in Roman times among the highest members of the patrician families. At the aristocratic Roman *confarreatio* the bride and groom not only ate together, but feasted the guests; and we are told that the cake of *confarreation* was broken over the bride's head as a symbol of plentifulness. Each of the guests took a piece of the cake to insure plentifulness for himself or herself.

Many of the American Indians used a bride cake in their marriage ceremonies. The Iroquois, for instance, have a peculiar kind of meal cake which plays a conspicuous part in the marriage festivities. The bride makes this cake and presents it to the groom. Traces of this custom still remain; and a similar custom is found also among the Fiji Islanders.

The early Anglo-Saxons had huge baskets of small dry crackers at their marriage ceremonies. Each guest pocketed one and took it home. Those that remained were distributed to the poor. Later it became the custom for the guests themselves to bring to the wedding small richly spiced buns which were piled in one huge mound on the table. It was a popular custom for the bride and groom to attempt to kiss each other over this mound, and if they succeeded they were assured lifelong prosperity.

We are told that the wedding cake, as we know it to-day, was the brilliant idea of a genius of a French cook who was travelling through England. Stopping for a while in London, he noticed the inconvenience of piling hundreds of small spice cakes into one mound, and he conceived the idea of icing this mound into one solid mass. So was the wedding cake born.

It is the traditional right of the bride to cut the first slice of cake. The superstition is that if any one else cuts into the cake first, the bride's happiness and prosperity are cut into.

Another old custom is to have a ring baked in the cake, the superstition being that the person who finds it will be the next to marry. And still another superstition is that if one takes home the piece of bridal cake and sleeps with it under one's pillow, the future husband will appear in a dream. Perhaps it is for that reason that slices of bride cake are conveniently packed in small boxes tied with white ribbon at modern marriages!

Origin of the Trousseau.—The word "trousseau" is from *trusse,* meaning a little bundle. In earliest times the trousseau was in the nature of a dowry and was an indirect way of compensating the bridegroom for the money or goods which he paid to the girl's father. During the later stages of marriage by purchase, these goods were handed over to the daughter as her marriage portion. Upon the decay of marriage by purchase, the bridegroom did not give money or goods to the father, but the latter nevertheless supplied the daughter with her dowry.

We can understand how the hope chest idea must have grown out of the custom of the dowry, among girls who realized the part money and possessions played in winning a husband. Thus in Roumania, for instance, girls begin at a very young age to make their bridal finery and the linens they will require for their homes. At one time the bridegroom had the privilege of examining the trousseau and deciding whether or not it was complete; and frequently, we are told, the choice of a suitor depended upon the worth of the girl's outfit.

In Greece it is not customary for sons to marry before all the daughters in the family have been married. Here we find sons helping provide the trousseaux and so speeding the marriage of their sisters.

In mediæval times trousseaux were elaborate and rich. We quote the following description of a bride's outfit from E. L. Urlin's book, "A Short History of Marriage." It concerns the wedding of Edward II to Isabella of France (1308), and though it describes a royal trousseau it reflects the trend of the times. Even the brides of the lower classes, we are told, were given rich and elaborate trousseaux.

> She [Isabella] brought two gold crowns ornamented with gems, gold and silver drinking vessels, golden spoons and fifty silver plates. Her dresses were made of gold and silver stuff, velvet and taffetas. She had six dresses of green cloth, six of rose scarlet, and many costly furs. For linen she had 419 yards, and the tapestries for her chamber were elaborate with the arms of England and France woven in gold.

No less elaborate was the trousseau of Lucrezia Borgia. We are told by an eyewitness that "In her wardrobe she had a trimmed dress worth more than fifteen thousand ducats, and two hundred costly shifts, some of which are worth a hundred ducats apiece; the sleeves alone of some of them costing thirty ducats each, being trimmed with gold fringe." Another eyewitness reported to the Duchess Isabella that Lucrezia had one dress worth twenty thousand ducats, and a hat valued at ten thousand.

There are various interesting superstitions concerning the trousseau. One is that if a bit of hand work—even one stitch—is placed by the bride-to-be on every piece that goes into the hope chest, happiness and good fortune will follow her throughout life. Because of this superstition many brides prefer to initial linens themselves, which is something to remember when making gifts.

Another superstition concerns the trying on of a garment belonging in the trousseau before the actual wedding day. There is a widespread belief that to do so will cause unhappiness and disappointment.

White for Purity.—So said the ancients. And they carried out this belief by making it a custom for brides to wear white as an emblem of their purity.

And even before it denoted purity, white denoted joy. The early Romans always wore white on occasions of rejoicing, such as birth and feast days. The white rose was an emblem of joy among the Greeks. And the ancient Patagonians, we are informed, were in the habit of painting their bodies white on every joyous occasion. The whole body was covered with white paint on the eve of the wedding ceremony.

Among various peoples white was not only the colour of purity, but it was considered a sacred colour. The natives of Central Africa, to give one instance, worshipped the white elephant as sacred.

Gradually all people accepted white as the colour denoting purity, and to-day white is considered most acceptable for the bridal gown. To quote "The Book of Etiquette":

From a study of the descriptions of bridal gowns at recent important weddings, we find that white satin is without doubt the favorite material. Crêpe-de-chine and heavy white brocade are also used; and the bride may select whichever material she likes best, something soft and clinging, unless she is inclined to be too slender, when taffeta is more suitable. Undoubtedly, no matter what the style of the gown happens to be, it should boast a train; and a draped skirt is always a popular wedding mode. The length of the sleeves and skirt is entirely governed by the fashion of the moment.

An excellent description of the bridal party which accompanied Lucrezia Borgia on her wedding day appears in Parsons' "Psychology of Dress." We quote, in part, the following, because it reveals the type of wedding dress of the period and various little customs:

> Leaning on the arm of an elderly cavalier dressed in black velvet, with a golden chain about his neck, Lucrezia went as far as the entrance of her palace to greet him. According to the prearranged ceremonial she did not kiss her brothers-in-law, but merely bowed to them, following the French custom. She wore a dress of some white material embroidered in gold, over which was a garment of dark brown velvet trimmed with sable. The sleeves were of white and gold brocade, tight, and barred in the Spanish fashion. Her headdress was of green gauze, with a fine gold band and two rows of pearls. . . . Refreshments were served and Lucrezia distributed small gifts—the work of Roman jewellers—among those present.

Miscellaneous Origins.—Among northern nations of Europe, in ancient times, it was the custom for newly married couples to drink metheglin or mead (a kind of wine made from honey) for a period of thirty days after marriage. Antiquarians say that from this custom grew the term "honey month," or "honeymoon." According to tradition Attila, the Hun, drank so much mead at his wedding feast that he died from the effects of it.

But whether the above origin of "honeymoon" is true or not, we know that in the days of marriage by capture it was necessary for the bridegroom to remain in hiding with his bride until her kinsmen tired of the search for her. And later, when love entered marriage and elopements were frequent, it was necessary for bride and groom to remain in hiding for a while. Both of these "hiding periods" seem to point to possible origins of the honeymoon.

In Luxon it was customary to seclude the bride and groom within the house for a period of ten days. No one was permitted to enter during this time. Among the Minahassas the newly married couples were secluded for three days and nights; among the Bedui for four days. In Bulgaria they are shut up for a week, during which time they may neither visit others nor receive visitors.

The exact opposite seems to prevail in Java. Here the bride and groom are secluded for forty days *before* the wedding, and during that time they are permitted neither to leave the house nor to perform hard work of any kind. After the wedding ceremony, however, they are expected to come forth from their seclusion and visit all their friends.

The name "bridegroom" was given to the newly married man because among various peoples it was customary for him, on his wedding day, to wait at table on his bride. "Groom" signified one who served in an inferior station. "Bridegroom" signified one who served the bride.

The custom of the bachelor dinner originated in ancient Sparta. It was customary for the Spartan bridegroom to sup with his friends on the eve of the wedding. This was known as the "men's mess."

It is an old custom for brides to wear gloves. In Egyptian hieroglyphics, the glove is the symbol of the hand. The name is TUT, and the word itself signifies to give, to honour. It means also distinction and ceremonial. Because of various ideas associated with the glove and with the hand, it became the custom in early times for the bride to wear gloves at her marriage.

We are told that white paper cut in the shape of gloves was hung up at the doors of houses at Wrexham, in Flintshire (England), as late as the year 1785. A surgeon and apothecary of the place was married to a popular young woman and the paper gloves were souvenirs of their marriage.

There are several old customs based upon the glove. If a man is caught sleeping and is kissed by a woman he is obliged to present her with a pair of gloves. (An old

English custom.) If a man manages to snatch a pair of gloves belonging to a woman, she must forfeit a kiss to retrieve her property. (Practised to a great extent in colonial times.) In early times the glove was also used in challenging. If a man felt that his lady had been insulted, he threw his glove in the insulter's face. This was the symbol or sign of a duel.

The custom of wedding bells originated in England. In mediæval times it was customary for the church bells to peal as the bride entered, and to peal once again as she emerged on the arm of her husband. The custom has survived and is still in use to-day.

Throwing the Bridal Bouquet.—The throwing of the bridal bouquet originated with the old custom of scrambling for the bride's garter. In the early 14th century in France it was considered a lucky thing to win the bride's garter, and everyone rushed for it at the conclusion of the ceremony. Brides wisely left one garter dangling where it could easily be reached, but nevertheless they were often hurt in the scuffle.

So the garter gave way to the stocking, and in the next century we find "stocking-throwing" the favourite bridal custom. But stockings aren't the easiest and most convenient things in the world to remove and cast to one's friends for luck, so some wise bride conceived the idea of throwing her bridal bouquet. The custom has prevailed, and lucky the maiden who catches the bouquet! Tradition says she will be the next to marry.

Everything has its significance. Each little custom that the bride observes links her to the long chain that stretches back across the ages. These customs continue from century to century; and though we sniff at them just the least bit contemptuously, though we say, in our 20th century sophistication, that they are superstitions and don't mean a thing, we know that we wouldn't ignore them for the world! Though we won't admit it, we know perfectly well that June's the month to marry in, and as for the day, well—

Monday for wealth, Tuesday for health,
Wednesday best day o' all;
Thursday for crosses, Friday for losses—
Saturday, no luck at all!

Wedding Superstitions.—"Happy is the bride the sun shines on," the poet sings. But why?

Primitive men recognized the fertilizing power of the sun. They believed, therefore, that the bride who married on a sunny day would be happy, prosperous. In Halmahera, boys were required as part of their initiation to expose themselves to the sun. Among the Hindus the bride was expected to rise early on the day before her marriage and "look into the face of the sun." In Central Asia both bride and groom greeted the rising sun together. If it rained on the day of the marriage, the superstitious people believed it to be a sign of evil, and interpreted it to mean that the wedding would not be happy.

Thus we have the old, old belief immortalized in the lines, "Happy is the bride the sun shines on."

You have probably heard many times the expression "lifting the bride over the doorstep." The bride in ancient Rome was lifted over the threshold, or lightly jumped over it, because it was believed a sign of ill-luck to stumble over it. To prevent stumbling, the bridegroom carried her into the house. The Romans held the threshold sacred to Vesta, the goddess of Virgins.

An old almanac by Andrew Waterman for 1559 furnishes a list of the days "good to marry or contract a wife (for then women will be fond and loving). Among us the fear of Friday is still a common superstition, and there is a marked preference for marriage in June. Superstitions such as these are groundless, yet they persist from generation to generation.

Concerning the Widow.—In primitive life there was a custom called *Levirate* by which the brother or nearest male relative of a man inherited his wife. She was like any other possession, and upon her husband's death she went to his brother or heir. There are records, comparatively late, of men bequeathing their wives while on the deathbed.

As civilization advanced, customs such as these faded into the background. But even to-day there is a great deal less ceremonial when a widow marries. There is a marked effort to keep the marriage simple and unostentatious. "White is for the girl bride only," the books on etiquette caution. And we are further advised that "When the widow marries, conspicuous display is in very bad taste."

Isn't it barely possible that in early life second marriages were simple and unceremonious because of the fear that elaborate ceremony and celebration would attract the evil spirit of the dead wife or husband? We know that among many savage tribes, when a wife dies in childbed it is believed that she becomes an evil spirit which haunts the home. Accordingly, when a wife dies in this manner, the husband instantly goes through the ceremony of divorce. If he marries again there is little ceremonial.

Our own custom of simple second marriages may have evolved from this primitive fear.

Customs of Divorce.—It is very probable that divorce is as old as marriage. The first divorces were just separations—the man and the woman found they could not be happy together and went their own way; or one or the other may simply have disappeared.

But many early peoples regarded separation after the birth of children shameful. The Iroquois never separated after children were born, nor did the Greenlanders. Among the Maoris, the natives of the Solomon Islands, and in New Guinea divorce is very rare. The Red Karens in Indo-China do not permit divorce if there has been a child. Among the Aztecs marriage was considered a tie that bound the man and woman together for life.

Quite the opposite condition prevailed among other peoples. The Athenians, according to record, permitted divorce upon the slightest excuse. But it was not permitted without a bill of divorce, specifying the reason. This the magistrate had to see and approve. It was rarely, indeed, that he disapproved. Early law, being made by man, was usually partial to man.

Among the early Romans dislike was considered ample reason for divorce. If a man found that his liking for his wife turned into dislike, he had no difficulty whatever in divorcing her, and remarrying at will.

Many curious systems of divorce prevail. In Tonga a man divorces his wife simply by telling her to go. In Yucatan a man at one time was able to divorce his wife for the merest trifle, and simply by leaving her and not returning. The Aleuts exchanged their wives when they tired of them, for food and clothes. Among the Eskimos there is no definite method of divorce. The man leaves the woman and goes to live by himself in another igloo. After a certain period the people realize that he is divorced, and he is at liberty to marry again whenever he pleases.

A curious custom prevails in Egypt. After a divorce, a man cannot legally take his wife again unless she has been married and divorced by another man. For this purpose it is the custom to employ a poor, ugly, or blind man, called *moostahhill.* He marries the woman, divorces her, and she is remarried by her first husband. We are told that this curious ceremony of marriage, divorce, and remarriage occurs frequently.

Prior to the 7th century an Anglo-Saxon husband could divorce his wife for various insignificant reasons. Walsh enumerates several of them. "A wife might at any time be repudiated on proof of her being barren, deformed, silly, passionate, luxurious, rude, habitually drunk, gluttonous, very garrulous, quarrelsome or abusive." Some of the reasons are not insignificant, of course, but think of divorcing a wife to-day because she is a little rude or quarrelsome!

(Courtesy of Metropolitan Museum of Art)

A wooden tablet covered with wax, used to teach children to write.

(Courtesy of Metropolitan Museum of Art)

Palette and brushes from a set of writing utensils, Egypt, 18th Dynasty.

Divorce was very rare among the North American Indians. They considered the marriage tie inviolable, and the man who left his wife without cause was ordinarily banished from the tribe. According to earliest records, it was disgraceful for a man to have more wives than he was able to maintain; and equally disgraceful for him to fail to maintain properly his wife or wives when he was able to do so. The Indians appear to have had a high sense of honour; they were fair to their women despite the fact that they are credited with having made drudges of them.

Wedding Anniversaries.—During the early periods of Christianity, every possible occasion for celebration or ceremony was seized upon. The wedding anniversary naturally presented itself as an appropriate occasion for merrymaking.

The wedding anniversary of to-day is not so much an occasion for merrymaking as it is for entertaining. Young people usually entertain at a dinner in celebration of their first anniversary; and there is a solemn banquet at the fiftieth. Following are the customary wedding anniversaries as they are accepted by modern society.

The Paper Wedding	First year
The Wooden Wedding	Fifth year
The Tin Wedding	Tenth year
The Leather Wedding	Twelfth year
The Crystal Wedding	Fifteenth year
The China Wedding	Twentieth year
The Silver Wedding	Twenty-fifth year
The Ivory Wedding	Thirtieth year
The Woolen Wedding	Fortieth year
The Silk Wedding	Forty-fifth year
The Golden Wedding	Fiftieth year
The Diamond Wedding	Seventy-fifth year

Through popular custom, the silver and golden wedding have become the two anniversaries that are celebrated more than any others. The anniversaries that come before the quarter-century mark are usually disregarded.

Wedding-lore of Many Lands.—Before leaving the fascinating subject of marriage and of wedding customs, let us glance at some of the lore that has been collected from various lands. Perhaps you will recognize some customs curiously similar to our own.

In Japan the bride is attired in white to typify her purity, and is covered from head to foot with a white veil. This veil is destined to be her shroud. Seated in a palanquin in all her finery, she is carried in gay procession through the town. Her family and friends are in the procession, the men in their dress of ceremony and the women in their richest gold-bordered robes. The spectacle is colourful and picturesque. Sometimes, according to age-old custom, two men run in front waving a red cloth, which is intended to ward off evil influences. In this manner the bride finally reaches the bridegroom's house, where a feast ensues and the bridal equipment is exhibited to the guests. It is customary, in Japan, for the bridegroom to send magnificent gifts to the bride which she gives to her parents in acknowledgment of their kindness to her. The parents in turn provide her with a handsome trousseau which is carried to the home of the bridegroom on the day of the marriage and there displayed.

In China single women always affect the utmost modesty and bashfulness. They seem to have a natural aversion to marriage. Thus, even though the bride may approve of her husband and of the marriage, out of modesty she must pretend that she does not. It is the custom for her to be locked in a sedan chair and the key and chair both consigned to the bridegroom. She is carried in this sedan chair to the home of the bridegroom, her dowry or trousseau accompanying her.

Among the Zulu Kaffirs, if a suitor has about twenty good-sized cows to give to the father of the girl he wishes to wed, he is considered "acceptable." The day is set for the marriage and all necessary arrangements made. On the marriage day, the bride advances with great dignity to the entrance of the kraal and falls upon her knees to receive from the young man the customary necklace of beads. This he places around her neck, and then raises her to her feet. Now he places a band of white beads, emblematic of his belief in her virginity, around her waist. She enters the hut and remains for a little while alone with him. During these few moments she is expected to decide whether she will take him "for better or for worse." If the decision is favourable she emerges hand-in-hand with him and her friends assembled outside strike up a song of congratulation. Then follows a dance in which everyone participates. If the decision is not favourable, the girl emerges alone, the guests disperse, and the marriage does not take place. But this rarely happens, as the girl who goes as far as receiving the necklace and entering the hut—as the girl who accepts an engagement ring to-day—knows whether or not she wants to marry the man.

In Russia it was formerly the custom for the father to strike his daughter gently with a new whip, and then give the weapon to her husband. It was, and is still, the custom to crown the bride with a garland of wormwood, to imply the bitterness of the married state. The priest sprinkles on her head a handful of hops to make her as fruitful as that plant. This handful of hops corresponds to our handful of rice.

The Italians have many wedding omens. They believe that the most fortunate time for weddings is the middle of June. The bride's dress must be a plain, long white robe; the face must be covered with a veil, and her hair must be crowned with flowers.

Many forms of marriage exist among the Australians. In some tribes traces of barter still remain. A woman is sometimes exchanged for so many silver bracelets or for so much land. Frequently we come across the custom, carried from one tribe to another through intermarriage, of symbolizing service to the future husband. This appears to be an important part of the marriage ceremony. The woman carries firewood to her lover's hut and builds a fire for him.

This same sort of custom prevailed among various North American Indians. The woman gathered together a small bundle of rods, piled them before the man's tent, built a fire, and made a meal cake for the husband-to-be. His eating of this cake constituted marriage.

The aborigines of Australia still practise abduction and capture of wives. This causes frequent trouble with other native tribes and sometimes results in blood feuds. And travellers tell us that the Australians are still in the habit of offering wives to visitors.

We encounter many such customs of offering wives to visitors, particularly among the South Sea Islanders. O'Brien gives us several instances of such offers made to him during his sojourn in the South Seas. Sometimes the wife was offered for a night, sometimes for his whole stay. Frequently she was the wife or the daughter of the host with whom he lived. To quote one instance from "White Shadows in the South Seas":

> When the time came for saying *apae kaoha* my kindly hosts sought to confer upon me the last proof of their friendliness. They proposed that I marry Vanquished Often.
>
> My refusal was incomprehensible to them, and Vanquished Often's happy smile in the moonlight quickly faded to a look of pain and humiliation. They had offered me their highest and most revered expression of hospitality. To refuse it was as uncustomary and as rude as to refuse the Alaskan miner who offers a drink at a public bar.

We cannot resist the temptation to quote from O'Brien's fascinating book this explanation of the kind of marriage that takes place among the Marquesans:

> No Marquesan can marry without the consent of his mother, and often she marries him to a girl without his even thinking of such a thing.
>
> A young man may bring home a girl he does not know, perhaps a girl he has seen on the beach in the moonlight, to stay with him that night in his mother's house. It may be that her beauty and

charm will so please his mother that she will call a family council after the two have gone to bed. If the family thinks as the mother does, they determine to marry the young man to that girl, and they do so after this fashion:

Early in the morning, just at dawn, before the young couple awake, all the women of the household arouse them with shrieks. They beat their breasts, cut themselves with shells, crying loudly, *Aue! Aue!* Neighbors rush in to see who has died. The youth and the girl run forth in terror. Then the mother, the grandmother, and all other women of the house chant the praises of the girl, singing her beauty, and wailing that they cannot let her go. They demand with anger that the son shall not let her go. All the neighbours cry with them, *Aue! Aue!* and beat their breasts, until the son, covered with shame, asks the girl to stay.

Then her parents are sent the word, and if they do not object, the girl remains in his house. That is often the manner of Marquesan marriage.

In New Zealand are still found definite traces of marriage by capture. According to the custom of this land, the more a bride kicks, cries, and struggles the more she is applauded by her friends. An eyewitness tells us that "even when all were agreeable, it was the custom for the groom to go with a party and appear to take her away by force, her friends yielding her up only after a feigned struggle." In New Guinea, we are told, the bridegroom carries off the bride or elopes with her, and afterward pays a compensation price to the parents.

Among the Todas and Osages the marriage contract resembles an act of barter. But it is not barter in its true sense. The Osage bride is stripped of her clothes and ornaments, which are made into one pile and carried to the groom's mother as a gift. She receives in exchange clothes and ornaments equally valuable. To conclude this exchange, which is merely a ceremonious custom with no definite significance, a family feast is given. A similar custom is noticed among the Chippewas, whose weddings always terminate in a feast at which gifts are exchanged between the bridegroom and the relatives of the bride. Among the Natchez it was the custom for the bridal pair to eat out of one dish. Later the bridegroom smoked the calumet, wafting the first fumes toward the parents of his wife and the second fumes toward his own parents, in ceremonious token of the alliance.

The Malay bridegroom is expected to remain under the roof and eye of his mother-in-law for a period of two years. After the expiration of that period he is permitted to remove with his wife to a house of his own. It is only then that he is considered actually married.

A glimpse at the marriage customs existing in Ceram reveals a bit of rare wisdom existing in the marriage compact. One reads, "What the husband wishes the wife must wish, and what the wife wishes, the husband must also wish; and let them not forget their parents." An excellent piece of matrimonial advice!

A curious custom is noticed in Uganda. After the marriage day the bride is permitted to remain idle for a full month. At the end of the month her relatives bring her a gift in the form of food. When the food has been entirely consumed, the bride begins housekeeping.

In Albania, which is a tiny country in the southeast of Europe, fire is regarded as one of life's sacred symbols. Therefore fire plays a large part in the marriage ceremonies. Wives are still abducted by the Albanians, and when a wife is "captured" she is taken to his home and placed before the fireplace. A huge fire is built and the girl is given a large pair of fire tongs. For three full days she is obliged to stand beside the fireplace, her head bowed, her hands grasping the fire tongs. She may not speak. She may not rest. Whatever food or drink she is given is brought to her. At the end of this ordeal she is considered married and she takes her place in the household. We are told that among the Albanians a heavy belt takes the place of our wedding ring. It is placed around the waist of the bride, after the three-day ordeal, and is preserved by her throughout life. Recent travellers in this faraway land tell us that even when a bride and groom are married at church by a priest, they go through this age-old ceremonial of the country and do not consider themselves actually married until they have done so.

There is probably no sect or class of people throughout the civilized world who use so little pomp and ceremony in their marriage customs as the Quakers. These people use no oaths. They have no elaborate feasting, no complex or complicated rites. They simply make assertion before witnesses that they will live together, and so they do.

No matter where our fancy may lead us, no matter with what people we may wander, we find interesting rites and customs based upon the old, old institution of marriage. In Spain we meet the *duenna* and her charge coming to meet the bridegroom promised in infancy. In the East we find sanctified prostitution; we see instances of legalized polygamy. We meet the girls of pleasure at Venice. We come upon a picturesque Tartar wedding. We walk in the shadow of a Turkish harem. We watch the dancing girls at Cairo. All age-old customs of the people. All the heritage of the centuries that have slipped from the shoulders of Life.

But we, who are concerned solely with the customs that relate to us in our daily life, must resist the great temptation to wander along the highways and byways of the Old World, glimpsing the customs of yesterday as they blend with the customs of to-day. Fancy, if we permitted it, would lead us into an intricate maze of facts, fears, superstitions, from which it would be difficult to escape.

And so we leave it here, recognizing with Sigmund Freud that "The man of prehistoric times lives on, unchanged, in our Unconscious."

CHAPTER IX

GIFT-MAKING

The friendly and flowing savage, who is he? Is he waiting for civilization, or is he past it, and mastering it? —WALT WHITMAN.

Every human being has two personalities: an archaic, primitive, childlike, unadapted personality, and a modern, sophisticated, adult, and to all appearances, adapted personality. —ANDRE TRIDON.

PRIMITIVE REASONS FOR GIFT-MAKING

SO simply and naturally has gift-making slipped into our scheme of things that we scarcely recognize its presence. Yet, like most human proclivities, it has a primitive background that reaches far back into antiquity.

From the very earliest periods, gift-making has existed in some form or other. Our savage ancestors made gifts habitually. But gift-giving in primitive life did not grow out of any thought or idea connected with generosity. It was not based upon the simple desire to give, or to please. There were other more selfish reasons, born of the circumstances and conditions of life in which early man found himself.

We know that primitive man was selfish. He was unutterably superstitious. He feared and distrusted strangers. He scorned the weak; he cringed before the strong. The conditions of his life made him so. And these conditions, as we shall presently see, gave fundamental reason for the custom of gift-making.

Whatever impulses primitive man may have had to share his possessions, or to make a gift of something which he would have preferred to keep for himself, grew out of fear. We can be pretty certain from what we know of the primitive nature that early man would not have parted with anything he wanted, unless he was afraid. It was usually some external condition, threatening his safety and well-being, that prompted the making of a gift. The whole principle of sacrifice in religious systems is based on this theory.

To Appease the Anger of the Gods.—There was probably nothing that primitive man feared more than the elements. He feared them because he could not understand them. The lightning ripping suddenly out of the sky and across the earth; the thunder rumbling angrily through the heavens; the wind tearing through the jungle in fury—all filled him with an overwhelming fear.

He did not reason that these were natural elements and that nothing he could possibly do would in any way affect them. He tried to control the wind and the rain by magic. He shot at the storm with his arrows. He chased the wind and shouted at the thunder. And when all his efforts failed, his fear increased.

What had he done to anger the gods? For surely the gods had sent these demons to punish him.

Out of this thought grew the idea of making gifts and sacrifices to the gods to appease their anger. Great mounds of earth were piled high and on them placed the offerings of the tribe. Sometimes food was the gift offered, and it was burned so that its fragrance might waft into the heavens and reach the nostrils of the gods.

So great a hold did this idea of gift-making to appease the anger of the gods take upon the primitive mind that even children were sacrificed. We are told that thousands of infants were sacrificed yearly to Moloch, hideous ox-headed god of the savage Phœnicians. The people gladly gave their children to the gods in return for safety, plenty, comfort.

Gifts to the Dead.—Early men feared the dead. Among some primitive peoples we find prevalent the thought that the dead send the thunder and the lightning. Among others we find the belief that the spirits of the dead haunt the homes of the living. Naturally, in his superstitious dread of those who were lifeless, primitive man gladly gave food and valuables as gifts, to keep the spirits happy. According to primitive reasoning, a spirit to whom gifts have been given will not do harm or injury to the giver.

Thus we find that, even in earliest times, it was a custom to bury with the dead valuable tribal possessions, great gifts of food, even clothing and implements. Of course, many people had the idea that the dead lived on in another world, and they buried food and necessities with the body so that the person who had died would not be in want on the journey. Nevertheless, it was a widespread belief that the dead could cause injury to the living, and we cannot fail to see that the element of fear must have entered into gift-making to the dead.

The Ahts bury gifts of blankets with their dead. The ancient Egyptians had precious ornaments and rich furniture buried with the men who died. The horse of a North American Indian was usually buried with him. Among the Comanches, when a man died it was customary to bury his favourite wife with him. Countless similar customs abound in savage life; and we cannot escape the fact that behind all these customs lurks the fear that perhaps the spirit will return to claim its possessions. And perhaps, in its anger, it will do injury to the living.

Therefore, among savage peoples, not only are the favourite belongings of the dead buried with them, but additional gifts are included to impress the spirits and keep them from haunting the spot.

Gifts to the Kings.—From gift-making to placate the angry gods and to appease the spirits of the dead, it would have been just a step to gift-making among the living. Kings must have been the recipients of gifts at a very early period.

We can imagine a tribesman making a gift of food or of implements to the tribal chief to win his esteem, and thus his protection. We can imagine a savage fellow sacrificing some treasured trinket to the Strong Man of the tribe, or the Wise Man, because of fear.

But more than all, we can imagine the people placing gifts at the feet of the king to insure happiness and prosperity for themselves. If they wanted sunshine and good weather, they probably sent a dozen sheep to the king. If they wanted a good harvest, they probably presented him with rare, costly skins and ornaments. If there was a famine, they possibly brought all their belongings in one great gift to win his approval and thus banish the curse of the famine.

Among many peoples, notably the early Egyptians, the king was considered a man-god with full control over the elements and the destinies of his people. Gifts would very naturally have suggested themselves to the people as a logical way to win the favour of the king, and thus be assured of peace and plenty. And in times of drought or famine, gifts would be made to appease the king, even as they were made to appease the gods in times of storm.

The Egyptians made great gifts to their kings. Others emulated the example thus set, and it became a widespread custom to make gifts to kings at various stated intervals. The Israelites, we are told, gave a tenth of all their grain, their wine, their cattle to the king. Others made gifts of pearls and fabrics, of gold, of sacred animals.

The custom of making gifts to kings spread everywhere, and even Christianity failed to wipe it out. Ambassadors, visiting foreign countries, brought valuable gifts to the regents. Kings visiting one another exchanged gifts. We are told that Queen Elizabeth received thousands upon thousands of gifts from her subjects at New Year. And even to-day, do we not hear frequently of gifts made to persons of power—our own President, for instance?

There is no doubt whatever that, no matter what other circumstances or purposes may have induced the making of the gift, there lurked behind it the unconscious desire to win the friendship of the person of power to suit one's own ends—even as the weak man of the primitive tribe made a gift to the tribal Strong Man in the desire to gain his friendship and protection.

The Bible gives expression to this thought. "A gift doth blind the eyes of the wise" (Deuteronomy, XVI, 19)—meaning, of course, that it is easy to obtain what one wants if one distributes gifts judiciously.

Ceremonious Aspect of Gift-making.—Among many peoples, the making of a gift became a sort of ceremony. We must realize that a gift meant far more to primitive man than it does to us. When he parted with a choice bearskin, or with a particularly sharp flint spear, he felt that he was parting with something akin to himself. In other words, he felt that the gift was actually a part of him.

Thus the exchange of gifts in primitive culture came to be a common way of ceremoniously binding two persons together. When the Dasuns of North Borneo exchanged weapons they were sworn friends. In central Celebes, even to-day, the exchange of gifts denotes lifelong friendship. In Baru the mere interchange of gifts is recognized as a ceremony for establishing friendship.

We are told that an elaborate etiquette exists among chiefs in Patagonia. One chief is prevented from entering the *toldo* of another until gifts have been exchanged.

In New Guinea the natives exchange slight gifts with visitors as a sign of friendship. In Tonga gifts are made to new arrivals, to visitors, to natives who have been away and returned. The Ceramese habitually make ceremonious friendship by exchanging gifts. The Greek host and guest, records tells us, broke a die, each keeping half in token of their friendship.

Travellers, coming in contact with strange peoples, habitually propitiate them by gifts. Two results are achieved. Gratification caused by the worth of the thing given tends to beget a friendly mood in the person approached; and there is a tacit expression of the donor's desire to please, which has a like effect. It is from the last of these that gift-making as a ceremony proceeds.

We can understand how, in primitive life, the ceremonious exchange of gifts would have been a symbol of peace and friendship (see p. 150). It has retained this character to the present day. We do not make gifts to people we dislike, as a rule. And we feel always a little more friendly toward the person who has made a gift to us. Though the exchange of gifts is no longer accompanied by ceremony—like building a huge fire among the Africans, or like smoking the calumet among the Indians—we still have certain forms of ceremonious survival. The banquet at which a loving-cup is presented, the graduation exercises at which the diplomas are presented, the military exercises at which medals are presented—all these are examples.

Gifts in Warfare.—Gift-making was a common method of settling disputes and making peace in early times. Among many African tribes, when peace was declared between two tribes, each tribe would contribute a gift of food, and a peace feasting would take place. Here we have two symbols of friendship—eating food together and exchanging gifts.

Among North American Indians it was a common custom for the chiefs to exchange gifts after a war. It was only after the exchange of gifts that the calumet was passed around.

Some peoples, upon making peace, required that the offending tribe or village send a gift to show their friendliness. Thus, when two villages in the New Hebrides culminate a term of warfare, peace cannot be declared until a gift is received by whichever village considers itself to have been in the right. The gift is usually in the form of pigs.

Gifts Become Obligatory.—"It is proof of great thought to separate thought from habit," says Cicero.

Spencer, in his "Studies in Sociology" (vol. III), separates thought from habit in gift-making. He tells us how little by little gifts which were at one time voluntary and one-sided, growing out of the first crude thoughts of man, became obligatory, reciprocal, habitual.

At first primitive man would have made a gift to the Strong Man or the Wise Man because he wanted to do so, because he felt safer and more secure after having done so. But later the Strong Man or the Wise Man would expect gifts, and if he did not receive them he would make it uncomfortable for the other fellow. Thus gift-making became, in a sense, obligatory, habitual. And it is only natural that the weak should have been the donors, the strong the recipients.

Early man made gifts to the tribal chief, to the gods, to the king, because he was afraid of what the chief, or the gods, or the king might do. Modern man very frequently makes gifts because he is afraid of what people will say.

With the ceremonious exchange of gifts to denote peace and friendship, gift-making became reciprocal. If a chief sent a dozen pigs to the chief in the next village, he expected a gift in return. If he didn't receive it, he very probably declared war upon that village. In certain sections of New Guinea, even to-day, visitors are expected to return trifles of some sort to the natives who present them with gifts, if they wish to be secure from harm during their stay.

Vanity undoubtedly enters, to some extent, into the exchange of gifts. One chief would like to feel that he can make as rich and impressive a gift as the other. To-day we do not like to feel that the Christmas gift we have received is more attractive and impressive than the one we sent.

GIFTS IN COURTSHIP AND MARRIAGE

Who knows what lover first stole through the night to leave a gift where his sweetheart slept? Perhaps a string of bear claws, perhaps a curious shell from the sea, perhaps a soft, warm skin—to tell his tale of love.

And who knows what maiden first fashioned a vessel that her lover might drink from the spring? Or fashioned a bag from the hide of some beast that he might carry his flints with convenience?

But all these fascinating sidelights are behind the pages of history; we cannot be certain whether or not they are true. However, we can be reasonably certain that gift-making between the sexes began when love began, and we know that love illumined some of the early pages in the book of life.

We can see, of course, why the exchange of gifts would have entered into courtship at at early period. One of the quickest and simplest ways to win a person's favour is to present him, or her, with a gift. There is a feeling of gratification. An attitude of friendliness is created.

This thought possibly took a strong hold upon the primitive mind, for among various peoples we find the mere exchange of gifts constituting the entire marriage ceremony. The acceptance of the gift by the woman implies the acceptance of the man. This type of marriage ceremony exists even to-day among the Khakyens.

Among the North American Indians, when a young man wished to court a young woman he made gifts, not to her, but to her parents. The gifts were usually blankets, a belt of wampum, a bracelet, etc. If the gifts were accepted by the parents, the betrothal was sanctioned. This is a form of modified marriage by purchase.

The same sort of custom prevails to a certain extent among the Japanese. The sending of specified gifts by the man to the parents of the woman constitutes an important part of the ceremony. Once the gifts have been received and accepted, the contract is considered complete. Neither party is at liberty to withdraw.

In Greece lovers courted their sweethearts with rich gifts. Flowers were a favourite gift from the man to the woman. We are told that the doors of some maidens were always banked high with flowers from their suitors.

The flower seems to be a widespread emblem or token of love. O'Brien relates this fanciful tale of love and the flower among the Marquesans in the South Seas:

If a man seeks a woman, he wears a white flower over his ear, and if his love grows ardent, he wears a red rose or hibiscus. But if he tires, he puts some green thing in their place. *Bon dieu!* That is the depth of ignominy for the woman scorned. I remember one girl who was made light of that way in church. She stayed a day hidden in the hills weeping, and then she threw herself from a cliff.

The Polynesian woman in love wears a red hibiscus behind her ear. As a rule, it is given her by her lover.

Flowers make acceptable betrothal gifts to-day. "The Book of Etiquette" says:

Expensive gifts should never be exchanged during an engagement, barring, of course, the engagement ring. The young man may present his prospective bride with books, flowers, or candy, but articles of wearing apparel are considered bad taste.

Friends of the bride-to-be are advised that they may send her, with their congratulations,

Pleasing bits of chinaware, glassware, and sometimes even silver. Odd pieces of bric-a-brac and quaint, unusual gifts and antiques are always acceptable. Markings on gifts are usually in the maiden name of the bride, but if any doubt be felt as to which she would prefer, it is best to ask her.

The Wedding Gift.—The exchange of gifts has always played a conspicuous part in marriage. For many generations it has been the custom in Sweden for the girl who is betrothed to be married to make a shirt as a wedding gift for her husband. He wears it on his marriage day, puts it away, and wears it again when he is buried. This seems to correspond with the custom of the bridal veil (see p. 242). If his wife dies first and he re-marries, custom demands that he burn the shirt on the eve of the second wedding.

In Java, when a woman marries she throws aside all her dolls and childish trinkets which are preserved for just this purpose. A fire is built and the trinkets thrown into it, in evidence of her determination to become a woman. The friends who have assembled for this ceremony of burning the childhood possessions congratulate the bride-

(Courtesy of American Museum of Natural History, New York)

How the Indians kept records on birch bark.
Each little figure carries an important message.

(*Courtesy of Metropolitan Museum of Art*)

Flemish, 15th Century. Model of a Carmelite scribe at work.

to-be and make several valuable gifts to recompense her for the things she has destroyed.

An exchange of gifts among the Aru Islanders constitutes marriage. The same is true of many other savage tribes. The man usually presents the girl with some trinket or ornament; she usually makes with her own hands something he can wear or use for decoration. A Timorese woman can bestow no greater mark of attachment upon her lover than to present him with something she herself has worn—a flower, a pin, a comb.

It is surprising that among certain peoples marriage is not considered complete until the bride and groom have exchanged gifts. There is a Kaffir custom, for instance, which prevents the bride from eating the food of the bridegroom's kraal "until her presents have arrived." As eating from the kraal constitutes marriage, we can see how important gifts are to the savage mind.

In South Celebes the marriage gifts between a bride and groom are very numerous. The favourite gift of the groom is a pair of ginger roots which have grown in the earth together. To the natives the "twin" ginger root is symbolic of marriage—the close union of man and wife.

It is still a modern custom for the bride and groom to exchange gifts before marriage. Somehow the very exchange of gifts seems to draw them closer. Though few realize it, and fewer still would admit it, the gift which the groom gives to his bride bears trace of the old form of marriage by purchase. He is more certain that the woman "belongs" to him when she wears his diamond wrist watch or his diamond lavallière. The thought exists in his subconscious primitive mind; it is there if he will search for it. "The man of prehistoric times lives on, unchanged, in our Unconscious."

As for the woman, who will deny that she does not have an instinctive sense of possession as she knits for her lover a tie, or purchases for him a wallet? We cannot escape it. We all have our share of the primitive personality; and though the mode of life has changed with the passing generations, the primitive instincts and impulses remain.

Gifts of the Guests.—Among the early Dutch, as among other early peoples, it was the custom to present the newly married couple with gifts of utility, and so start them out in life. The custom of presenting wedding gifts is to-day firmly established in our social code and "everyone who receives an invitation is expected to send the bride a gift."

The savage tribes of Africa and of Australia are in the habit of making gifts of food to the newly married pair. Among the early Anglo-Saxons a rich spice cake was considered an appropriate gift from a wedding guest. In Colonial America the governor presented the newly married couple with a certain amount of grain and flour. Food, being a prime factor in the business of living, has always suggested itself as a sensible and appropriate gift.

But in modern times, among civilized peoples, food holds a place of lesser importance, because it is ordinarily available to everyone.

The wedding gift is the prettiest and most useful article within one's means. China and silver are always appropriate, and cut glass, linen, books and even checks or gold pieces are most acceptable.

It is interesting to note that people of the upper classes threw goldpieces to the peasant bride and groom when Europe was young; that concealing goldpieces on the person of the bride was part of the marriage ceremony among certain North American Indians; and that there are even to-day, in Mexico, people who cast money to the bride and groom.

There is a slight prejudice against giving money as a present at a wedding or at any other time [says "The Book of Etiquette"] but one has only to see the joy that the bride and groom get out of spending the money over and over again before they finally do spend it to have this prejudice dispelled.

Silver and linen are usually marked with the initials of the bride, more often than not with the initials of her maiden name. If there is any doubt as to which she prefers and one is not able to find out indirectly, it is permissible to ask her.

Gifts should always be accompanied by the cards of the donors, but these should be removed when they are on display.

The custom of displaying gifts, however, is falling into disuse. People of better taste object to this old custom which has been handed down to them from an earlier and less conservative generation. It was once the universal custom to display all gifts on the day of the marriage; royalty and peasantry alike practised the custom. It crossed the ocean to the United States and prevailed for a while in fashionable society. But it is practically obsolete to-day.

Perhaps it was out of this distaste for publicly displaying wedding gifts that the idea of the private Trousseau Tea evolved. The bride-to-be simply invites her most intimate young women friends to her home, and tea is served informally. The gifts, and the trousseau if she likes, are on display in an adjoining room so that her friends may see them. But after the tea the gifts are packed away and are not "on display" to any one who may call.

OTHER KINDS OF GIFTS

In early life, gift-making among the sexes was regulated with great precision. Certain gifts were tabu to the woman; others were tabu to the man. As we advance in the social scale, we find that the same sort of regulation in gift-making exists between the various castes or classes.

For instance, among the Israelites it was the custom to give a tenth of the grain and wine and cattle to the king. Among the Egyptians, only the finest fabrics and the most elaborately wrought ewers might be presented to the king. Among various African tribes, only a pure white elephant made an acceptable gift to the chieftain. Even in religious sacrifice, which is a form of gift-making to the gods, definite animals or articles are specified.

Very possibly the custom of making gifts at definite times grew out of the custom of making gifts of a definite kind. For instance, in early Rome it was the custom for the people to carry small trinkets as gifts to the senators under whose protection they found themselves. It became a definite custom to present definite gifts to the senators. But when? Naturally, a definite time had to be arranged to avoid confusion and to make the little ceremony of gift-making impressive and effective.

The New Year's Gift.—The Romans decided upon the first day of the new year as an appropriate time to make their presentations to the senators. And it has been the custom ever since for friends to exchange gifts on New Year's Day.

Let us see why this day was chosen. There are two possible explanations. In the first place, New Year's Day was a time of celebration and thus a propitious time to make gifts. But perhaps the main reason for making gifts at this time was to invite protection from the senators during the ensuing year.

Suetonius and Tacitus both mention the custom of making gifts on New Year's Day. Claudius made it a law that presents could actually be demanded on this day, but on no other day during the year. According to the records that have come down to us, the gifts were usually trinkets of some sort—the fancy of the moment, no doubt—although there are some instances of exquisite fabrics and of wearing apparel being presented to men in high office. There are also instances of gifts of flowers and fruit, usually in pretty baskets.

The Romans who settled in Britain introduced to their neighbours the custom of making gifts on New Year's Day. It became the custom among the early English to clean the chimney on this day so that luck could descend and remain all year. Among us, instead of "cleaning the chimney" we "clean the slate," and make good resolutions for the following year. Perhaps this custom of cleaning the chimney so that good luck might descend has something to do with the Santa Claus myth. Surely Santa Claus with his pack of gifts brings "good luck" to the household!

From Britain the custom of making gifts on New Year's Day spread all over Europe. In Spain and in France the habit took firm hold. Even in faraway Persia it became the custom to exchange eggs as gifts on New Year's Day. Here we see another significance: The beginning of life, of creation, is symbolized by the egg. New Year's Day is the beginning, or creation, of a new year. Thus, it seemed to the Persians, no gift could be more appropriate at this time than the gift of eggs. The same significance is seen in our gift of coloured eggs to children at Easter-time.

History records that during the reign of Queen Elizabeth the custom of presenting New Year's gifts was carried to great extremes. Gifts of extravagant value were presented to the Queen, and the people made many gifts among themselves.

One authority tells us that not the least valuable of the gifts which the Queen received was a pair of black silk knit stockings. Such stockings were rare, indeed. Until that time the Queen had worn cloth hose. But the gift so delighted her that she vowed never to wear cloth hose again. Nor did she!

It was during this period of extravagant gift-making that gloves became a popular New Year's gift. Like the inevitable box of candy of modern life, the pair of gloves became the obvious gift when one was unable to make another selection.

The Christmas Gift.—With us, the New Year's gift is not quite as popular as the Christmas gift. Everyone—except a Scrooge—exchanges gifts at Christmas-time.

It was a custom among the Romans for the priest to put a box on all outgoing ships. The people were required to put something into it—a gift in the form of a trinket or a piece of money. It was known as the Priest's Box.

When the ship was ready to sail, the box was sealed and went to sea with it. Among the Scotch and the Irish it was a custom to throw a shoe after the ship to insure its safe return; perhaps this Priest's Box was intended to serve the same purpose.

But authorities tell us that when the ship returned the box was given to the Priest; it was placed aside until Christmas, at which time mass was said and it was opened. Sometimes the money was kept by the church; sometimes it was distributed among the poor. It is related that frequently, at the opening of the Priest Box—which later became known as the Christmas Box—those who had not placed anything in it came forward and offered gifts in the form of money or jewellery. The purpose was to supplicate the saints and win forgiveness for sins. If the truth be known, it is for very much the same reason that Christmas gifts are often exchanged to-day. We feel a little better, a little more self-sacrificing, a little nobler when we have made others happy through gifts.

During the early period of Christianity it was the custom for poor men and women to sing carols in the streets at Christmas-time. They would be given food, clothing, and money not because it was of the carols they sang, most likely, but because it was the custom to do so. And custom, among superstitious peoples, is sacred. They were afraid that evil would befall them if they did not make gifts to the singers who carolled Christ's praise.

Another custom was for men who were skilled in carpentry to make miniature reproductions of the Christ child in the stable. Some really remarkable reproductions were made, showing the cradle, Mary, the Child, even the Wise Men bringing their gifts. There are several such reproductions still in existence.

The makers paraded the streets at Christmas showing their handiwork to the people. They even went into homes to show their "cradles," as they were called. If by any chance some clever fellow had added a new little twist—such as painting the whole thing or illumining it in some way—he was surrounded by an admiring crowd who carried him around in triumph. If he were as clever an actor as he was a carpenter he could make the superstitious people believe that he was a prophet—divinely inspired. And his gifts were rich accordingly!

The exchange of gifts at Christmas-time possibly grew out of the desire to emulate the amazing unselfishness of Christ. In later life, of course, the exchange of gifts would have become traditional, customary. And a certain joyousness, induced by the exchange of gifts and the merry-making accompanying it, inspired a genuine generosity.

The custom was nurtured in Germany. Here it became the habit to make periodic exchange of gifts among friends, relatives, acquaintances. It became an obligation, and to escape it the man with many friends sometimes took a trip abroad at this period.

From Germany, the custom of Christmas gift-making spread over Europe. It crossed the sea and was brought to the struggling colonists who had tried to cut loose from all the Old-World influences. It has become more and more an institution, as the generations have slipped by, and to-day we exchange gifts at Christmas as a matter of course.

Gifts to Children.—We know from actual records that gift-making to children goes far back into prehistory. There are at various museums actual dolls, animals, and other toys which have been taken out of the long buried tombs of infants.

Love of offspring appears to have been prevalent even in primitive times, despite the records of infanticide. The Fijians, famous for cannibalism and savagery, are greatly attached to their children, and the children to their parents. The Tongans and New Zealanders are said to be extremely fond of, and kind to, their children. Among the Greenlanders, passed by in the march of civilization, the bonds of parental love seem stronger than with almost any other people.

We can very easily picture a savage father of long ago bringing a curious shell for his child to play with. We can see a savage mother carefully whittling a flint or bone toy that her child might have something with which to be amused. Among these primitive peoples, marriage was not considered binding until a child was born. The birth of the child, therefore, must have been an occasion of great celebration, and perhaps all the clansmen or tribesmen presented gifts to the new-born child. It would have been a ceremony—to show the child he was welcome and among friends.

But as we have said, there are actual records to prove that gift-making to children existed at an early date. It is not necessary to peer behind the unknown and try to fathom the primitive mind.

Painted clay puppets—some in the form of humans, some in the form of animals—were given to early Egyptian children as playthings. We know that these were toys, and not amulets or fetishes, for they are found only in the tombs of infants or young children. (See illustrations.) There have also been found in the tombs of Egyptian children small wooden carts, houses, and ships. An ancient Egyptian ball is in existence which has small stones inside of it, so that when one shakes it, it rattles. This was probably the forerunner of the rattle as we know it today.

The early Romans had a method of adoption in which the birth of the child was simulated. The man who adopted the child gave it rich gifts, to prove that he was able to take care of it.

In ancient Greece a great ceremony took place on the tenth day after the birth of the child. A feast was given by the parents—the purpose, we are told, was to imply the father's acknowledgment of the child's legitimacy—and the friends and relatives who were invited brought toys of metal or clay for the infant. The mother was presented with rich painted vases.

Gifts have always accompanied christenings. During the Middle Ages the child was usually presented by its godparents with silver or gold spoons. It is very possible that the phrase "born with a silver spoon in his mouth" arose from this old custom.

The custom of presenting the children with gifts at Christmas was most pronounced among the Germans in early life. *Kris Kringle* is their name for Santa Claus. It is derived from *Krist Kindli* which means Christ Child. We can understand why the holiday would have been recognized as being particularly a child's holiday.

Saint Nicholas, or Santa Claus, is regarded as the patron saint of Christmas. The old nursery myth is that he comes down the chimney with a pack on his back to leave gifts for good children.

It is possible that this myth originated with the custom of cleaning the chimney at the beginning of the new year to enable good luck to enter the household (see p. 280). A housewife, busy cleaning the chimney at about the Christmas period, might have whispered to her children, to keep them out of mischief, that if they were good Santa Claus would come down the chimney and bring gifts for them. Tremendously impressed, the children would have hurried with the news to their little friends. And so it would have spread, becoming finally the popular nursery myth that it is to-day.

CHAPTER X

Correspondence, and the History of Writing

As the art of writing and reading spread, came that old desire, that pathetic desire so common among human beings, to astonish some strange and remote person by writing down something striking, some secret one knew, some strange thought, or even one's name, so that long after one had gone one's way, it might strike upon the sight and mind of another reader. Even in Sumeria men scratched on walls, and all that remains to us of the ancient world, its rocks, its buildings, is plastered thickly with the names and the boasting of those foremost among human advertisers, its kings.

—H. G. Wells.

THE BEGINNING OF WRITTEN RECORDS

THE communicating of facts, thoughts, ideas, or fancies through writing belongs to an advanced stratum of development.

We know that the world has had a long, dim history which has been left practically unrecorded. We know that it has had an intermediate history which has bequeathed to us a wealth of material relics, but still no written records of what man thought or felt. The third great period of social development, of which we to-day are a part, is illumined by the invention of writing and its astonishing development. We can scarcely conceive of the tremendous influence which writing, and its sister art, printing, have had upon human affairs.

Of course, we cannot be certain when writing began, any more than we can be certain when speech began, or faith, or art, or any other human quality which is based upon long ages of development. Not even the historian can definitely tell us when writing began. Nor can the archæologist go back any farther than the records which he understands.

We can only *guess* that some early dreamer sat on the bank of a river and with experimental twig or finger made curious, fanciful patterns in the wet clay. We can only *guess* that some Palæolithic caveman, drawing bears and buffalos on the wall of his cave was attempting to express some crude thought that crowded through his mind—a thought lost to us for ever. We can only *guess* that infant systems of writing lie buried with forgotten civilizations, and that at some future time they may yet be discovered.

But let us see what we do know about the origin of writing and the first written records of mankind. We know that before any genuine sort of writing made its appearance, a kind of picture writing existed. The North American Indians appear to have been highly advanced in this art. Examples of their picture writing show us how even the most elaborate messages could be conveyed through this simple means.

Picture writing is merely a system of conveying thoughts or facts through pictures. There is in use in Europe to-day a timetable which has small black signs or pictures on it for the purpose of guiding tourists. A tiny cup on this timetable indicates a place where refreshments may be had. Various other signs indicate things of importance to the traveller.

This simple and elementary method of conveying ideas constituted the first kind of writing. It existed among the early Egyptians, the early Babylonians, the Chinese, the American Indians. It exists to-day among savage and untaught people all over the world. It is the simplest, crudest, and most elementary way of recording ideas. It bears the same relation to writing as gesture and imitative sound bear to speech (see p. 126).

At first picture writing was a device rather than a system. It helped man express his ideas, not only to his fellows but to himself. He devised the method of drawing pictures for his own convenience and satisfaction.

There could have been no attempt, at this early stage, to create a definite system. That would have come later. At first each picture would represent one thought in itself. The person who saw the picture would be obliged to supply by imagination what was lacking. We are inclined to believe that there is a long train of thoughts and ideas behind every crude drawing found on the walls of Palæolithic caves.

Systems of Complex Picture Writing.—But gradually, as picture writing developed, it grew into a system of signs for expressing ideas; that is, two or more pictures were combined into what we call "words" to express, not one simple idea, but a trend of thought. The Chinese to this day employ this type of "pictographic writing."

A form of complex picture writing is found in Egypt. It is familiarly known as hieroglyphic writing, and many excellent specimens are to be found on monuments, mummy cloths, temple walls, etc. Photographs of hieroglyphic writing are reproduced on these pages.

Another form of hieroglyphic writing which existed in Egypt and which was used by the priests is known as hieratic writing. It is much simpler and the characters take on a flowing form, like our script. This type of writing was used in letters, in the keeping of accounts, the writing of psalms, deeds, etc. The hieroglyphic writing was used on the monuments and the temples, and wherever a decorative effect was required.

The Egyptian hieroglyphic writing is one of the finest survivals of picture writing we have. Some monumental examples date back almost to 5000 B.C. The discovery of the Rosetta stone by the French engineers attached to Napoleon's expedition to Egypt in 1799 was the master key to the reading of this hieroglyphic writing.

While the Egyptians were developing their kind of picture writing, still another kind was developing among the Babylonians. At first these people had a crude and primitive picture writing which shows signs of having

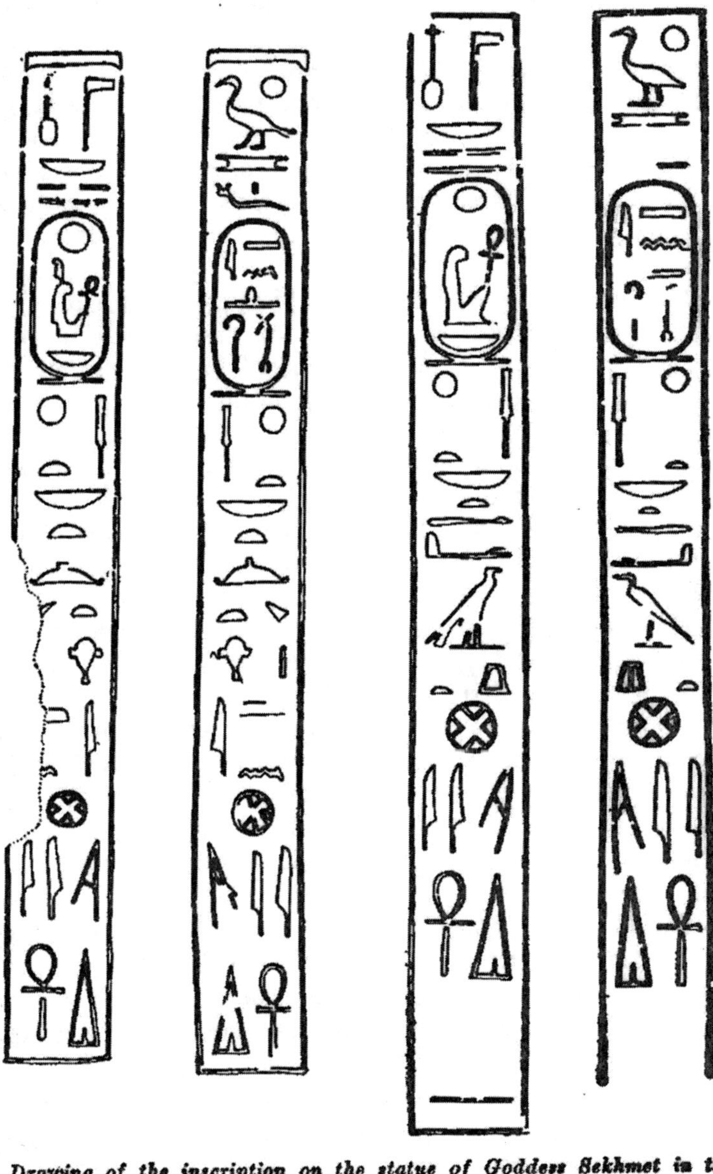

Drawing of the inscription on the statue of Goddess Sekhmet in the Metropolitan Museum of Art. A fine specimen of hieroglyphic writing.

emerged, very possibly, out of hieroglyphic writing. Existing specimens in no case show more than half-a-dozen lines.

The now famous cuneiform writing (from Latin, *cuneus,* a wedge) replaced the simple picture writing of the Babylonians. It was invented by a people known as the Sumerians. They used the pictures to represent sounds apart from ideas—the first people to do this. With a wedge-formed implement they wrote first on stone, later on clay.

This cuneiform writing of the Sumerians spread with amazing rapidity. It was adopted by the Babylonians and by them passed on to the Assyrians. The latter simplified some of the characters and conventionalized many. Its influence passed even to Egypt and hieroglyphic writing ceased to be simply pictographic; it became a sound-sign system. This method of writing became widespread; it was used as a means of correspondence among most of the Mediterranean peoples, and as far inland as the Persian Gulf.

The word "cuneiform" was used for the first time in 1700 by Thomas Hyde, well-known as a professor of Hebrew in the University of Oxford. The term has found general acceptance among historians. But another familiar and popular name for this type of writing is "arrowhead writing."

The Origin of Alphabetic Writing.—It is to the eternal glory of the Phœnicians that they invented alphabetic writing.

The word "alphabet" itself is from the Greek names for the first two letters, "a" and "b"—*alpha* and *beta.* But the Phœnician alphabet existed long before the Greeks attempted to write their traditions and their mythology for record.

Cuneiform writing was, of course, the great impetus that led to the origin of the Phœnician alphabet. The Egyptians, the Babylonians, the Assyrians, and other peoples were using a method of writing whereby articulate sounds were being represented to the eye by complex forms and figures. But we can understand how unwieldy this system of writing must have been. It did not lend itself to ordinary or extensive use; it was cumbersome and complicated.

The Phœnicians took the one feature of Egyptian writing which could be universally applied, disentangled it from the jumbled mass of signs and pictures, made of it a unit, and created therefrom a system, or method, of writing based upon an alphabet. They achieved the greatest step forward in the art of writing.

Because of its obvious simplicity and its universal application, this form of alphabetic writing quickly spread. It was carried everywhere. It spread over the whole Asiatic continent. It found its way to Crete, to Thera, to Greece, to Italy. It passed on into Europe and firmly established itself there. It became, in a word, the writing system of the whole civilized world.

Early Writing Materials.—Before proceeding with the further development of writing, as it concerns correspondence, let us glance at the materials which were being used. With what did early man write? And on what did he record his thoughts, his ideas?

Sculptured records on stone are, of course, the earliest records we have. Much of the literature of the old civilization was written on clay baked into stone. Photographic examples are given.

When portable manuscripts became desirable, many materials were pressed into service. The skins of animals, the leaves of plants, linen, fragments of tile—all were used. There is a charming Pompeian wall painting which shows a girl holding a double tablet of clay in her hand, her "pencil" to her chin as though she is pondering. She is evidently writing a love letter.

For writing on clay tablets a slender, four-sided piece of wood was used. It was a forerunner of our pencil.

The ancient Egyptians wrote chiefly on linen or wood

with a brush or reed pen. But for literary work, for official documents and for the "Book of the Dead" they used papyrus. The papyrus is a tall, graceful plant, the pith of which was pressed flat and thin and joined with others to form strips. On these strips of papyrus records were written and painted. Fragile though it may seem papyrus

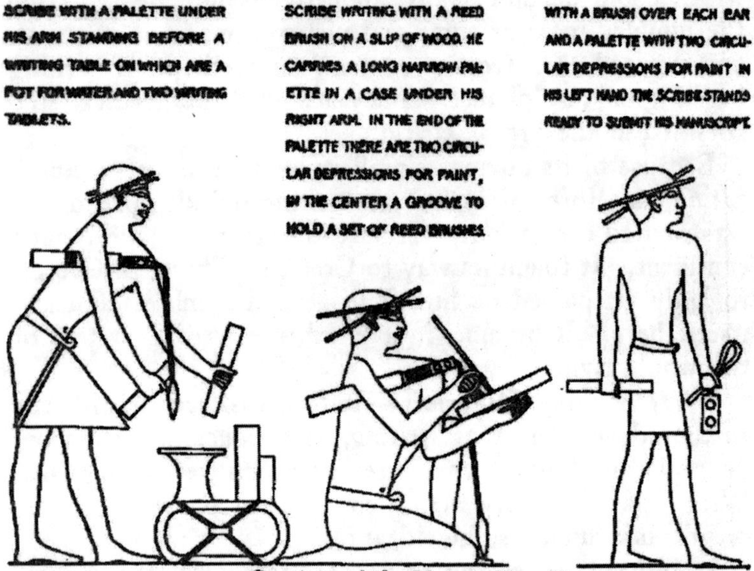

Courtesy of the Metropolitan Museum of Art.

FROM WALL-RELIEFS IN THE TOMB OF KAGEMNI AT SAKKARA. DYN. V (ABOUT 2730-2625 B.C.)

FROM A WALL-RELIEF IN A MASTABA-TOMB AT GIZEH. DYN. IV (ABOUT [illegible] B.C.)

SCRIBES

is very enduring and there is a piece in existence which is said to date back to 3500 B.C. Some priceless records, indeed, are preserved for all time on the papyrus pages of Egypt's literature.

The use of papyrus descended to the Greeks and Romans. From its name comes our word "paper"; and from the "roll" or *volumen* of papyrus manuscript comes our word "volume" as applied to a book.

The Greeks and Romans wrote upon papyrus, which

(Courtesy of Metropolitan Museum of Art)

Interesting assortment of antient Egyptian scarabs 12th to 18th Dynasty.

(Courtesy of Metropolitan Museum of Art)

A beautiful old Greek vase, figured. The exterior shows three women preparing wine to serve.

they burnished with a polishing stone, with a reed cut to a point. This reed writing instrument was very similar to our pen. They used an ink made from cuttlefish. The early scribes were well-equipped to write enduring records of the things they did, and thought, and felt, and wondered about.

The Greeks originally followed the example of the Phœnicians and wrote from right to left. But later the priests decided to write the oracles in the opposite direction, because they believed that the direction toward the right was of good omen. They reformed the habit of writing, and originated the custom of writing from left to right. We still observe this custom, or habit, and undoubtedly always will.

It is interesting to note the antiquity of carrying the pen or pencil behind the ear. We notice the following passage in the life of S. Odo: "He who saw a pen sticking above his ear, in the manner of a writer." By the 7th century feather pens were common, and double inkstands, for red and black ink, were being used.

The First Books.—With language, alphabet, and materials, with reasoning faculties and imagination, man was beginning to write of the things that interested him. The long pent-up desire for self-expression found outlet in crude attempts to write down the thoughts and ideas that crowded through his mind. There was born the overwhelming wish to tell, to confide, to record, to astonish. Man became distinctly conscious of his own imaginative and creative faculties; he found keen pleasure in writing down, as far as he was able, the traditions which formerly he had orally related.

The influence of writing upon human thought cannot be estimated. Man's experiences no longer died with him, unless he so desired. He was able to record his thoughts and his secrets. He was able to communicate those thoughts to men hundreds of miles away. He was able to share his own knowledge, and share in the knowledge of others. Slowly, gradually, surely, writing exerted its magic influence upon the mind of man, and priceless treasures of knowledge were being stored for us who were fortunate enough to come at a later day.

But we must not imagine that the full benefits of writing were flashed all at once upon a waiting world. At first writing was a slow and painful process. Books were written word for word by the author, and his copy was the only copy. There was no way of multiplying it, except by

A monk of the 10th century laboriously copying word for word the text of the Bible. This was the only way of multiplying the number of books.

copying it all over again. Naturally, such books were rare and costly.

And we must remember that the book must at first have been a sort of mystery to the ordinary person. Only the priest and the student understood it. For a long time the benefits of writing were denied the world as a whole; but with the discovery of paper a tremendous stride was taken.

Concerning the great impetus to thought which writing had upon mankind, H. G. Wells says:

From the first writings onward, a new sort of tradition, an enduring and immortal tradition, began in the minds of men. Life, through mankind, grew thereafter more and more distinctly conscious of itself and its world. It is a thin streak of intellectual growth we trace in history, at first in a world of tumultuous ignorance and forgetfulness; it is like a mere line of light coming through the chink in an opening door into a darkened room; but slowly it widens, it grows. At last came a time in the history of Europe when the door, at the push of the printer, began to open more rapidly. Knowledge flared up, and as it flared, it ceased to be the privilege of a favoured minority.

The Discovery of Paper.—Papyrus, of course, was a form of paper. But the supply of papyrus was limited. It had to be fastened strip by strip, and there was neither a uniform size nor quality. Learned men, eager to set down and record their thoughts and experiences, began to dream of better materials and easier methods of writing.

Paper as we know it originated in China. It was in use as early as the 2d century B.C., but it was not until the 8th century A.D. that the secret of making it was learned from the Chinese. During an encounter with the Arab Moslems several Chinese who were skilled papermakers were taken, and they taught the art to the Arabs. Paper manufacture flourished in Arabia from the 9th century onward. But it was not until close to the 14th century that really good paper was made in Europe, Italy leading in its manufacture.

Origin and Development of Printing.—Now we come to one of the most fascinating phases of human development—the discovery of the printing press and its effect upon the world. It must have been like the rise of a glorious new sun. What one read before, thousands were now able to share. What was once the privilege of a few became the property of all. Schoolbooks were cheapened and placed within the reach of everyone. Mankind entered upon a new intellectual era.

You can see the immediate result, of course. As the books now being made were easier to read, simpler to understand, infinitely cheaper to buy, more people began to read. Quickly the art of printing spread. Quickly books were multiplied. And quickly the firebrand set intellectual flames burning brightly all over Europe.

At first an abundance of Bibles made their appearance. Then the first great European literatures began. Language lost a great deal of its dialect; it became polished, literary. More and more books made their appearance; they became still easier to read, still less like the student's mystery they once had been. And the world read.

The first printing from movable type appears to have been achieved by Coster in Haarlem (Holland) at about 1445. At about the same period the famous Gutenberg was printing at Mainz. Almost simultaneously printers began to turn out books in Italy and when, in 1477, Caxton set up his press in Westminster, printing was established as a new and remarkably useful art.

Like all other great advances, printing permeated the social fabric and its influence coloured the lives of the people. In all the great ages, or stages, of development, intercommunication was the great impetus toward the strengthening of the social life of the multitudes.

Gesture, the very first kind of intercommunication, made two savage fellows friendly when they might otherwise have fallen upon each other. Speech separated man for ever from the lower animals; it bound men together in common intercourse. And it brought into being the story-teller, the myth-maker, the wanderer from clan to clan, from tribe to tribe, from people to people, carrying the folk tales and traditions wherever he went. Writing, as a means of intercommunication, broadened the intellectual horizon, made it possible for man to share his thoughts with another many miles away, made it possible for him to record his experiences to entertain or enlighten others.

Printing made mass thought possible. It set the mind of mankind free. It placed knowledge within the reach of the lower classes. It enabled one part of Europe to know what the other part was doing, saying, thinking, planning. It gave to all of mankind a better, clearer, saner knowledge of itself and of the world.

To the present generation, printing is no longer the marvel, the astonishing achievement, it seemed to earlier peoples. Like so many other of the good things of life, it is simply accepted. Yet printing has, directly and indirectly, done more to change the manners and customs of man than any other one development. Out of printing grew advertising, and advertising is subtly, surely, inevitably changing the mass mode of living. Advertising seeks out the most remote corners of the globe, discovers what is needed by the people there, and supplies the demand. It turns its searchlight upon the smallest town, the tiniest community, and tells the people there precisely what the woman in the metropolis is wearing, doing, saying, how she is entertaining, where she is going.

With this influence constantly and increasingly at work, it is inevitable that many age-old traditions be at last discarded—or at least changed sufficiently to accord with the new order of things as portrayed in the advertising pages. No history could give to posterity a clearer knowledge of our daily life and our customs of living than the advertising pages of our modern newspapers and magazines. They are a precise record of what we are doing and wearing; how we are entertaining; what we are using—*what we want.*

We cannot leave the subject of intercommunication and its influence upon the manners and customs of man without mentioning the moving pictures. They, too, have changed to a certain degree the mode of living. When the slum girl is able to see how her millionaire sister lives, and when the millionaire girl is able to see how her slum sister lives, there is bound to be a reaction of some sort. But the influence of the moving pictures has, as yet, scarcely been felt. It will be the pleasant task of some later writer to record the effect of the moving pictures upon mass life.

The telephone, the telegraph, the radio, the wireless—all are modes of intercommunication. But they are merely like links in the great chain of intellectual progress set free by the printing press.

THE SOCIAL INVITATION

Writing very early became a device for making social affairs run more smoothly. Writing in the sense of books, newspapers, records, stories is one thing; writing in the sense of social correspondence, invitations, cards of greeting, congratulation, and condolence is quite another.

The North American Indians were among the first to use actual invitations. They burned their message on buckskin and sent it by a runner to the person for whom it was intended. Tribes also had a smoke message which they used to call their people together for purposes of feasting, celebrating, etc. This smoke message was used sometimes in warfare.

It appears that among the Indians, ever a hospitable people, the development of the invitation was rapid and marked. Long before 1600 the Algonquins were sending out "dinner invitations" in the form of specially cut blocks of wood about the size of the little finger. All those who received the bit of wood with its curious picture message knew that they were invited to attend the feast and celebration being given by the Algonquins. They came from far and wide to join the merrymaking.

Among early European peoples the invitation developed slowly. The peasantry, of course, had no need for any such thing as an invitation; if one of their number wished to celebrate at the public bar or in his home, he merely called all his friends together with as much proud noise as he could command. Among the upper classes a private messenger was sent to give the information orally.

By the time of Shakespeare the invitation had reached a fairly high point of development. The mode of the written invitation first found favour at court and then spread to the people in the cities. These invitations were written on huge sheets of white paper, by hand, the initial letters usually made by stamp and decorated with colour.

"So many guests invite as here are writ," says Shakespeare. The invitations were carried by pages or messengers to the homes of the people for whom they were intended, and usually an answer was required, in the manner of our acknowledgment.

The development of the wedding invitation was particularly marked. In small villages the wedding bells ringing sweetly from the church belfry were the only invitation. All the friends and neighbours gathered together to greet the bridal party. But in large towns and cities it became necessary to invite by written word those who were to attend the wedding ceremonies.

The following rare old invitation, written in 1786, was clipped by William Hone from a Cumberland (England) newspaper and incorporated by him in his famous "Table Book." Here is an exact reproduction of the invitation:

INVITATION

Suspend for one day your cares and your labours,
And come to this wedding, kind friends and good neighbours.

Notice is hereby given that the marriage of Isaac Pearson with Frances Atkinson will be solemnized in due form in the parish church of Lamplugh, in Cumberland, on Tuesday next, the 30th of May inst. (1786); immediately after which the bride and bridegroom with their attendants will proceed to Lonefoot, in the said parish, where the nuptials will be celebrated by a variety of rural entertainments.

Then come one and all,
At Hymen's soft call.
From Whitehaven, Workington, Harington, Dean,
Hail, Ponsonby, Blaing, and all places between;
From Egremont, Cockermouth, Barton, St. Bee's,
Cint, Kinnyside, Calder and parts such as these;
And the country at large may flock in if they please.

Such sports there will be as have seldom been seen,
Such wrestling and fencing, and dancing between,
And races for prizes, for frolic and fun
By horses and asses and dogs will be run,
That you'll go home happy—as sure as a gun.
In a word, such a wedding can ne'er fail to please;
For the sports of Olympus were trifles to these.

Nota Bene—You'll please observe that the day
Of this grand bridal pomp is the thirtieth of May,
When 'tis hoped that the sun, to enliven the sight,
Like the flambeau of Hymen, will deign to burn bright.

This specimen of an 18th-century wedding invitation is doubly valuable. Not only does it reveal to us the kind of wedding invitations that were being written and publicly printed in those days, but it gives us an excellent picture of the kind of weddings that were then in vogue. Can you imagine races by dogs and horses at the modern marriage? Can you imagine fencing and wrestling and the "country at large" flocking in?

Compare the above invitation with this example of the correct invitation of to-day:

Mr. and Mrs. John Grey Taylor
request the honour of your presence
at the marriage of their daughter
Helen Marie
and
Mr. Raymond Mitchell
on Friday, the fourth of June
at six o'clock
at the Presbyterian Church
Boston

The custom of posting invitations did not come until comparatively late. Not because posting was unknown—a royal post system existed even in ancient Persia. But for a long time a popular superstition made it an insult to send an invitation any other way than by personal messenger. But gradually this superstition passed out of favour, and soon everyone who entertained was posting invitations—recognizing this as a simple expedient toward getting guests together.

Ceremonial Announcements.—When anything of importance happens the natural impulse is to announce it to everyone. If we are unhappy, we want others to know of, and share in, that unhappiness. If we are joyous or proud, we want others to know of it, and be joyous or envious according to the circumstances.

To announce a death, the Singhalese, even in earliest times, sent out a lock of hair cut from the head of the dead and twisted around a small stick, the whole wrapped in a leaf or bit of cloth. Our announcement card, with its black border, is fundamentally the same in purpose.

In Uganda it has been the custom for ages to announce births and deaths by the boom-boom-boom of the war drums. A certain number of beats announce a birth; an entirely different number and variety of beats announce a death.

People everywhere, since early times, have had ways and means of announcing to others the things that interested them. The festive dance of the Indians is a method of announcing a wedding, just as it is a method of celebrating it. The crêpe on the door is a method of announcing death.

Writing, to a large extent, did away with pantomimic and dramatic forms of announcement. The transition was slow and gradual, of course, and many of the dramatic survivals are still noticeable in modern life. But slowly, surely, the written announcement gained its foothold and has been in social use ever since.

To-day cards are sent to friends and relatives to announce the birth of a child. Cards of announcement are issued by the bride's parents to those who have not been invited to the wedding. Mourning cards are issued upon the death of a member of the family. These written announcements are social devices pure and simple; they expedite the social affairs of the family.

Letter-writing.—In the development of social life it became necessary to write notes of congratulation, sympathy, appreciation. The receipt of a card of announcement would require some sort of acknowledgment. Each age has had its needs, and always those needs have been supplied.

The development of the art of letter-writing is a fascinating study in itself, and a fair discussion of it would fill a book. It was born in very early times but was confined at first to students, priests, and learned men. It followed painfully in the wake of writing, and received its greatest impetus with the discovery of a good and cheap paper. It was nurtured in France and England; it was developed to its highest point of development in the 17th and 18th centuries. It entered social life and found a peculiar place for itself in the heart of the hostess. It swept with a flourish through the 19th century. It waned perceptibly with the discovery of the telephone, the telegraph. But it still holds an important place in the social scheme.

On a certain occasion Lord Chesterfield's son sent some Arquebusade water to his aunt. She sent him a letter of thanks and enclosed in it a letter from the Lord. In this letter, Lord Chesterfield gave a draught of a letter which he recommended that his son write in answer to the aunt. To avoid hurting his feelings, he wrote:

> I hope you will not be offended at my offering you my assistance upon this occasion; because I presume that, as yet, you are not much used to write to ladies.
>
> A propos of letter-writing, the best models that you can form yourself upon are Cicero, Cardinal d'Ossat, Madame Sévigné and Comte Bussy Rebutin. Cicero's Epistles to Atticus and his familiar friends are the best examples that you can imitate, in the friendly and familiar style. The simplicity and the clearness of Cardinal d'Ossat's letters show how letters of business ought to be written; no affected turns, no attempts at wit, to obscure or perplex the matter, which is always clearly and plainly stated, as business always should be.
>
> For gay and amusing letters, for *enjouement* and *badinage*, there are none that equal Comte Bussey's and Madame Sévigné's. They

are so natural that them seem to be the extempore conversations of two people of wit, rather than letters which are commonly studied, though they ought not to be so.

I would advise you to let that book be one in your itinerant library; it will both amuse and inform you. I have not time to add any more now, so good-night.

To Lord Chesterfield's excellent advice we will add a word more. If you wish to learn not only a crisp, excellent style for letter-writing, if you wish to glean a wealth of valuable anecdotes, witticisms, paradoxes, for use in conversation, by all means read and *study* Lord Chesterfield's letters to his son. But do not pattern yourself after him or after any one else. Remember this paragraph from "The Book of Etiquette":

Letters should be written *personally*—that is, they should represent the sender. Be sure, first, that you know exactly what you want to say and how you want to say it. Then put it down on paper as though you were speaking; make no pretense at being so very highly educated that you must use flowery language and poetical phrases. Simplicity in wording and in form is the most effective and graceful method. It is a greater mark of learning and intelligence to write a simple, ably expressed, cordial letter, than to write one that shows an obvious effort to cover, by extravagant and highly figurative language, the reserve and dignity that are the foundation of all good breeding.

Concerning the Salutation.—Forms of salutation in letter-writing were originated to a very great extent in France, although some forms of salutation originated in the English court.

For a long time the only form of salutation used in letter-writing was "God keep you!" or its equivalent. The use of "Your humble servant" first came into use in England at the marriage of Queen Mary, daughter of Henry IV of France. It was derived from *Votre très humble serviteur.*

Such forms as "Your obedient servant" and "Your humble servant" are still used in letters of importance. In 16th-century France they were used by everyone; no other form was used. That the English still have survivals of this salutation emphasizes the importance with which French manners and customs were regarded by the social world.

Much etiquette concerns the salutations in letters to royalty. Garrick Mallery, in an article which appeared some time ago in the *American Anthropologist,* says:

A private person writing to royalty used the largest sheet of paper procurable and only four written lines at the bottom of the first page could be used to commence the communication, the remainder of the page being left blank after the form title, which should be distributed through at least five lines. Six lines of the epistle to a prince might appear on the first page, and so on in graduation. Wars have been occasioned by the breach of this etiquette. The enmity between Cardinal Richelieu and the Duke of Buckingham arose because his haughty eminence addressed the Duke without leaving any space open after the title of Monsieur, which insult his Grace returned in the same paper-sparing manner.

At this period France was making the social laws for all Europe. Madame de Genlis records that "all men, even princes of the blood, must place the word 'respect' in letters written to any woman." The English copied this form of courtesy, and both French and English still use to-day such phrases as "respectful homage" and "respectful regard." Our phrase "respectfully yours" appears to have been borrowed from them.

The etiquette of correspondence is very much simpler in the United States than it is anywhere else.

There are two distinct forms of the social letters—the formal and the informal [says "The Book of Etiquette]. The formal social note is used only for invitations, announcements, and their respective acknowledgments. It is always written in the third person, and always requires an answer. The informal note has no definite formula, except that it can be generally compared to all the informal trend of correct social usage.

Whether formal or informal, the social note always bears the name of the person to whom it is addressed. When writing socially to Mrs. Joselyn, for instance, one does not use the expression "Dear Madam," but "Dear

Mrs. Joselyn." The form "my dear" is considered a trifle more formal than just "dear," although in England the reverse is true. "Dear Madam" and "Dear Sir" are forms reserved exclusively for use with business letters.

In closing the letters, the forms "Very truly yours" and "Yours truly" express a certain formality. Friendly letters are closed with such expressions as "Yours most sincerely," "Cordially yours," "Very affectionately yours." The pronoun "yours" should not be omitted as it leaves the phrase unfinished and is not complimentary to the person addressed.

Flowery forms have entirely disappeared from correct letter writing, and a dignified simplicity prevails instead.

Crests and Monograms.—Elaborate crests, seals, and monograms were at one time considered an essential part of social correspondence. Fashionable stationery to-day bears neither crest nor seals; and the monogram if used at all, is simple and inconspicuous.

"The monogram," says Symmachus, "is a name set forth in an abbreviated form, and so compacted by certain intertwinings of the letters as to be more easily understood than read."

The Greeks are supposed by most authorities to have been the first to use monograms. Beautiful combinations of letters are to be found on old Greek coins; and elaborate seals and monograms are found on ancient rings. The Romans, copyists of the Greeks in almost everything else, adopted the device of monograms. They were possibly the first, however, to use monograms to express family names. As one writer says, "Greece was the seed-ground of arts, but it was in Rome that they flowered."

The early kings of France and emperors of Germany used monograms because they were not able to write, and their signatures were required on documents. Eginbard, the biographer of Charlemagne, tells us that this was precisely the case with the great ruler. He was unable to write, so he had a monogram made and he used it whenever his signature was required.

King Theodoric (A.D. 493–526) was extremely illiterate, according to all accounts of him. He was unable to write his name and therefore unable to sign his edicts. Because of this he had a plate made of gold, perforated with the letters of his signature. He used this as a stencil and traced his initials through it. In this manner only was he able to sign his documents.

The early French kings, it appears, did not always sign their court documents or write their monograms themselves. They had secretaries to perform this duty. There are in existence several rare old characters which bear the words "The King orders his monogram (*nominis karacter*) to be written under it." And sure enough, there under it appears the King's monogram, carefully sealed or stamped by the secretary. William I, the Norman Conqueror of England, made use of just such a device to sign his documents.

The French kings invariably used black ink in the stamping or drawing of their monograms. The exception to this rule, however, is Charles the Bald who was not only King of France but Emperor of Germany. The documents of Germany he signed in vermilion, and they were countersigned in black by the Chancellor.

The Saxon kings not only signed with a monogram, but added a cross to make their signatures still more sacred. One writer tells us that they diluted the ink with the wine of the Eucharist.

During the 15th and 16th centuries the use of monograms became general. Merchants began to adopt them as signs or trademarks. They found their way into social life and were used on stationery. "Monograms came to mean to the middle classes what the coat-of-arms meant to nobility."

There are many examples of 16th-century monograms in existence. They are interesting and beautiful. They are based, with few exceptions, upon Gothic forms; some are grotesque, some indistinct and scarcely readable, some charming and truly artistic.

Crests are quite as old as monograms. But while monograms developed largely because of the illiteracy of persons whose signatures were important, crests grew out of vanity and the love of symbols.

From the earliest times men have used emblems to indicate their nationality. The Egyptians carried images of bulls and crocodiles into battle. Each of the twelve tribes of Israel had its special ensign. The Indians of British Columbia had crests of their totem poles, usually in the form of a frog, or wolf, or eagle. The subjects of Demiramis adopted doves and pigeons as their emblems. They selected the dove in deference to their queen whose name meant "dove."

Athens used, as its public sign, an owl. This was a compliment to Minerva. Carthage used a horse's head; Corinth, a winged horse; Persia, the sun; Rome, an eagle. All peoples appear to have used some sign, some symbol, to distinguish themselves from others. These symbols were the original crests.

As a form of ostentation and vanity, the crest is quickly falling into disuse, except with royalty. The monogram, however, is still in good taste and may be used on social stationery. To quote "The Book of Etiquette":

> The monogram should be decorative without being elaborate. It should be placed in the centre at the top of the page when no address is given. It should be omitted entirely when the address appears at the top of the page. The space occupied by a monogram should not cover more than the approximate circumference of a silver dime. A monogram is usually stamped in black, dark green, or dark blue. Vivid colours must be avoided.

The most correct stationery to-day bears simply the address engraved in Gothic or Roman lettering in the upper centre of note and letter sheets and on the reverse side of the envelope.

CHAPTER XI

Calling Customs

Let us respect the ancient manners and recollect that, if the true soul of chivalry has died among us, with it all that is good in society has died.

—Gladstone.

Since custom is the principal magistrate of man's life, let men by all means endeavour to obtain good customs.

—Lord Bacon.

HOW CALLS ORIGINATED

In early life there could have been no regular visiting, no established calling customs. The condition of life would have been too uncertain, too hazardous, for any such thing.

Mankind must have been fairly well advanced in the social scale before the idea of visiting his neighbours even occurred to him. At first he would have been suspicious and distrustful of any attempts toward friendliness. He would have avoided his neighbours as they avoided him. He would have been satisfied simply with his cave home for shelter, his meat and his fruits for food, his woman for companionship. The first primitive existence must have been absolutely devoid of any sort of social element.

But as we follow in the footsteps of man, painfully and slowly developing, we see that it was by a series of very natural steps that the custom of calling grew in his life. With the use of spears and flint implements to kill beasts, man was able to supply himself with an abundance of food. With his cave well filled with food he was not afraid to welcome some wandering fellow and sit with him under the stars. His attitude toward his neighbours changed. He had plenty of food and they had plenty of food. Why need they fear one another?

(Courtesy of Metropolitan Museum of Art)

Chinese guests returning from a banquet, carrying with them the food they could not consume. A painting by Ku Hung-Chang.

(Courtesy of Metropolitan Museum of Art)

Tea-pot of the 18th Century, Dutch, Delft.

Tea-pot and stand, France, 19th Century.

And so we find them joining one another as they sit silently before the fire. First it would be just one fellow, coming over timidly and making known by gesture his desire to be friendly. Then another would wander close in his loneliness. They would discover that it was good to gather thus in company. The fire was warm and bright; the stars winked like thousands of tiny eyes; the trees whispered softly, and far away some beast howled to the sky. Man moved closer. Like called out to like, and a slumbering social instinct was awakened.

Then came speech and its great influence upon the life of man. Speech meant coöperation. It meant exchange of thoughts and experiences. It meant binding together of man to man in the common desire to express hopes, joys, sorrows, fears. It meant a great impetus to the social instinct.

Story-tellers and myth-makers followed in the wake of speech. And there evolved the need for an audience.

And so it continued through long ages of development, one custom growing up out of another, mankind gradually being drawn closer and closer in a social fabric that has patterned itself with all the human instincts. Not the least of these instincts is the desire to be respected and admired by one's neighbours, to be a person of worth and importance. Out of this instinct, undoubtedly, came the custom of making and returning ceremonious calls.

The First Calls.—It is always at a point like this that fancy tempts us, and we feel strongly the urge to wander along forgotten ways and poke curiously into the unknown.

Could not some primitive mother have called upon a neighbour mother to show her round, fat baby? Could not some savage youth, ages and ages ago, have called upon some other youth to match his skill and strength?

Visits, we are told, began among the ancient Israelites. The rabbis visited one another constantly for the purpose of sharing their wisdom. And they visited the people to teach, to comfort the sick, to console the bereaved. They wandered among the Egyptians with their custom of making calls, and the Egyptians copied the fashion.

But even before this time, which, after all, was a period of early civilization, men were making calls upon one another; but these calls were intrinsically of a homage-paying nature. As has been noted in a previous chapter, early men made gifts to the Strong Man, the Wise Man, the tribal gods, the kings, to win their approval and hence their protection (see pp. 270-271). Making a gift necessarily meant going to the person for whom it was intended.

We can see how, by association, the very act of coming came to be looked upon as a mark of homage and respect. Eventually it would have acquired the character of a reverential ceremony, and a man would call upon a superior for the same reason that he presented him with gifts.

The early tribesman, for instance, would have come personally with his gift for the tribal chief, to see that he received it and no one else. Gradually it would have become the established or traditional custom in the tribe to call upon the chief at stated, definite intervals, to do him homage.

We saw how presents which were once voluntary and entirely one-sided gradually became obligatory and reciprocal (see p. 273). In the same manner the custom of ceremonious visiting became gradually obligatory and reciprocal.

To Make the Marriage Bargain.—Simultaneously with this ceremonious and reverential type of visiting there was developing an entirely different kind of visiting which had nothing whatever to do with homage. It concerned marriage bargains and the settlement of marriage prices.

Thus, when a man had a daughter for whom he wished to receive a dozen or so of his neighbour's pigs, he called upon the neighbour and indicated to him his willingness to make the exchange. If the neighbour were agreeable, the bride price was settled and the marriage celebration planned.

Or, if a man had a son of marriageable age he probably called upon his neighbour and discussed with him the benefits to be derived from a union between that son and the neighbour's daughter.

The custom of calling grew out of such natural steps as these in the development of man. When it became necessary to call upon his neighbour, he called upon him. When there was absolutely no reason for calling, he didn't.

Visits between Kin.—Possibly the first visits made for the purpose of the simple pleasure to be derived from them were the visits between kin. We can imagine a young bride returning to her own clan or tribe to visit her mother. We can imagine the mother visiting her son who lives with his wife in another hut. These visits would not have been ceremonious in the least. They would have been simple calls for the sake of seeing the person from whom one has been separated.

Yet we can see how, out of this custom of calling upon kin, grew the more general custom of visiting one's friends and neighbours. Perhaps two old mothers, whose children were all married and far away, called upon each other frequently to find sympathy and solace in each other's company. Perhaps two old men, no longer able to fight or work, called upon each other to relate brave tales of their youth, of their lost strength, of their one-time skill in the hunt.

This form of simple, unceremonious visiting between kin and between friends, gradually exerted its influence upon peoples everywhere. It found a foothold for itself in the social scheme and it has maintained that foothold ever since. We call it the "informal call." But it means simply the friendly little visit that one neighbour makes upon another.

Caste, and Calling Customs.—It is inevitable that caste should have entered the custom of calling at an early period. One tribal chief would feel that the other ought to call upon him first. One class of people would feel that another class ought to do them homage. It has always been so, for man has always been conceited.

In early life conquered chiefs were obliged to do homage to the new chief. When we read of a certain conquered people of ancient Peru, for instance, we notice that the chiefs were "ordered to reside at the court of Cuzco during certain months of the year." This was regarded as a fitting way to do homage.

You remember the story of Charlemagne. He not only forced subject kings to remain in his presence and so indicate their subservience to him, but he actually forced them to serve him at table.

In feudal Europe vassals were obliged to make periodical visits to their suzerains, to show their subjugation to them. The suzerains, in turn, were obliged to make visits to the lords. And the lords were obliged to do homage to the king. So was visiting a method of showing respect and homage between the castes.

Where caste exists, visiting becomes ceremonious. It cannot be the friendly or "informal" visiting that exists among equals. Thus caste affects the calling customs of many countries. In the Orient, where there are many castes, "ceremonial visits are regulated with great precision." The same is true in India. In England there were at one time about fifty classes or castes of people before reaching the commoner, and the visits of all these castes were carefully regulated. In France and in Spain matters of precedence relating to diplomatic calls at court appear to have been of great moment and sometimes occasioned actual battles (see p. 109).

We have not escaped, even to-day, the influence of caste in our calling customs. Concerning the first call—that is, asking a new acquaintance to call—"The Book of Etiquette" says:

> You cannot, except under special conditions, invite people to your home unless you have called on them in formal manner and they have returned the visit. A young woman, and an unmarried woman, wait for an invitation to call from an older woman and matron. It

is not advisable for a young woman to ask a gentleman to call until she has met him several times. . . . A married woman does not leave a card for an unmarried man. . . . It is expected of a young matron or of a débutante that she request being permitted to call upon an elderly matron or an old lady after the two have met at a watering-place or in the home of a mutual friend, and after having exchanged cards, etc., etc.

Then there is the matter of the first call which "is often a very delicate matter. Frequently sensitive people are offended by some unconscious slight on the part of a friend." We are told that an unmarried woman must always pay the first call of the season upon a matron. The bride does not make the first call, but waits until her friends and neighbours have called upon her. The elder of two women is always entitled to the first visit.

Rules such as these, which are to be found in every book on etiquette, prove without a vestige of a doubt that caste consciousness still exists among us, although in greatly modified form.

Calls of Condolence and Congratulation.—We cannot be certain when the custom of making calls upon friends or neighbours for the purpose of sympathizing with them or congratulating them originated. The custom is very probably an old one. We know that in ancient Greece neighbours and friends gathered together on the tenth day after the birth of a child to congratulate the parents and present gifts. Other peoples must have had similar customs.

That calls of condolence are of great antiquity we can be reasonably certain. In the face of death we are all afraid, and it is but a human instinct to sympathize with those who have felt death's hand.

Calls of condolence existed in ancient China. Confucius says:

Generally guests who come to condole are first saluted by kneeling toward them and knocking the head on the ground to manifest one's grief. However, the process of knocking the head on the ground before bowing to the guests is a more expressive manner of showing grief, and I prefer the latter way in cases where mourning lasts for three years.

In China to-day condoling visitors bring mock money which is buried with the dead. There are elaborate funeral repasts, attended by relatives and friends.

Among the Irish it has for generations been the custom to call at the home of death and sit for hours with the bereaved. There are drinking, feasting and chatting, for all the world as though it were a social function.

Civilization brings understanding and kindliness, and to-day "when the call of condolence is made ten days or two weeks after the funeral, the intimate friends of the family should be careful to avoid all subjects that would cause pain. The call should be brief. It is poor form to remain longer than fifteen minutes unless one is a particularly intimate friend."

The Ceremonious Calls of Modern Life.—The ceremonious call is quickly becoming obsolete. With the minuet and the high handshake, it belongs to yesterday. But distinct traces of the ceremonious type of visiting still prevail and are to be found in our modern life.

The "at-home" day, for instance, is a survival.

> There was a time when fashionable districts of New York were divided into regular sections wherein on a given day in the week a whole neighbourhood was "at home." Ladies in visiting dress, with trains and bonnets and tight gloves, carrying card cases, tripped into this house, out of that, and again into another.

During the heydey of the "at-home" call, huge quantities of visiting cards were left at every house. The number of cards was regulated with precision and care. These calls were not based upon civility or friendliness. Visiting, under this system, was purely a ceremony.

Both card-leaving and the "at home" are to-day practically obsolete, though our so-called "duty calls" are a survival. For instance, two weeks after having been entertained at a formal dinner one is expected to call and leave cards. When one is notified of a death, one is expected to call and leave cards. A bride in a new neighbourhood expects her neighbours to call and leave cards. Every book on etiquette has a list of these obligatory calls. They cannot very well be regarded as friendly or informal; they are more or less ceremonious.

The morning call was at one time a very popular social institution. It appears to have been a remote but distinct sequence of that system under which subordinates were required to call from time to time and show loyalty to their superiors. It existed principally in court systems under which courtiers were required to present themselves at stated intervals to do homage to the king.

In the 17th century, for instance, in the empire of Mogul,

> All those that are at Court are obliged, under a considerable penalty, to come twice every day to salute the King in the assembly, once about ten or eleven o'clock in the morning when he renders justice; and the second time about six hours at night.

The morning call, which is now practically obsolete, but which still exists in Washington and in certain small towns, appears to be a survival. Persons of lesser rank in the social scheme call upon their superiors before noon any day except Sunday, and leave cards to show they have been there. It is another way of "doing homage."

In the United States caste consciousness is not as pronounced as it is abroad, and the call is a social pleasure rather than a social device. The only calls that still carry with them a flavour of ceremoniousness are those previously enumerated, concerning condolence, congratulation, inquiry, etc.

The Informal Call.—During the early periods of Christianity it was the custom of neighbours to call upon one another at Christmas, New Year, and other important holidays. Ricard tells us that "everyone called upon everyone else" exchanging the good wishes of the season.

When the Dutch came to settle in New York they brought with them the custom of making friendly, informal

New Year calls. This custom has remained with us, and to-day the New Year call is usually one of the jolliest and most delightful of the season.

When visitors call informally it is customary to serve refreshments of some sort. Usually tea and cake are served to callers in the afternoon. In Manila native fruits are offered the visitor. In New Mexico the customary refreshment, when they are in season, is piñon nuts. In Sicily liquor is served the guest.

The phrase for hospitality in the Society and Sandwich Islands is, "Let us eat together." These people are most hospitable and they will share their last bit of food with a guest.

In Japan calls are usually made in the morning. Dainties are served to the guests on white paper—confectionery and little cakes, ordinarily—and they are eaten with chopsticks. What he cannot eat the visitor carefully folds in the paper and deposits in his pocket sleeve to carry away with him.

Among most peoples, eating together is the greatest sign of hospitality, and to refuse to eat with a host is regarded as a serious insult. Among us, a hostess dislikes to be refused the cup of tea or the dainties she offers.

"The Book of Etiquette" is partial to the friendly informal call and recommends it to those who want to entertain simply and unostentatiously. It says in part:

> If you feel that, because you are not fortunate enough to own a pretentious dwelling and to hire impressive butlers and maidservants to welcome your guests, you should not make calls and have them returned, you are depriving yourself of a pleasure infinitely greater than all elaborate display and ostentation. Simple, informal calls made for the purpose of creating and developing friendships, and made with a feeling of genuine cordiality and friendliness, are even more gratifying than the stiffly formal social calls.
>
> Do not feel that you are obeying etiquette's decrees when you neglect your friendships merely because your home and facilities do not warrant extensive social intercourse. True etiquette is universal in its appeal and reaches the country woman in her little cottage as directly as it reaches the stately dowager in her city mansion.

The ceremonious call of the 19th Century, now practically obsolete. This type of call was a survival of the homage calls of early life.

Origin of the Visiting Card.—Early peoples, calling upon one another, always felt that it was polite to announce their arrival beforehand. They felt that the owners ought to be warned of their approach.

We can see the origin of this, of course. Earlier in the

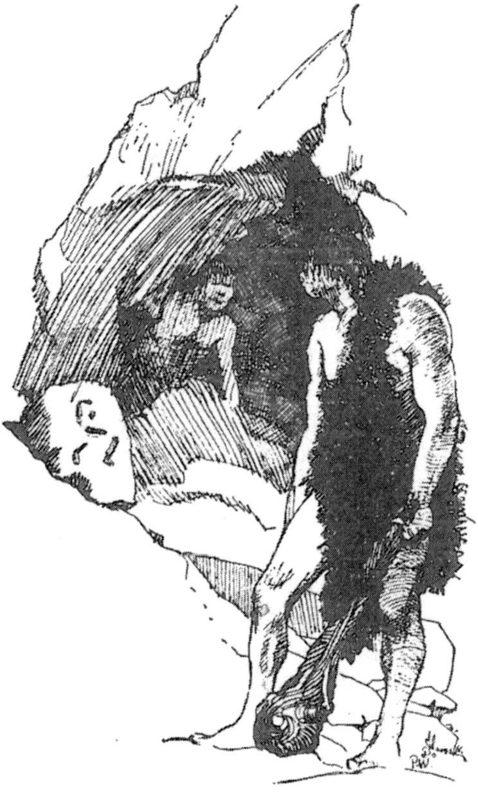

Primitive man placed a bit of carved rock at the entrance to a cave. If it were taken in, he knew he was welcome; if it remained untouched, he hurried away. We use a bit of inscribed pasteboard—the visiting card.

stage of social development, when one tribe approached another it would not know at first whether the approach were hostile or friendly. But if that tribe announced its approach, it must naturally be friendly. Otherwise it would approach silently, secretly, to steal upon them unawares. Through obvious association, it became a form of early politeness to make known one's approach.

Thus in Australia, before coming within a mile of the fires of the natives of another village, it is customary to announce the approach by loud "cooeys." In other sections of Australia it is the custom, when one tribe approaches another in peace, to carry burning sticks.

A Blackfellow would not think of breaking in suddenly upon the privacy of the horde he is about to visit. He warns them of his arrival by building a fire a little distance off. Several peoples, in widely separated parts of the world, use this method of making known their approach.

Among the ancient Israelites it was considered good form, when visiting friends or strangers, to send a servant ahead to announce their coming. This corresponds to our custom of sending a card or note several days in advance when we are planning to visit someone and we wish him or her to be at home.

It was not until the late 17th and early 18th centuries that the visiting card, as we know it, came into general use. Its development appears to be most marked in France, as are, indeed, most social developments. During the 18th century in France we find a whole generation of artists and designers devoting themselves entirely to the creating of visiting cards for the fashionable world.

Many of the elaborate visiting cards of this period are still in existence. We have seen one, for instance, decorated with a wreath of roses bordered with olives and bearing the name "Marquis de Llano." The decorations were made by the artist Raphael Mengs.

Another card bears the picture of a spaniel holding a miniature card in his mouth on which appears the name "Adam Bartsch" (celebrated author of the "Peintre Graveur," a work published at Venice in twenty-one volumes). Another one of his cards reveals a savage dog tearing a roll of paper which bears the date 1795. Beneath it is the legend: "Adam Bartsch has the pleasure of presenting his compliments and good wishes for the New Year."

Ornamented cards such as these were used for various purposes. They were sent with gifts. They were left at homes to show that the owners had been there. Invitations were written on them.

It appears that men had their cards ornamented to harmonize with their professions. Thus the architect Blondel had his name inscribed above the cornice of a ruined monument; an artist had a palette on his card; the landscape gardener, a bit of pretty landscape.

After a period of great ostentation in cards, the pendulum seems to have swung to the other extreme. During the late 18th and 19th centuries, ordinary playing cards were used and the names were written in pen or pencil on the back. Several such cards, of about the period of 1850, were found in a house in Dean Street, Soho, under repair. One of them bears the name of Isaac Newton.

As they proved useful and convenient in the matter of visiting cards, the playing cards were next used for invitations. Invitations to dinners and parties were scribbled on their backs. But toward the close of the 19th century such social carelessness was frowned upon, and the simple pasteboard card which we know came into favour.

Our custom of using white cards bordered with black for mourning purposes possibly originated with the Chinese. They have used cards of various kinds from a very early period. And they have been among the first to use a different colour to indicate mourning. The Chinese visiting card is a strip of vermilion paper printed in black. For mourning purposes the paper is white printed in dark blue.

The formula on the Chinese visiting card is as ornate as its appearance. The card bears not only the name of the visitor, but an address of respect to the host. One card, to give an example, bears this inscription:

The tender and sincere friend of your Lordship, and the perpetual disciple of your doctrine, presents himself in this quality to pay his duty and make his reverence even to the earth.

The correct card of to-day is engraved with the name only, or with the name and address. To be absolutely correct it is pure white engraved in black. Cards for mourning are white edged with a narrow border of black. (See pp. 588-589 for the origin of black as the color of mourning.)

Before leaving on a long trip to some distant place, it is customary to call upon one's friends, not for the purpose of making a visit, but merely to leave one's visiting card on which one has written in one corner the letters P. P. C. The cards may be mailed if preferred.

This is a rather old French custom. The letters P. P. C. mean *Pour prendre congé* (To take leave). The card is purely a courtesy card, to inform one's friends of one's departure, and no acknowledgment is necessary.

CHAPTER XII

Hospitality and Entertainment

And when ye reap the harvest of your land, thou shalt not wholly reap the corners of thy field, neither shalt thou gather up the gleanings of thy harvest. And thou shalt not glean thy vineyard, and the single grapes that drop in thy vineyard shalt thou not gather up. For the poor and the stranger shalt thou leave them. I am the Lord thy God.
—Leviticus XVIII, 9.

THE CORNERSTONE OF CIVILIZATION

"THE hospitable reception of guests procures wealth, fame, long life and heavenly bliss," says Manu, the maxim-maker.

As we ride back across the ages, peering here into a palace, there into a hovel, sometimes into a cave on the hillside, sometimes into a tent on the edge of a desert, we are inclined to shout, "You are right, old Manu!" Wherever history traces the tale of hospitality, there too it traces the tale of man's greatest development. Hospitality appears to be one of the cornerstones upon which the city of civilization has been built.

Of course, there was no hospitality when mankind was young, when life was lived from day to day with no thought of a past or a future. All that mattered was to-day—food and shelter and comfort for the one little life from dawn to dark.

But hospitality came early into the life of man. When food was scarce, man ate furtively and alone in some corner; but when it was plentiful, he shared.

This sharing of food grew, undoubtedly, more out of a sense of vanity than from any feeling of generosity. The man who killed the ox or the bear was proud of his achievement. Here was food, good food. Come and taste of it.

He had killed it. *He* had made this food possible. And he felt, as he strode around the spot watching the others timidly tear bits of the beast away, that he was superior to them, that they were obligated to him.

We trace the same sort of personal vanity and pride in the great feasts given by tribal chiefs and kings. It gave them a sense of power and importance to gather people around them and give them food. The chief who could feast fifty tribesmen felt mighty. No one else could feed fifty men. No one else had so much food, so many good things. And hence, no one else was so powerful, so important.

It is not difficult to parallel this in modern life. The fashionable hostess strives to give the most brilliant function of the social season. Magnificent dinners are given, frequently, not out of any mistaken sense of generosity but because the host and hostess like to feel that they *can* give magnificent dinners.

Yet in early life it was just this sort of selfish vanity that aroused in man the first slight inclination toward hospitality. He found a peculiar new kind of pleasure in sharing, in being generous. It was probably different from any instinct he had ever sensed before. He felt warm and comfortable as his friends came from all around to share in his kill. Good people. They honoured him. They respected him. And there was plenty of meat for all!

So he played generous host, and the part pleased him. It has pleased king and vassal, lord and peasant, duke and commoner in all the ages between. There is no satisfaction that can be likened to the satisfaction of giving.

And so hospitality came into the darkness of early times and helped to broaden the shaft of light that already indicated the path of human progress and development. It became a step upon which mankind climbed to reach a higher and better place for itself. It became a cornerstone which mankind used in building the foundation for civilization.

Relationship of Food to Hospitality.—Like a deep-sea pearl, hospitality has taken on many rich and beautiful hues. But in early life hospitality meant just one thing—sharing your food with your neighbour or with a stranger. Later it meant sharing your sleeping place with him, giving him shelter and protection for the night. But the hospitality that threw open the hut or the tent to the stranger was delayed until mankind could be sure that not every stranger who approached was an enemy, that not every wanderer was an evil spirit.

Among almost all savage tribes, once you have broken bread with a man or taken a drink with him you are considered on peaceful terms with him. You are under obligations to protect him if he is in danger; he will protect you if you are in danger. This act of hospitality, of eating together, is a tie that binds in close relationship.

Thus, in the villages of Leti, Moa, and Lakor friendship is expressed by eating together. In Sumatra the guest is presented with betel (a nut which when chewed makes the teeth black) in token of friendliness. In Java a superior pays the inferior a high compliment if he offers his half-chewed betel.

From the earliest times, eating and drinking together has been a tie of relationship. Writers like to call it food kinship. It was widely prevalent and was usually of a ceremonious nature. This food kinship was an elementary form of hospitality; it exists to-day in various modified forms. Its influence can be traced even in modern hospitality.

The traveller among savage peoples finds that many of them have actual formulæ for hospitality based upon the old principles of food kinship. The Tahitian formula for hospitality is *"Haëre maï ta maha"* (Come and eat with us). Among the Koniagas visitors are presented with a cup of water as a ceremonial mark of friendship and the customary phrase is, "Let us be friends." Among us it is the custom to serve tea or refreshments of some sort to the visitor.

We know that in modern life the refusal of food or drink is not always taken in good grace. It is considered an act of common politeness to accept it, whether one wants it or not. This, too, appears to be a survival. Among the Bedouin Arabs it has, from the very earliest times, been considered a serious breach of etiquette to ride up to the front of a man's tent without stopping and eating his bread. According to the code of manners prevalent among the Arabs, the man in the tent has reason to consider himself insulted, and hence an enemy of the other.

Among the Iroquois the regular act of courtesy and friendliness toward a visitor was to present him with a dish of hominy. To refuse it would be a great breach of courtesy and would cause instant enmity. In Sumatra a similar custom prevails. The guest is offered betel and he must accept it whether he likes or not. To refuse would be an inexcusable insult to the host.

"To the primitive mind, eating together produced identity of substance, of flesh. Therefore those who ate together were kin. (See p. 250). And therefore those who ate together were friendly toward each other, on peaceful terms. Through association of ideas, eating together became inseparably linked with hospitality.

Among the North American Indians, tobacco-smoking took over all the ideas attached to food in primitive life. Just as eating and drinking together was one of the earliest ties of relationship among the peoples of early times, passing around the calumet became the regular custom of making peace and alliances, of indicating friendliness and hospitality, among the Indians. You know how, in modern life, a man does not light his cigar or cigarette until he has first asked his companions to join him.

So through the ages hospitality has always associated itself with the act of eating and drinking together, or, as in the case of the Indians, smoking together. We, too,

(Courtesy of Metropolitan Museum of Art)

A bronze strainer; Etruscan, about 6th Century, B. C.

(Courtesy of Metropolitan Museum of Art)

Dining hour at Penhurst Castle, England, in the 14th century. Model of the Great Hall.

(Courtesy of Metropolitan Museum of Art)

A bronze strainer; Etruscan, about 6th Century, B. C.

(Courtesy of Metropolitan Museum of Art)

Dining hour at Penhurst Castle, England, in the 14th century. Model of the Great Hall.

show our hospitality by inviting our friends to teas, to luncheons, to dinners.

Early Hospitality.—It seems that hospitality, in early life, found expression in great feasting. Tribal chiefs gave great feasts in honour of some important event or to do homage to a visiting chief. The Greeks and Romans gave great banquets to which they invited everyone of importance. The Israelites had a simpler hospitality, but they too gave great feasts. And we know that the Egyptians always feasted in great halls, offering food to their gods before they themselves touched a morsel.

There is no doubt whatever that the Israelites were a hospitable people, and that others emulated their customs of hospitality.

> And if a stranger sojourn with thee in your land, ye shall not vex him. As one born in the land among you, shall be unto you the stranger that sojourneth with you, and thou shalt love him as thyself; for ye were strangers in the land of Egypt. (Leviticus XIX, 33, 34.)

We know from Homer's Iliad that the Greeks were great entertainers. There are descriptions of magnificent banquets and extravagant feasts. It appears that the Greeks gave feasts to celebrate all important events in their lives—births, marriages, holidays, victories in warfare; and practically everyone was invited.

The Roman feasts were greater than any, because they had the food products which enabled them to give great feasts. What they lacked they usually sent for, and their messengers went far and wide to obtain choice fruits and viands. The Romans were noted for their hospitality. Nothing was too rich or too costly for the entertainment of their guests. They had elaborate tables, beautiful ewers and drinking vessels. They appear to have been highly advanced in the art of entertaining.

The Egyptians of 4000 years ago were fond of dinner-giving as a form of entertainment. We are told that their dinners lasted several hours, and that both men and women were invited, which was an unusual thing. In early life women did not usually attend feasts or dinners with the men. Dining couches and small tables were provided, and the guests regaled themselves with geese, game, fish, bread, and wine. During the progress of the meal household slaves stood behind the guests waving ostrich plumes.

This luxurious type of hospitality and entertainment lasted for many generations among those people who could afford it. The lower classes knew no hospitality in the sense of feasting. They shared their bread when they had bread. They celebrated their marriages and births

GUESTS AT FEASTS WITH ATTENDANTS

as best they could. But they were too vitally concerned with the business of living to develop among themselves the art of hospitality. It would appear that for a long time there were only two great classes—the wealthy and the powerful who entertained lavishly; and the toiling classes who knew only the simple kind of hospitality that comes from the heart.

With the coming of Christianity there was a great impetus toward simple, unostentatious hospitality. Christ preached against luxury and display. He taught simple kindliness and generosity. Feasting and lavish entertaining continued unabated among those who were accustomed to it, but something seemed to have happened in the lives of the people. A new, wholesome kind of hospitality permeated their social fabric and made its influence very definitely felt.

It became the custom to "share one's bread with the stranger at the gate." Hospitality was extended for the sole purpose of being hospitable, and not because of vanity or the desire to impress.

Among the early European peoples simple hospitality took a firm hold. The Anglo-Saxons "invited all the countryside" to the wedding feast, to the celebration. The French shared wine and bread at the tavern, and helped one another make merry. In Spain, in Italy, in Germany, in Russia, wherever we wander, we find traces of the new kind of hospitality that had marched, like some pioneer, at the head of Christianity.

Hospitality is such a vast subject, it has so many beautiful threads that reach out across the tapestry of life, that we cannot do justice to it in a book of this nature. Perhaps some day someone will write of hospitality alone, and tell of its great and far-reaching influences upon civilization. But we who discuss it here must be satisfied with the briefest kind of outline. We let our eyes rest but for a moment upon the beautiful design it traces on the tapestry, and then—on again to mankind, its habits, its customs, its instincts, its manners!

A Curious Custom of Hospitality.—A widespread custom of hospitality in early savage life, and a custom still prevalent in various spots throughout the uncivilized world, is that of "lending" the wife to the visitor (see p. 264). The Eskimo, the Australian aborigines, and almost all South Sea Islanders still practise this age-old custom, regarding it as one of the most essential duties of the hospitable host. This sexual hospitality has its parallels in modern life, in highly modified form, of course.

The books on etiquette tell us, for instance, that "the hospitable host mingles with his wife's guests and tries to make them feel 'at home.'" When going in to dinner "the host does not offer his arm to his wife but to the most important woman guest. The hostess enters on the arm of the most important man guest." On the golf links or tennis courts the hostess who plays well should not join her husband but "play with the man she feels will be most pleased to have her."

Modern life abounds with just such laws of hospitality

The names and symbols of important guests at the Pharaoh's palace were engraved upon the "guest wall." This was accounted a high honour, as it is accounted an honour to-day to sign one's name in the guest book of a famous hostess.

as these. We do not realize, as we observe them, that their origins lie buried in the dim past of yesterday.

Possible Origin of the Guest Book.—Browsing for a while in old Egypt, we stumble across an old custom which is startlingly like a custom observed to-day.

It seems that it was customary for all important guests at the Pharaoh's palace to have their names and symbols engraved on the "guest wall." This was accounted a high honour. Modern guests inscribe their names in the guest book. The more fashionable and important the hostess, the more honourable the guest accounts it to inscribe his name in the book. One cannot fail to see the strange similarity between these two customs, separated by so many ages of civilization.

The Favoured Guest.—It has always been the custom to show deference to the favoured—that is, the most important—guest. In savage feasts the most important guest sits at the right of the chief. When Europe was young, the favoured guest always sat at the right of the host, at feasts, and was helped to the choicest joints, the rarest fruits, the costliest wines.

It seems that there have always been methods of showing deference to the favoured guests, even in the earliest times. Among the Romans there was one place at the head of the table reserved for the host, the hostess, and one guest of honour. Among the Egyptians the highest in rank sat with the host at the head of the table. Among the Greeks the highest in rank had their hands washed first, the lowest in rank last.

With us, "The host leads [into the dining-room] with the lady who is to sit at his right. If the dinner is in honour of a married couple, the host goes in to dinner with the wife of the honoured guest; the hostess goes in with that lady's husband." We see here the same inclination to show deference to the guest of honour by extending to him, or her, the place of importance at the table.

The Arabs welcomed their guests by pouring melted butter on their heads, to refresh them. The Greeks instantly showed their guests to the public baths. The Egyptians anointed their guests with oil upon their arrival. With us, as soon as the house-party guest arrives, "he is shown to his room and not disturbed until he has rested and refreshed himself."

Among the Ainu the guest is always given the most honourable and comfortable seat—the east or sacred end of the hearth. In Persia the guest is given the favourite *sadr* or floor space opposite the door end of the room. It is customary, among modern civilized peoples, to offer the most comfortable spot and the most comfortable chair to the guest. We often see a host insisting that his guest take his own favourite seat, because it is more comfortable than any other.

"It is the height of rudeness for any one to go to an entertainment given in honour of someone and fail to meet him." We quote from a recent book on etiquette. This custom of "meeting" the guest of honour is not very different, fundamentally, from the custom that existed in ancient times. Each guest at the chief's feast, or the king's magnificent banquet, was obliged to kneel down before him and pay him homage.

The "Bread-and-Butter" Letter.

When a traveller arrives at a village in Arabia, the sheik or chief sends him perhaps a present of milk and bread and fruits, begging him to accept it as a mark of his hospitality. The stranger receives it, but before he leaves the place he is sure to be visited by the chief in person, and then the traveller is expected to make him some present in return for what he has received. Not a word is said about pay for his entertainment, for that would be a breach of the laws of hospitality; but the traveller, if he has been long in the country, knows quite well the object of the visit, and if he is wise, will make the sheik such a present as will satisfy him. If he does not, he may find after he has left the place that something has been stolen from him; or he may, perhaps, be waylaid and robbed by some persons employed by the very man who has entertained him. (From "Customs of the Bedouin Arabs," pg. 83)

A brief survey of the customs of hospitality of various peoples indicates the prevalence of just such customs as these. All peoples appear to have some mode of showing gratitude for hospitality received. The Awemba send a gift to the person who has entertained them. The prince of Congo dedicates one of his wives to the tutelary god of his host. The Andaman Islander, to indicate his gratitude, asks to be given one of the children of the family to bring up as his own. Among us the "bread-and-butter" letter is sent to the hostess.

This is simply a grateful expression of appreciation for the hospitality enjoyed during one's stay at the home of the hostess. It derives its name from the idea of eating "the bread and butter" of the hostess' home, and has become acceptable through constant usage.

The "bread and butter" letter is written only when one has been a guest at a house party. One is expected to write it within ten days after departure. We are cautioned to write the letter promptly, for "it would be gross neglect to fail in so obvious a duty." A typical "bread-and-butter" letter is reproduced herewith:

TERRACE REVAIN,
June 23, 19—.

DEAR MRS. BEVANS:

This is to tell you again how very much I enjoyed the week-end at Pine Rock. We got into the city at five and Morgan brought me out home in a taxi. Mother is giving a small bridge this afternoon and so I found everyone busy, for while there is not a great deal to do it is impossible to get any one to help do it.

Tell Mr. Bevans that I am arranging for three or four tennis games next week, so that when I come again, if I don't win, I shall at least not be beaten quite so shamefully.

Let me know when you come to town on your next shopping trip. Perhaps we can arrange for lunch together somewhere.

Very sincerely yours,
HELEN R. JANIS.

This is simply the polished, 20th-century way of saying that one is grateful for hospitality received, and that one hopes at some future day to repay it.

Concerning Precedence.—Matters of precedence have always been of great importance. We have seen how simple matters of precedence have occasioned diplomatic battles (see p. 109), and if we could glimpse behind the pages of history, we would see that such matters have actually precipitated wars.

With us a guest is expected to go through a doorway first. The host holds back saying, "After you" or merely indicating by nod and gesture that he wishes the guest to enter before him. But among the Chinese, the guest is supposed to refuse firmly to enter before the host and then enter with him. This is a custom of politeness very sacred to the Chinese. The host who invites his guest to enter first would consider it an insult if the guest actually did so. Thus they go through the little ceremony of refusal and of entering together.

In Arabia the host remains outside while the guest enters. He acts as a sort of "lookout" for enemies. When all seems safe and sound, he too enters the tent.

The Comanche host is offended if the guest does not enter first and take the place pointed out to him. This custom appears to exist among many peoples. Perhaps it originated in the fear of the guest to enter first—fear that the host was not friendly and might do him harm when his back was turned. If this is true, entering first would be a form of politeness on the part of the guest. It would indicate his absolute trust of the host.

Announcing One's Arrival.—The Blackfellow, about to visit a neighbouring horde, pauses while he is yet some distance off and builds a fire. This fire is supposed to warn the people of his coming. After a few moments he rises, approaches the horde, and when he is outside of the camp and within sight of everyone, he sits down. He does not enter or mingle with the people until he has been invited in by the chief or someone of importance.

Throughout the Orient it is considered a form of simple politeness to send a servant ahead to announce one's coming.

A quarter of a mile or so distance from an encampment which he is planning to visit, a Veddah stops and shouts.

He continues shouting and does not proceed until an answering shout is heard.

Many similar customs exist all over the world. It has always been regarded as polite to warn of one's arrival. Even savage peoples consider it a great discourtesy to break in upon the privacy of others.

To-day we knock on the door, ring a bell, or send in our card, as the case may be.

The Ceremonious Leave-Taking.

"The Book of Etiquette" says:

> The guest must seek out the host and hostess and thank them cordially for their hospitality. It is customary to shake hands upon taking leave.

The custom of taking ceremonious leave of one's host is an old one. In the Andaman Islands it has been for generations the custom to blow into the host's hand when leaving. One writer gives the following dialogue between a host and guest among these half-savage people:

> GUEST: Indeed I go.
> HOST: Very well, go; when will you come again?
> GUEST: I will bring away something for you one of these days.
> HOST: May no snake bite you!
> GUEST: I will be watchful.

Then they blow into each other's hands and part, shouting promises, cautions, and invitations until beyond earshot. Some partings are no less brief to-day!

The Blackfellows and other peoples had the custom of hand-blowing and used it as frequently as we use our custom of hand-shaking. The Blackfellow to-day always blows upon his host's hands when he wishes to make known his intention of leaving. If the host is satisfied to let his guest depart, he blows upon the guest's hand in return. If not, he merely shakes his head and draws back his hand, and the guest extends his visit.

But to-day, "It is not civil or courteous to attempt to prolong the presence of any guest after he has made known his desire to leave." And instead of being ceremonious, lengthy, and stilted, the leave-taking is brief, cordial.

THE INDIAN—PIONEER OF AMERICAN HOSPITALITY

Curiously enough, the North American Indians have always been highly advanced in the art of hospitality. While they were yet in a state of savagery they had customs of hospitality which were an inspiration to the white people who first came among them.

We must recognize the North American Indians as a race highly in advance of other savage races. We know that for ages the Indians were forced to remain savages because lack of metals made it difficult for them to battle with the forest. How could they clear the land for agriculture with only a stone ax for tool? As Widney says:

> Any one who has helped, even with the steel implements of an advanced civilzation, to hew out a home amid the beech woods of Ohio will realize the almost hopeless struggle which would lie before a savage race making its first start with stone ax and sharpened stick towards subduing a densely wooded land.

So the Indians slipped behind in the march of progress and civilization, as we regard progress in the sense of material things; but in many of their manners and customs they were amazingly advanced.

A study of the American Indians cannot fail to impress you with the hospitality which characterized their daily life. Few people were as open-hearted and generous as they. Their unaffected kindness and their willingness to share a last morsel astonished the early white settlers who came into contact with them. Some of the tales of English and Indian intercourse, as recorded by these early white people, are touching.

In the summer of 1584 an expedition under the auspices of Sir Walter Raleigh landed on the island of Wocoken, off Albemarle Sound. They invaded the land of the Algonquin tribes and made themselves comfortable.

Yet "there came down from all parts great stores of people" bringing ducks, hares, fish, fruits, nuts, and many good things for the newcomers. The wife of the chief, Granganimeo, came personally and invited the two leaders of the expedition (Philip Amidas and Arthur Barlow) into the house. She washed them, gave them every comfort, "and served roasted fish and venison on a board that stood along the side of the house."

In 1525 Cortes, the Spanish explorer, visited an island in Lake Peten where he was lavishly entertained by the chief of the tribe, Canec. Cortes reports that they "sat down to a dinner in stately manner and Canec ordered fowls, fish, cakes, honey and fruit."

Captain Clark, of the famous Lewis and Clark expedition, wrote with enthusiasm of the hospitality which he encountered. He told how the Indians of the Columbia Valley boiled salmon and served it on a platter of rushes, neatly made. "It is the custom of all the nations on the Missouri to offer every white man food and refreshments when he first enters their tents."

And this despite the fact that the white man was stealing their land, cheating them of their possessions, ousting them from their homes! This kind of generosity, this whole-souled and simple hospitality, cannot be found among any other people, savage or civilized.

We have borrowed many things from our Indian brothers, but nothing more valuable than their custom of generous hospitality. They paved the way for the hospitality which has become so peculiarly associated with this country. We owe them, as we owe all peoples of the world from whose manners and customs we have borrowed, a debt of gratitude.

William Thomas dwells at some length upon the hospitality of the Iroquois. We have borrowed so many little customs from these people that we feel it is worth while to quote this passage which sums up, not only the hospitality of the Iroquois, but of all North American Indians:

Among the Iroquois, hospitality was an established usage. If a man entered an Indian house in any of their villages, whether a villager, a tribesman or a stranger, it was the duty of the women therein to set food before him. An omission to do this would have been a discourtesy amounting to an affront. If hungry, he ate. If not hungry, courtesy demanded that he should taste the food and thank the giver. This was repeated at every house he entered, and at whatever hour of the day. As a custom it was upheld by the rigorous public sentiment.

The same hospitality was extended to strangers from their own and from other tribes. Upon the advent of the European race among them, it was also extended to them. This characteristic of barbarous society wherein food was the principal concern of life is a remarkable fact.

The law of hospitality, as administered by the American aborigines, tended to the final equalization of subsistence. Hunger and destitution could not exist at one end of an Indian village, or in one section of an encampment, while plenty prevailed elsewhere in the same village or encampment.

MODERN HOSPITALITY

With a background such as Thomas describes above, it is not strange that the early colonists should have acquired the habits of simple hospitality. They patterned themselves somewhat after the people on the other side of the ocean from whom they had escaped; somewhat after the red people into whose midst they had come and who set them the eloquent example of simple and kindly hospitality.

The early pages in the history of our country, darkened by the pathetic struggles of the colonists to master the conditions in which they found themselves, are brightened here and there by tales of jolly entertainments and generous hospitality. We read with quickening heart-beat of a pathetic little wedding feast in Plymouth. We read with a sudden warmth of tenderness of a Thanksgiving dinner in the wilderness. We follow a train of covered wagons westward and rejoice with the pioneers when they reach at last their destination and every man, woman, and child gladly helps in clearing the grounds for the great celebration.

Torn from their native homes, banished from their places of birth, alone in a strange new world, these pioneers were yet held together by the bond of hospitality. They were kind to one another, generous, hospitable. They shared alike the hardships and the pleasures of their experiences. *And they built strong because they built together.*

In the centuries between, many conflicting influences have moulded themselves upon the American consciousness. Many customs and fashions have crossed the ocean and patterned themselves upon our lives. But we have never wholly lost that heritage bequeathed us by the early colonists—a love of simple kindliness and hospitality, a love of sharing with our neighbours and having them share with us.

Home Entertainments.—In modern life, hospitable entertainment divides itself into two kinds. There are the formal entertainments on occasions of moment; and the jolly informal entertainments that go the round of the social clock.

Formal entertainments include the large dinner, the ceremonious luncheon in honour of a visiting guest, the débutante tea, the elaborate garden party, the musicale, the début dance, the costume ball.

At one time the word "reception" included everything intended to be formal and ceremonious in the nature of entertainment. Whether a dance, a tea, a dinner or a garden party, it was known as a "reception." But the "reception" went out during the reign of Queen Victoria, and now the word is used merely to indicate a public affair presided over by a committee.

Informal entertainments include the simple dinner, the simple luncheon and afternoon tea, the card party (unless it is very large and ceremonious), the simple dance, the supper, the Christmas, New Year, or birthday party. The bachelor dinner and the shower tea are invariably informal in nature. Wedding anniversaries are usually celebrated in an informal manner, but the dinner which celebrates the golden wedding anniversary is always formal.

Dinners Large and Small.—Dinner-giving as a form of entertainment is as old as—well, as Methuselah, at least! And we can imagine its going back very much farther, when some cave fellow, out of the goodness of his heart, invited one or two of his neighbours to join him in his feast. Since eating and drinking together appears to have been one of the earliest forms of hospitality (see p. 324) dinner-giving must be included among the earliest forms of entertaining.

Generations of culture separate the dinner-giving of early times from the dinner-giving of to-day. Let us glance for a moment at the early dinners and see what they were like.

Early savages, we have seen, simply gathered about a huge fire and tore choice morsels of food from the roasted bear or ox. The honoured guest sat to the right of the host, or the chief, and was given the very choicest bits. They ate until they could eat no more, and then slept side by side in stuffed exhaustion.

Among the American aborigines, the floor was the table and the guests ate from a common dish. Unlike the savage races of Australia and Africa, the red Indians did not stuff or gorge themselves, but ate only to satisfy their hunger. They feasted on occasions of importance, but even then with moderation. After the dinner, or the feasting, they entertained with dancing and pantomime, with feats of skill and strength.

The Greeks and Romans were fond of dinner-giving. They were both surprisingly advanced, and they had elaborate table appointments. Guests were entertained with wrestling, races, feats of strength and daring. The Roman guests came with their servants and remained for several hours. They ate reclining on couches, gorging themselves with game and fruits and "washing down the food with huge draughts of wine."

The Egyptians, we know, were fond of dinner-giving as a form of entertainment (see p. 325). Their dinners, like those of the Romans, lasted several hours, and the guests ate during most of that time. The Egyptians had some rich table appointments, but not nearly so rich and elaborate as those of the Romans; and unlike most peoples of early times, the Egyptians invited both women and men to their entertainments.

In the East guests not only were feasted but they were expected to carry away with them the food they were unable to consume. Among some Eastern peoples, if the guests did not carry away food with them it was regarded as a reflection upon the host's generosity. Among us the hostess sometimes insists upon the favoured guest carrying away a piece of the birthday cake; the country hostess frequently prevails upon her city guest to take away a jar of home-made preserves, some maple syrup, or some other city rarity.

Women were usually barred from feasts and dinners in the East, but this was not true of the Japanese women. From the earliest times, their position was unlike that of any other women of the East. Their minds were cultivated as the men's were. They were not secluded. And the result is that they are, as they always have been, excellent hostesses.

Formal dinner-giving is one of the most difficult of all modern social entertainments in the home. It is not enough to set a well-appointed table, to serve a correct and delectable dinner. As Emily Post says:

> If the great world of society were a university which issued degrees to those whom it trains in its usages, the *magna cum laude* honours would be awarded without question, not to the hostess who may have given the most marvellous ball of the decade, but to her who knows best every component detail of preparation and service, no less than every inexorable rule of etiquette, in formal dinner-giving.

The "groaning board" is a thing of the past. Hospitality is no longer judged in terms of over-stuffed larders,

No matter how formal a dinner may be, it should under no circumstances consist of more than a *hors d'œuvre*, soup, fish, entrée, roast, salad, dessert, and coffee. The dishes should be selected with a regard for balance; there should be as many simple foods as there are rich ones.

A well-balanced guest list is as important as a well-balanced menu. And after the right guests have been assembled, one must place them properly at the table. To quote from a recent book on etiquette:

> It is usually a mistake to invite great talkers together. Brilliant men and women who love to talk want hearers, not rivals. Very silent people should be sandwiched between good talkers, or at least voluble talkers. Silly people should never be put anywhere near learned ones, nor the dull near the clever, unless the dull one is a young and pretty woman with a talent for listening, and the clever, a man with an admiration for beauty and a love for talking. . . . The endeavour of a hostess, when seating her table, is to put those together who are likely to be interested in each other.

Entertainment or amusement of some sort appears to have followed eating even in the earliest times. Greeks, Romans, Egyptians, all had dancing, games, or entertainments after dining. As we thumb the pages of life it is curious to note how modes of entertainment have changed, even as the mode of living has changed.

The whim of the moment is to gather about the bridge tables as soon as dinner is concluded. Hostesses deliberately invite guests upon their qualifications as bridge players. Sometimes dancing follows the formal dinner; sometimes a musicale. Frequently the guests gather in the drawing room for conversation. At large formal dinners, professionals are sometimes brought in to entertain with dancing or singing.

The little dinner, or the simple, informal dinner, is quite a delightful social function. It has less of the dignity and elaborateness of the formal dinner, but more of a jolly, informal joyousness. It follows in the wake of Christmas and Thanksgiving. It conjures in one's mind pictures of turkey and stuffed potatoes and all good things to eat. And

340 B—1 (Courtesy of Metropolitan Museum of Art)

A marble table with bronze fittings. Roman, 1st Century, B. C.

(Courtesy of Metropolitan Museum of Art)

Part of a couch, restored as seat with stool. Decorated with bone carvings and glass inlay. Roman, 1st Century, A. D.

(Courtesy of Metropolitan Museum of Art)

A domestic scene showing the table manners of the early 17th Century. Flemish school; boxwood.

somehow, such impressive appointments as silver candlesticks and finger bowls fade into nothingness!

The success of the small dinner depends very largely upon the hostess. She must not become "flustered" over trifles; she must not be ill at ease if she does not want her guests to be ill at ease. If she is jolly, calm, poised, happy; if she is satisfied with things as they are and not disturbed because her home and her appointments are not elaborate; if the food is well cooked and well served, the guests will vote the dinner a success.

Origin and Evolution of the Afternoon Tea.—George Eliot earnestly inquires, "Reader, have you ever drunk a cup of tea?"

There seems to be something peculiarly heart-warming in a fat, friendly teapot. And gossip over the steaming teacups can be most enjoyable, you know! Perhaps that is why the afternoon tea has become so popular a form of feminine entertaining.

We associate the afternoon tea with merry England. Pepys, in his much-quoted diary, records that he sent for a cup of tea—"a China drink of which he had never drunk before"—on the 25th of September, 1660. Another writer tells us that tea was not introduced into England until 1661 and that the East India Company thought so much of it that they presented a few pounds to the King, regarding it as a gift worthy of his royal acceptance. Dr. Johnson declares that Earls Arlington and Ossory were the first to import tea into England in 1660.

Perplexed by these conflicting facts, we search the sources and find that it was a forgotten gentleman of Holland who introduced tea to the English. History never recorded his name. No one seems to know precisely who he was. But they know that he was a dreamy-eyed fellow who had lived long in the Orient, and who came to England at a very early date bringing with him a peculiar little leaf.

To this curious leaf the dreamy-eyed Dutchman added hot water and sugar. And he drank. But England refused to drink with him. They would have none of him and his funny hot drink, until one or two of the curious tasted it. Instantly those who tasted the tea were converted, and begged the stranger for one of the little packages of green tea leaves he had with him.

As is the way with imagination, the story spread that the drink from China contained drugs. And as is the way with human nature, everybody began tasting it!

It was good, this tea from China. England took notice. Great quantities of the leaves were imported. Nobility adopted the tea fad. At once, everyone followed suit. To drink tea was to be fashionable. So England drank.

We do not know what clever English hostess first conceived the idea of the ceremonious afternoon tea. We presume that it followed closely upon the introduction of tea as a beverage. It would appear that fashionable hostesses took to serving tea to their guests in the afternoon; and thus evolved the custom of the afternoon tea as we know it. To-day practically the whole world sits down to its cup of tea, and in the United States, as in England, clever hostesses entertain at the tea table.

How to Entertain with Tea.—The afternoon tea, in the sense of a cup of tea and a muffin at five o'clock, is unquestionably an English institution. But the tea interpreted in the sense of social entertainment is largely of our own development.

The ceremonious tea is given for a débutante daughter, for a son returning from college, for a visiting guest, for a noted celebrity. Refreshments are served in the dining room, instead of in the drawing room or on the lawn as at simpler teas. Trays of thinly sliced bread are on the table, and dainty sandwiches in large variety. Sometimes fruit salads are served; sometimes cakes and bonbons. But the refreshments are never so substantial that they interfere with dinner.

The fashionable tea for the débutante usually includes dancing. This same type of tea is given by a hostess to introduce a new daughter-in-law to her circle of friends. The formal garden party is simply a ceremonious tea out-of-doors.

Simple teas are delightful. With her hissing tea urn and jolly conversation, the hostess makes each guest feel happy and at ease. The occasion carries no hint of formality, of restraint. The purpose of the simple tea is to see one's friends and be seen by them, to enjoy a chat, and, if the truth be known, to show one's new tea gown!

Somehow, drinking tea together seems to strengthen the bonds of friendship. Strangers who meet for the first time at the home of a mutual friend and sit down with her for the inevitable cup of tea feel themselves friends of long standing. It brings to mind the Ardras who, from earliest times, had the custom of drinking together as a sign of peace and friendship; the Seminoles and their famous drink which establishes the tie of friendship; the many other savage peoples of early times who drank together as a symbol of their friendliness.

The trousseau tea is a modern adaptation of the tea party. The young woman who is about to be married invites her friends to an informal tea at which she displays her trousseau and gifts (see p. 279). Tea, cinnamon toast, muffins, and fruit are usually served.

The Japanese tea party is becoming a popular form of informal entertainment. The home is decorated with Japanese lanterns, rugs, incense burners, etc., and the guests are required to wear Japanese kimonos. Real Japanese tea and rice cakes are served, with almonds and cookies in tiny lanterns to delight the guests. The latter, by the way, do not sit on chairs, but cross-legged on cushions in the approved Japanese fashion. At a recent Japanese tea the women guests were presented with miniature parasols as souvenirs.

The high tea is a favourite form of tea entertainment when one wishes to invite eighteen or twenty friends without undertaking the trouble or expense of a dinner. Sunday evening seems to be the popular time for the high tea. Small tables are used, four guests being placed to a table. These little tables are covered with tea cloths and decorated with a sprig of flowers in a coloured vase. At this type of tea one serves salads, sandwiches, cold cuts, tea or coffee, and cake.

Coffee as a beverage was introduced in England as early as 1662. It made its appearance in France in the same year. But long before the French and English had learned to know and love the rich aroma and pleasing flavour of coffee, the Persians and Arabians were using the beverage. The Arabian writers of very early times mention coffee as a drink. And the Persians are said to have drunk coffee as early as A.D. 875!

The Turkish coffee party is a novel and interesting method of entertaining. The coffee is brewed at the table in a tall Turkish coffeepot and served in Turkish cups. The delectable Turkish paste candy and cookies are served with it. Among coffee lovers, the "afternoon coffee" has taken the place of the afternoon tea. In Germany "afternoon coffee" is indeed a social entertainment and is known as the *kaffee klatsch.*

In the summertime, hostesses like to serve iced drinks to their guests. An iced-tea party would be good fun. The clever hostess would send out an unusual invitation—something like the one that follows—and make the party live up to the promise.

> Brrr, it's cold! The tea, of course. There's going to be plenty of it at Ridgefield Terrace on Monday afternoon. And some other cooling things to make you forget the weather. Shall I expect you at five? I have a very special little surprise for you.

The "other cooling things" can be chilled fruit, ice-cream, and peppermints. Or one might serve image ices and cookies. The "little surprise" might be a pretty fan or some similarly appropriate souvenir.

With a little originality the clever hostess can make even

the simplest entertainment charming and delightful. There is absolutely no reason why the hostess with but a small home and limited equipment should feel that she is handicapped. She may not be able to give elaborate dinners or large formal teas, but she can certainly give jolly, informal teas and parties that her guests will enjoy.

In the chapter on Holidays are various suggestions for entertaining on specific occasions. This chapter will prove helpful to the reader who is planning such entertainments. Similar suggestions will be found in the chapter on Games and the chapter on the Dance.

The reader is urged above all things to remember that true hospitality is of the heart, rather than the purse. A cordial handclasp and a cup of tea can give more comfort and happiness than a stiffly formal and extravagant dinner party.